TELL MY MOTHER I GONE TO CUBA

TELL MY MOTHER I GONE TO CUBA

STORIES OF EARLY TWENTIETH-CENTURY MIGRATION FROM BARBADOS

Sharon Milagro Marshall

THE UNIVERSITY OF THE WEST INDIES PRESS
Jamaica • Barbados • Trinidad and Tobago

The University of the West Indies Press
7A Gibraltar Hall Road, Mona
Kingston 7, Jamaica
www.uwipress.com

A catalogue record of this book is available from the
National Library of Jamaica.

ISBN: 978-976-640-594-6 (print)
978-976-640-595-3 (Kindle)
978-976-640-596-0 (ePub)

Cover and book design by Robert Harris
Set in Minion Pro 10.5/14.2 x 27
Printed in the United States of America

This work is dedicated to the kind and generous people of Baraguá, who still offer hospitality to strangers, and who keep the British West Indian culture alive in Cuba. It is dedicated in particular to Joseph Atwell, who inspired me to begin this search.

And to my mother, her sisters and brothers and – most of all – to my maternal grandparents, Miriam and Isaac Marshall, who made the adventure of Panama and Cuba a very special part of my life.

CONTENTS

FIGURES

TABLES

PREFACE

SINCE THE POST-EMANCIPATION PERIOD, MIGRATION HAS BEEN A significant factor in the social and economic life of mostly working-class citizens of the island of Barbados, and the Barbadian reputation for ubiquity is one that is well earned.

The early movements were to neighbouring islands such as Trinidad, and to British Guiana as well. But Barbadians were also to be found much farther abroad. Barbadians were present among the labourers in the first attempt by the French to construct the Panama Canal, although not in as large numbers as in the subsequent American-financed construction.

When the canal was completed in 1914, many Barbadians and other West Indians went on to Cuba to work in that country's expanding sugar industry. Others had gone there directly from Barbados and the other islands, and many more would continue to do so until the migratory flow was staunched by restrictive legislation enacted in Cuba and at home.

But all this I would eventually come to learn and appreciate, quite by chance. I initially came to this research topic as a journalist, rather than a historian, when I first visited Baraguá – a small town in central Cuba inhabited by the descendants of Barbadians and other British West Indian immigrants. I was then part of a Caribbean Broadcasting Union television crew which went on assignment to Cuba in 1993.

Interviewing these people who spoke in the accents of their parents, even though they had never visited the islands from which their parents came, suddenly put my own family history of migration to Panama and Cuba into a wider context. My maternal grandparents had been part of the migratory wave of West Indians to both these countries.

Cuba is where my mother, Delcina Esperanza Marshall, and some of her siblings were born. It was only following the death of her husband in May 1936 that my grandmother returned to Barbados with her younger children, leaving two older daughters who had already married and were starting their own families in Cuba.

The Caribbean Broadcasting Union assignment inspired me to find out more about this period in Barbados's history and the forces which had influenced my own family history. This led me to register in the Department of History at the Cave Hill campus of the University of the West Indies to pursue a graduate degree in the subject.

In addition to what I could glean from the library at the Cave Hill campus, this research journey led me to the Barbados Public Library and the Barbados National Archives. It also included a trip to Jamaica and the library at the Mona campus of the University of the West Indies. Several research visits took me to Cuba: to the Biblioteca Nacional José Martí, Casa de las Americas and the Archivo Nacional in Havana; Casa del Caribe in Santiago de Cuba; and the British West Indian Welfare Centre in Guantánamo. On visits to the United States, I gathered valuable material at the Schomburg Center for Research in Black Culture in New York, and in Florida, from the Cuban Heritage Collection at the University of Miami and the Special Collections and the Latin American Collection of the University of Florida, Gainesville. In London, the Public Record Office proved to be a trove of Colonial Office and Foreign Office records and correspondence, including an original letter from Marcus Garvey.

I would discover that it was the ultimate aim of annexation of Cuba to the United States which led to American investment in Cuban sugar estates, particularly in the eastern part of the country. This investment had created the conditions for the West Indians to migrate from the harsh conditions in their home countries, as had been the case during the construction of the Panama Canal. Even though they were able to earn higher wages than at home, the welcome they received in Cuba was sometimes hostile, and some of them were subjected to serious exploitation and ill-treatment. As British subjects, they appealed to His Majesty's consular representatives in Cuba, and this would put them at the centre of a diplomatic storm involving Cuba, Great Britain and, to some extent, the United States. This historical context to the Barbadian migration story is told in part 1 of this book. It is by no means intended to be a definitive history of British West Indian migration to Cuba, or Anglo-Cuban or Cuban-American relations of the period. Others have already chronicled aspects of this research area far more eloquently and authoritatively than I possibly could. I am indebted to them, as I rely on their assistance in "setting the scene" in which the British West Indian migrants became actors.

Throughout this process of discovery, the most precious sources were the poignant oral histories gathered through personal interviews conducted with respondents in Barbados and Cuba. They were invaluable in helping to put a human face on the data gathered from *Blue Books* and censuses and other official documents. These respondents included a few of the original migrants and some first-generation descendants. This publication is a medium for them to tell their own migration stories to a wider audience.

Their stories are made even more significant by the fact that several Barbadians can tell of relatives who returned from Cuba in the early years of the migration and refused to speak of their experiences there. People who were subjected to discrimination on the basis of race and nationality; people who had lost their savings in the 1920 bank crash; and who were disappointed by the harsh reality of the so-called Promised Land were not keen to relive those experiences. This might be one possible explanation for the paucity of documentation on this chapter of Barbados's history.

Kathryn Walbert opines, "oral history has several unique benefits that no other historical source provides", stating, "Oral history allows you to learn about the perspectives of individuals who might not otherwise appear in the historical record. While historians and history students can use traditional documents to reconstruct the past, everyday people fall through the cracks in the written record."[1]

Another important advantage of oral history identified by Walbert is that it "provides historical actors with an opportunity to tell their own stories in their own words. Through oral history, interviewees have a chance to participate in the creation of the historical retelling of their lives."

I concur wholeheartedly with these sentiments. During the course of my research, I conducted at least fifteen interviews with some of the original British West Indian migrants to Cuba, as well as some of their descendants, to afford them an opportunity to "tell their own stories in their own words". The respondents were asked a basic set of questions, depending on their status as either migrant or descendant.

These in-person interviews were recorded and transcribed between April 1993, when I made my first visit to Baraguá, and August 2000, at the time of my final research visit to Guantánamo. Some interviews yielded richer material than others. Responses to the questions were consolidated to form a continuous narrative.

Some of these narratives are offered in part 2 of this book. They relate eloquently and vividly the escapades of a young stowaway, the excitement of setting out from Bridgetown by ship, the hazardous sea journey and the first sightings of Cuba from afar. They also tell of a train ride to Baraguá after arriving from Panama and to Ciego de Avila after arriving from Barbados, a chance meeting with an old acquaintance on a railway platform, reuniting with family members, the joys and difficulties of daily life in Cuba, interactions with other West Indians, Cubans and Americans, and the return to Barbados after many years.

Jorge Giovannetti suggests that there is still much research work and analysis to be done in order to gain a proper perspective of the British West Indian experience in Cuba and elsewhere in the Hispanic Caribbean. He expresses the view that "it will also benefit from examining the experiences of the various islanders, rather than resting on generalisations such as 'the Antilleans' or 'the British West Indians' that, while having some heuristic value, do not provide insights into the particular histories of, say, the Barbadians, the Saint Lucians, or the Jamaicans".[2]

It is my sincere hope that this book will add to the body of knowledge regarding this migration experience and help to perpetuate the memory of those who made the journey from Barbados to Cuba.

The recent rapprochement between Cuba and the United States brings with it the prospect of a new era of American investment in Cuba. This is an opportune time to reflect on the period in the early twentieth century when US investment in sugar plantations in Cuba lured thousands of foreign labourers there.

Little did I know that embarking on this research project would also change my life in an unexpected way. While on a research visit to Guantánamo City, I would meet the man who would become my husband, himself the grandson of a Barbadian man who was among those who had migrated to Cuba.

ACKNOWLEDGEMENTS

THIS WORK WOULD NOT HAVE BEEN POSSIBLE WITHOUT the very kind assistance of a number of persons, whose contributions I wish to acknowledge.

In Barbados, the staff of the Barbados Public Library – especially Sylvia Reynolds – the Barbados National Archives, and the University of the West Indies library at the Cave Hill campus. In Jamaica, the staff of the library at the Mona campus of the University of the West Indies, particularly Judy Rao.

In Havana, Elliot Nelson and the staff at the Biblioteca Nacional José Martí, Casa de las Americas and the Archivo Nacional. In Santiago de Cuba, the staff of Casa del Caribe. In Baraguá, Olivia "Beba" Nelson and Teófilo Gay. In Guantánamo, the members of the British West Indian Welfare Centre – most notably Roberto Claxton, Jorge Derrick and Thelma Audain.

In New York, the staff of the Schomburg Center for Research in Black Culture. In Florida, the staff of the Cuban Heritage Collection at the University of Miami – especially Lesbia Varona – and the staff of the Special Collections and the Latin American Collection of the University of Florida, Gainesville.

In London, the staff of the Public Record Office.

I especially wish to acknowledge all the persons who consented to interviews and shared their stories, and those who read and critiqued my work.

I am also indebted to Janis Clarke-Marville and Selwyn Smith for their practical support, and to Professor Sir Hilary Beckles and George Lamming for encouraging me to continue with my research when it seemed that I would never make headway. Desmond Brunton, Carlos Moore and my husband, Pedro Hope Jústiz, are to be thanked for their persistence in persuading me to bring the work to publication.

ABBREVIATIONS

BWIA	British West Indian Airways
CO	Colonial Office
FO	Foreign Office
PIC	Partido Independiente de Color
PRO	Public Record Office
UNIA	Universal Negro Improvement Association

PART 1

~~~~~~~~

HISTORICAL BACKGROUND TO BARBADIAN MIGRATION

CHAPTER 1

EARLY TWENTIETH-CENTURY BARBADOS

BARBADOS AT THE TURN OF THE TWENTIETH CENTURY was a society only sixty-six years removed from the official end of slavery in the then British colonies, when the Emancipation Act came into force on 1 August 1834. The jubilant chant of the former slaves in appreciation to Queen Victoria was, "Lick an lock-up done wid, Hurray fuh Jin-Jin. / De Queen come from England to set we free. / Now lick an lock-up done wid, Hurray fuh Jin-Jin."

The apprenticeship system, which many abolitionists considered slavery simply under a different name, had lasted another four years. It was ostensibly a means of training the newly freed slaves, who were not used to independence, how to be free men and women. Their jubilation would turn to frustration with the realization that their circumstances had not changed appreciably.

The labour-intensive cultivation of sugar cane, which dominated Barbados's economy since it was introduced to the island in the first half of the seventeenth century, had fuelled the slave trade, a forced migration from the African continent. After emancipation, the planter class in this primarily agrarian society could – and did – dictate terms in a market where labour was plentiful.

The House of Assembly was dominated by the planter class, which enacted legislation to keep these descendants of slaves in subjugation. The criteria for qualification as an elector of representatives to the House of Assembly excluded the overwhelming majority of the working class. Qualified electors were men who earned a salary of fifty pounds per annum, or who owned land which yielded five pounds a year, or who had a university education. By 1911 only 1,986 Barbadian citizens met these qualifications. It would not be until 1951 that universal adult suffrage was achieved.

LIFE AFTER SLAVERY

The sugar industry, the island's major employer at the time, could not provide many of these recently freed black labouring-class citizens with adequate earnings. The vast majority of black Barbadians of that era lived in rural plantation tenantries. They kept small subsistence gardens which were normally rented from the estates, and their access to these garden plots was contingent on their working for the same estates. The "located labourer" statutes, which bound individual workers to specific plantations, survived well into the twentieth century and kept the black population in conditions not too far removed from slavery.

The former slaves had been allowed to remain in their houses and allotments, and were required to give their labour to the plantation in return for this benefit. Bonham Richardson points out that the tenant was required to sign or mark a written contract, which also bore the mark or signature of the planter or his agent. F.A. Hoyos describes the consequences if the tenant objected to the terms:

> If the "located labourer", as he was called, refused to give his services on these terms, he could be ejected from his house and land and the crops he had grown on his allotment could be taken over at what was generally less than their current value. If the located labourer left of his own accord, seeking higher wages on another plantation, his crops were taken over without any compensation at all.[1]

Betsy Cleaver, an estate labourer attached to Neale's Plantation, was one such who was summarily ejected after she ran afoul of her estate manager, as Hilary Beckles documents.[2] Her "crime" was not that she refused the terms of service, but rather that she sought to protect her interests.

> As part of the labour arrangement established with the manager of the estate, Betsy rented half an acre of the land belonging to the estate. Her husband was a located labourer on a neighbouring plantation. When the time came to cut her canes, the manager of the estate insisted that they could not be harvested until the estate had completed its own harvest. Betsy's argument was that this would destroy the value of her canes, and proceeded to make arrangements with the neighbouring estate where her husband was employed for the harvest and grinding of her crop.[3]

The manager regarded this show of initiative on Betsy's part as an act of insubordination. He had her house unthatched and her belongings thrown into the road. After Betsy sought shelter in her infirm uncle's house, a similar vengeful act was inflicted on his house one night while he slept. The manager told the magistrate that this was the punishment which should be enforced on every estate in Barbados against any labourer who committed a similar offence.

WORKERS' WAGES AND NUTRITION

The *Barbados Blue Book* for 1909 to 1910 gives the average wage of an agricultural worker as eight pence a day, and suggests that an able-bodied labourer could earn from eight pence to one shilling "within the ordinary working hours". Masons, tradesmen and carpenters earned between two shillings and two shillings, six pence a day. Domestic servants were always hired by the month, their monthly wage varying from eight shillings, four pence to one shilling.

The 1878 Education Act had provided for education, rather than employment, for Barbadian children under twelve years old. However, as Richardson notes, "necessities of survival, produced by landlessness and low wages had traditionally driven black children into child labor gangs ('third-class gangs') on the plantation in the nineteenth century and well into the twentieth".[4]

Table 1.1. Prices for Selected Grocery Items in Barbados, 1909

Commodity	Price
wheaten bread	3d
milk, per gallon	1s
butter, fresh native, per lb	1s 3d
cheese, per lb	1s 3d
beef, per lb	9d
mutton, per lb	10d
pork, per lb	5d
rice, per lb	2d
tea, black and green, per lb	2s
salt, per lb	½d
sugar, refined, per lb	3d
codfish, salted, per lb	5d

Source: Barbados Blue Book, 1909–1910.

Even with children in the household being employed, these workers would have found it challenging to provide proper nutrition for themselves and their families. They would have been confronted with the prices shown in table 1.1 for these selected grocery items at their neighbourhood shops.

Richardson comments that "a combination of poor nutrition, crowded and unsanitary conditions, and a lack of control over any but the tiniest parts of their island meant disease and early death for many black Barbadians at the turn of the century".[5] He points to the high infant mortality rate at the beginning of the twentieth century as one measure of the general ill-health of the black labouring class, and asserts, "Compared even with the similarly depressed sugar cane colonies of the Commonwealth Caribbean, Barbados stood out. The average number of deaths of infants under one year per 1,000 live births for the years 1900–4 was 282. Comparative data for other places were Jamaica, 171; Nevis, 197; Dominica, 185; Trinidad, 162; British Honduras, 139; British Guiana, 85; St. Kitts, 247."[6]

The vestry system, which was introduced in Barbados in 1630 when the island was first divided into parishes, persisted well into the twentieth century. Each vestry had the authority to levy taxes on land, buildings, animals, vehicles and the pews of Anglican churches in its parish. It was then responsible for the repair and maintenance of parish church buildings, remunerating church officials, repairing the public roads and paying annual stipends to sanitary inspectors of the parish. Vestries were also obligated to provide for the education and maintenance of the parish poor. They maintained almshouses where food and medical care could be obtained.

Richardson notes that, "because estate wages were so pitifully low, many black laboring families of Barbados in 1900 had first-hand experience with parish almshouses". He observes that "a rural black Barbadian 'belonged' to a particular parish just as he 'belonged' to a particular estate. And vestrymen made sure that parish funds were not being used to support outsiders from beyond the district's boundary line, who were thereby the financial responsibility of others."[7]

He explains that for the urban labouring classes, "conditions were even worse in the pockets of lower-class black housing scattered throughout Bridgetown and the suburbs of St. Michael parish"[8] than those of the rural districts. However, young black men and women were attracted to the city in search of work and excitement. They were sometimes sent back to their own parishes if they sought to obtain poor relief in St Michael, but often found their way back into town, sending for other relatives from the countryside if they were able to obtain work. But they looked outwards too. Barbadians began migrating to neighbouring British Guiana, Trinidad, St Croix, Surinam, Cayenne, Brazil and farther afield.

BEGINNINGS OF A MIGRATION TRADITION

These conditions at home rendered the prospect of migration, with an opportunity to earn wages much higher than could be obtained in Barbados, an attractive one for thousands of working-class Barbadians. Migration from the island was the means by which black working-class Barbadians could pursue opportunities to attain a better standard of living, especially since there was not an abundance of Crown lands to provide alternative sources of generating income. The population and vital statistics segment of the 1909 to 1910 *Blue Book* records that for 1891 to 1909, male emigrants from the island were estimated at 15,820, while the number of female emigrants is given as 8,817, for a total of 24,637.

For many years British Guiana was an important destination for Barbadians in search of work. A 1919 edition of the *Barbados Herald* carried an article, "Emigration from Barbados to British Guiana", that discloses that G.D. Bayley, Guiana's Commissioner of Lands and Mines, had recently written a précis of the history of immigration into the "Magnificent Province" from Barbados. The article states, "according to that account, emigration to that colony dates back to the time of emancipation".[9]

The 22 August 1919 edition of the *Port of Spain Gazette* chronicled the arrival of one contingent from Barbados, which was reproduced in the Inter-Colonial News column of the *Barbados Herald*: "More than one hundred Barbadians, including some women, passed through San Fernando by the Wednesday evening's train on their way to work under contract of the Sainte Madeleine Usine. A crowd assembled about the railway station to see the industrious strangers."[10]

At the turn of the twentieth century, Barbadians were described as being "in the habit" of "finding employment as butlers and servants in northern Brazil, mainly Belém".[11] Richardson also explains that, between 1907 and 1912, "as many as 2,000 were engaged as railroad construction workers on the Madeira–Mamoré railroad, more than 2,000 miles upriver from Belém near the border of Bolivia".[12] Of this period, Elaine Pereira Rocha relates, "West Indian workers arrived in Brazil from several islands of the Caribbean, but predominantly from Barbados. In the Amazon region they became known by the generic denomination of 'Barbadianos'."[13] Transported there by ships of the Booth Steamship Company Limited, which called at Barbados on the journey from New York to Manaus, the workers were employed by British companies which had been awarded contracts to build not only railroads, but also tramlines and telegraph and electricity infrastructure, and to upgrade harbours in northern Brazil.

Richardson also records that, as early as 1890, "large numbers of Barbadians in Surinam and Cayenne [were] reported [to be] in destitute and diseased condition".[14] Barbadians were to be found much earlier and farther afield from their island home; Richardson relates an incident which occurred in September 1892, in which 270 Barbadian men, along with 23 others from Martinique and St Lucia, "were responsible for a disturbance aboard a German steamer at Boma, a tiny downriver port town of the Belgian Congo".[15]

Under the headline, "Barbadian Ubiquity", the *Herald* carried another item reproduced from the *Port of Spain Gazette*. It was a report from a Trinidadian in England on peace celebrations in the British capital at the end of World War I, which, as the *Herald* said, "gives an instance of Barbadian ubiquity and the recognized characteristics of being everywhere and in everything".

> I had a great good laugh yesterday. Two New Zealand soldiers came up to me and asked the way to Buckingham Palace – one of them was a tall white and handsome fellow, the other short and coloured. I asked the coloured fellow; "Are you a New Zealander?" to which he affirmatively replied. I said, "No man you are a Barbadian." He owned up at once that he was from Bridgetown, and we had a hearty laugh. We went to Buckingham Palace and became friends.[16]

So there is evidence to suggest that at least one Barbadian travelled to New Zealand and joined that country's armed forces in the early part of this century.

GOVERNMENTAL ATTITUDES TO EMIGRATION

Governmental attitudes towards emigration varied according to the social and economic circumstances of the period. In the immediate post-emancipation period, the planter class feared a shortage of labour on the sugar plantations if large-scale migration were encouraged, and they acted to keep the labourers at home.

For example, G.W. Roberts observes that as early as 1838, an act was passed which, although ostensibly dealing with the prevention of bastardy, carried a veiled deterrent to migration. Under the terms of this act, legal action could be taken against a mother or "putative father" of a bastard child who left the island. A warrant could be issued for their arrest, and, if apprehended, they could be put in a "house of correction".[17]

More direct legislation would soon follow. In 1839 the House of Assembly passed two acts specifically designed to restrict emigration. The first was entitled "An act to prevent the clandestine deportation of young persons from the island". The second was "An act to regulate the emigration of labourers from this island and to protect the labourers in this island from impositions practised on them by emigration agents".[18]

The labourers did not share the planters' views on the subject, and did not appear to be appreciative of these efforts to protect them. According to Roberts: "Opposition to emigration was however confined to the planters; the workers viewed the efforts being made to curtail migration as undue restrictions on their freedom of movement. Vigorous protests against these attempts to limit migration formed the major part of a widely supported petition to the House of Commons in 1840."[19]

Pedro Welch takes the view that while the passage of legislation such as the Masters and Servants Act of 1840 was designed to tie freed persons to the former place of employment, it appears to be more applicable to the rural than the urban context, where the work experience was more individualized: "However, despite some differences between the rural and urban conditions, the aim of the former owners was consistent – control of the working class by all means necessary. Attempts by freed persons to seek better working conditions elsewhere were bound to run into white opposition."[20]

Mary Chamberlain observes that for the first time, some members of the House of Assembly began to consider seriously the notion that Barbados could not sustain its population adequately after the cholera epidemic of 1854 and a series of droughts in the 1860s. This gave rise to an act passed in 1864, which legislators hoped would encourage emigration. Chamberlain, however, states:

The encouragement was more in the letter than the spirit of the law, for although the House of Assembly may have been unanimous in fearing the disruptive consequences of poverty; they were not entirely convinced by the argument equating over-population with poverty nor with emigration as a solution. It was still only thirty years since the abolition of slavery, less since the end of apprenticeship, and access to an unlimited supply of labour was still perceived as essential for the profitable production of sugar.[21]

Nevertheless, as Elizabeth Thomas-Hope notes, during the century after emancipation both government and people grew increasingly reliant on emigration – but for different reasons. She describes the value of this outlet for both the former slaves and their descendants, as well as for the governments of these colonies:

> To the colonial government, the loss of potential labour, which was at first economically disastrous, later became the principal factor on which they depended in the face of increasing populations. To the emancipated agricultural labourers and peasants, the fact that their labour was in demand was nothing new, and certainly provided no incentive to stay when the availability of employment overseas gave the opportunity for freedom from the system at home.[22]

The project to construct the Panama Canal, first by the French from 1881 to 1889, and later by the Americans from 1904 to 1914, served as a magnet to draw large numbers of British West Indian labourers who sought to improve their economic fortunes. Between 1904 and 1914, some nineteen thousand Barbadians emigrated to Panama under contract, during the construction of the Panama Canal. Apart from these documented workers, many others also went to Panama to work. Velma Newton suggests that there might have been as many as forty thousand of these undocumented Barbadian labourers who made their way to Panama independently.[23]

Thomas-Hope notes that there was a general lack of governmental intervention in the migration process for the West Indian colonies, but Barbados was a notable exception: "During the Panamanian migration, not only were male labourers encouraged to leave, but the Victoria Emigration Society sponsored the emigration of women, probably to discourage the men's return by stabilizing the community abroad."[24]

The Victoria Emigration Society had been formed in 1897 to assist the emigration of women in "reduced circumstances" who found it impossible to earn their living in Barbados. The suggestion for its establishment came from a committee appointed by the governor to consider suitable ways to mark the sixtieth anniversary of the reign of Queen Victoria.

Roberts too remarks on the official attitude to the Panama migration: "The Government of Barbados moved promptly to put this large scale emigration under rigorous control. The Emigration Act of 18th March 1904, not only strengthened the conditions governing recruitment of labour in the island, but also continued the modest provisions for assisting emigration originally introduced in 1873."[25]

The fact that they had other avenues through which they could market their labour brought about a growing self-confidence among the labourers. A popular chant of the emboldened workers was:

> We want more wages, we want it now
> And if we don't get it, we going to Panama
> Yankees say they want we down there,
> We want more wages, we want it now.[26]

Richardson reports that as one group of men bid farewell to the plantation for brighter prospects in Panama, one of their members shouted to others working in the cane field, "Why you don't hit the manager in de head, and come along wid we!"[27] He observes, "For many Barbadians who emigrated to the Canal Zone, the exodus to Panama was simply a first step for movement further afield. Many veterans of the canal moved on to Cuba for sugar factory and cane-cutting jobs with the Americans there."[28]

According to Richardson, "Barbadians in Panama had found that relatively high American wages were ample compensation for serving gruff Yankee supervisors, conditions they rightfully expected at the giant American sugar estates in Cuba and Santo Domingo. Many Barbadians had travelled directly to Cuba from Colón when the Panama Canal was finished."[29]

Among those who travelled first to Panama and then to Cuba was a young man who was born on 7 June 1880 in Ben Hill, St Andrew. Isaac Newton "Bonnie" Marshall had learned the blacksmith's trade and no doubt expected that his skills would have been useful in the grand construction project. At age twenty-five, he first left for Panama on 19 November 1906.

He had courted a young lady, Miriam Delcina Lawrence, who was born on 24 August 1884 in Market Hill, St George. The courtship saw him walking from St Andrew to St George to see his sweetheart. On his return to Barbados, they were married on 19 December 1907 at St Augustine's Chapel in the same rural parish where she resided. Bonnie would return to Panama with his wife. Their eight children would be born in Barbados, Panama and Cuba. The daughter whom they named Delcina Esperanza was born in Central Hershey, Cuba, where they eventually settled. She would become my mother.

FROM PANAMA TO CUBA

The United Fruit Company Steamship Service, an American corporation, transported hundreds of these British West Indian citizens from Panama to Cuba. Among the ships plying that passage were the SS *Toloa* and the SS *Ulua*. Cryptic entries on a passenger list do not convey the fears, hopes and aspirations of the human cargo on board. From the reader's perspective, we can only try to imagine the emotions which they experienced on the journey.

For example, the passenger list of the SS *Toloa*, which sailed from Cristóbal to Havana via Limón on 22 June 1921, included carpenters, domestics, dressmakers and housewives in the prime of life. Apart from this personal information, these deck passengers were listed simply as "British".

Women migrated in their own right to seek work, but they were also important agents in the maintenance of the family unit. Apart from the labouring migrants, there were also young passengers transported in the company of older relatives on these ships.

The SS *Ulua*, which also sailed from Cristóbal to Havana on 22 June 1921, carried among the "British" deck passengers at least three women – Mrs Galloway, Mrs Goddard and Mrs Maxwell – who were travelling with young children.

These women were more than likely going to Cuba to be reunited with husbands or partners who had gone on ahead, as was the case for Maradell Greene's mother. In chapter 10, Greene shares her recollection of the family's journey to be reunited with the father who had gone on ahead to Central Baraguá. The

Table 1.2. Selected British West Indian Passengers on Board SS *Toloa*, 22 June 1921

Name	Age	Gender	Status	Occupation
Lucilla Brown	34	Female	Married	
Samuel Brown	46	Male	Married	Carpenter
Frances Bryan	36	Female	Married	Dressmaker
Arthur Benjamin	33	Male	Single	Carpenter
Robert Clarke	32	Male	Married	Labourer
Ellen Crichlow	30	Female	Married	Housewife
Richard Jordan	28	Male	Married	Carpenter
Olivia Little	29	Female	Single	Domestic

Source: SS *Toloa* ship's register, Archivo Nacional de Cuba.

Table 1.3. Selected British West Indian Passengers on Board SS *Ulua*, 22 June 1921

Name	Age	Gender	Status	Occupation
Elizabeth Galloway	28	Female	Married	Dressmaker
Matilda Galloway	1	Female	Single	None
Peter Galloway	6	Male	Single	None
Lillian Goddard	24	Female	Married	Dressmaker
Joseph G. Goddard	10/12	Male	Single	None
Josephine Maxwell	29	Female	Married	Domestic
Eleanor Maxwell	4	Female	Single	None
Clementina Maxwell	3	Female	Single	None
George Maxwell	1	Male	Single	None

Source: SS *Ulua* ship's register, Archivo Nacional de Cuba.

family had been separated for three years. She and her two sisters sailed to Cuba from Panama with their mother, in the company of two of her mother's female friends, one Barbadian and one Jamaican.

Similarly, when the SS *Toloa* sailed from Cristóbal and Puerto Limón to Havana on 1 June 1921, the deck passengers included a number of young women – Mrs Callender, Mrs Meade and Miss Thompson – travelling with their young children.

The number of Barbadians who travelled to Cuba from the British West Indian colonies was second only to migrants from Jamaica, which had a larger population and closer proximity to Cuba. Because of this, all the British West

Table 1.4. Selected British West Indian Passengers on Board SS *Toloa*, 1 June 1921

Name	Age	Gender	Status	Occupation
Ruth Callender	39	Female	Married	Housewife
James Callender	13	Male	Single	None
Margaret Meade	38	Female	Married	Domestic
Gertrude Meade	7	Female	Single	None
James Meade	2	Male	Single	None
Naomi Thompson	25	Female	Single	Dressmaker
David Thompson	6	Male	Single	None

Source: SS *Toloa* ship's register, Archivo Nacional de Cuba.

Indians there were often referred to as Jamaicans – *jamaicanos* or *jamaiqui-nos*, just as the West Indians in Brazil were called *barbadianos*. They were also called *antillanos, anglófonos* and *ingleses*. It is estimated that fifty thousand Jamaicans sought work in Cuba during 1919 to 1920, the peak years of Jamaican migration there.

William Theodore Mullings of Mountainside in the Jamaican parish of St Elizabeth made ten trips to Cuba, travelling to Santiago de Cuba and Camagüey in the early 1900s. His son, Rupert, explained that his father went initially to work on the sugar estates. While he did cut canes there, he also worked as a lumberjack, he drove the locomotive that pulled the canes to the factory, and pulled sugar and produce between the estate and the port, and he also operated a commissary.

Mullings stated that his father was one of several relatives and neighbours from the community of Mountainside who went to Cuba to find work:

> I can remember from my village the names of them. I mentioned my mother's uncles, two of my mother's uncles – her mother's youngest brother and her father's youngest brother. (Sammy was my grandmother's youngest brother, and Isaac was my grandfather's youngest brother.) There was my mother's cousin, George. There was her cousin, Surgeson. Two other cousins, Bertie and Willie, and another one who was called Captain, and I can never for the life of me remember what was his real name. And then my granduncle, Isaac, his two sons – Cleon and Deliman – they lived there for several years, and then they returned and managed his farm. It was quite an extensive farm he had adjoining the house plot that my father had. My first introduction to Spanish was to listen to those two brothers speak Spanish, my mother's first cousins. They came back and they were always practising Spanish, and they would practise with my father, who kept it to his dying years. I can remember there were two Blake brothers, and there were the Chisholms – James and his brother, Oswald, who was married to my mother's aunt. It was a village where they specialized in going there.

Mullings's father told him that a lot of Jamaicans stowed away to Cuba, and some paid money to stowaway and never got there: "My father told us about one who was caught on the ship on which he went on one of his trips. They took him to Santiago, and they sent him back on the next boat out."

On their return to Jamaica, the men from Mountainside would share stories of their experiences in Cuba, as Mullings recalls from his childhood days:

They used to stay close to each other. That was another thing. The guys from the village, they kept in contact with each other. You could hear them talk about. . . . Oh, I didn't mention the guy who lived right next door to us, my mother's first cousin also, the older brother of Surgeson. He also went. He kept telling us stories, including Cuban duppy [ghost] stories. He used to come across and tell us these stories at nights. He used to tell us that the Cuban duppies are afraid of Jamaicans. That the baby duppy was crying one night, and the mother duppy said, "Shhh, shhh; *jamaiquinos, jamaiquinos*." "Keep quiet; Jamaicans around."

FROM BARBADOS TO CUBA

At the end of World War I, the Barbados government was still disposed to supporting migration. Richardson states, "In November 1919 the assembly authorized funds for bicycles, house repair, tools, and driver training for returned soldiers. More significantly, the legislators paid for the emigration of 152 war veterans, 133 to Cuba."[30]

By 1919 the *Barbados Herald* published an article on emigration stating:

A natural taste for travel and outside exploration – encouraged further by local conditions of congestion and consequent economic hardship – is a well-known Barbadian characteristic, and but little inducement is needed to make sons of the soil hurriedly pack their kit and be ready for any opportunity offering by which they can improve their position and that of their dependents for whom they always retain their affection and deep regard whatever be their financial success.[31]

The voluntary movement to Cuba was fuelled by the expanding sugar industry, particularly in the eastern provinces. American businessmen made this expansion possible through injections of capital. Many of the recruits for the Cuban sugar industry were engaged by agents operating in Barbados, but hundreds more also found their way to "the promised land" on their own. The agents were acting on behalf of large, powerful sugar corporations, which were largely American-owned.

The voracious demand for sugar had fuelled fundamental changes in the organization of the production process. It had given rise to the growth of the *central. Centrales* were complex organisms where money, machinery and men were combined with the sole aim of producing sugar. They consisted of much more than the central mill to which the cane was brought. The land, the houses, stores and railways were owned by the *centrales*. Many of them even had their own police forces. Some controlled their own private ports, where many of the West Indian immigrants were landed, totally outside of the normal processes of the national government. In short, the *central* has been described as a state within a state.

The organization of the Cuban *centrales* differed from the system which Barbadians had left behind. As Jerome Handler describes:

> The heart of the plantation and the focus of operations was the area known from an early period (until the present) as the plantation yard, mill yard, or simply and most frequently, the yard. Plantations of any consequence had in their yard at least one windmill, occasionally two or three, for grinding sugar cane. Situated close to the mill were other buildings essential to the processing and manufacture of sugar, molasses, and rum, e.g. the boiling house, curing house and distillery, storerooms, workshops for tradesmen, stables, houses for white staff (if a larger plantation), and owner's or manager's residence, variously called the mansion house, dwelling house, or simply the house (today called the great house). Very close and usually adjacent to the mill yard was the slave settlement itself.[32]

After emancipation, the plantation system had continued to function in a manner largely similar to that which had previously existed during the days of slavery. As Beckles, Hoyos and Welch illustrate, the former slaves did not become free and equal citizens in rural and urban post-emancipation Barbados. They were subject to indignities as they remained on the estates, and were severely limited in negotiating adequate wages for their labour. Migration, as Roberts and Richardson demonstrate, became a viable option for many as they sought to improve their economic lot. However, the facility with which they left home depended on changing economic circumstances at home and governmental attitudes towards the loss of a potential source of manpower, as well as opportunities available in foreign fields of labour.

Prior to the abolition of slavery in the islands, there is evidence that black West Indians had been in Cuba well before the twentieth century. They had been pressed into service for the British Empire. During its attempt in the eighteenth century to capture Cuba from Spain, Britain looked to some of the smaller islands in the Caribbean archipelago, which it already possessed, to augment its fighting forces. During the siege of Havana by the British in 1762, the provincial troops listed in the diary of Major Joseph Gorham were "5,300 Negroes from Jamaica, Barbadoes, and the Windward Islands".[33]

Forced labour from British colonies in the region operated new steam machinery in Cuba's plantation economy in the 1840s to maintain production. Some planters in the colonies, worried about losing their investments as the anti-slavery campaign gained momentum in Britain, relocated themselves as well as their slaves to Cuba and other Spanish colonies in the region. Even freed slaves – mainly from the Bahamas and Jamaica – were either caught up in the traffic through deception or by kidnapping. The British consul in Havana, David Turnbull, was an ardent abolitionist and devoted much time and effort to securing the release of these hapless slaves and former slaves.[34]

While that prior travel to the Spanish-speaking country had not been within the control of the "negroes", in the first decades of the twentieth century, black working-class Barbadians and their West Indian counterparts voluntarily migrated in appreciable numbers, in answer to the call of Cuba. This time, they would be venturing out as masters of their own destiny.

CHAPTER 2

AMERICAN SUGAR BARONS
AND THE CALL OF CUBA

THE BRITISH WEST INDIAN WORKERS, PROPELLED OUT OF their home environments, which offered limited opportunities for them to profit from their labour, were attracted by the possibilities which Cuba promised. They would become cogs in the wheels of a great American industrial enterprise, caught up in the exercise of US imperial and capitalist ambitions in Cuba.

The British West Indians were interjected into a complex situation in which they were forced to navigate black Cubans' struggles for recognition and equality of opportunity, Cubans' growing sense of nationalism, and their own sense of identity and relationship with the British colonial power. As Daniel Bender and Jana Lipman acknowledge, "When historians place labor and working people at the center, empire appears as a pivotal dynamic of U.S. history, rather than as a brief chronological blip or a moment of European envy."[1] In their words, "Working men and women often navigated multiple empires in their search for employment."[2] The West Indians also had to confront competing manifestations of British and American empires on Cuban soil.

SUGAR CULTIVATION IN CUBA

Cuba – the Pearl of the Antilles – is the largest island in the Caribbean archipelago. The sugar industry had been introduced in Cuba soon after the Spaniards settled the island early in the sixteenth century, but it was not until 250 years later that significant expansion would take place.

Cuba's sugar industry developed rapidly following the collapse of the economy of Saint-Domingue, occasioned by the Haitian Revolution of 1791 to 1804. In the mid-1840s Cuban trade with England and the United States surpassed the island's trade with the colonial power, Spain. In the 1860s, Cuba produced more than 30 per cent of the world's cane sugar.

Cuban sugar planters looked to the British West Indies for ideas on improving the industry. In 1795 Francisco Arango y Parreño and Ignacio Montalvo y Ambulodi made the first official trip abroad on behalf of other leading Cuban planters. The trip took them to England, Portugal, Jamaica and Barbados. Franklin Knight states that this was a precedent-setting mission. "Arango's fact-finding tour to Barbados and Jamaica in 1795 became the first of a frequent general practice. To any Cuban sugar producer, the grand tour of the British West Indies became a source of personal prestige, establishing the traveler as an authority on the subject of sugar production. In some cases, the trip became the prerequisite for the founding of an *ingenio* (sugar estate with factory)."[3] Among the techniques which these travellers imported were the "Jamaican train" boiling process for the manufacture of sugar, a process which was developed originally in Barbados in the mid-seventeenth century.

Slavery was abolished in Cuba in 1886. Around this time the *central* began to make its appearance. The *central* was a complex system of land, labour and capital geared to the production of sugar, which had been appropriated from Martinique. As stated by Leland Jenks in *Our Cuban Colony*, "The bulk of the less efficient, poorly located plantations ceased to mill their cane. They concentrated upon raising it for sale to mills of greater efficiency and financial resources."[4]

Jenks asserts that "the idea of industrial units of large capacity and improving mechanical and chemical efficiency was thus not an American innovation after the war with Spain. The American contribution was to apply the idea with greater resources."[5]

The *colono* system was another development which accompanied the introduction of the *central*. It decentralized the management of large sugar estates and enabled new areas to be brought into production. The small farmer or *colono* was usually bound by contract to plant a certain amount of cane, and deliver the cane to the *hacendado* or mill owner. The *colono's* farm was also known as a *colono*.

AMERICAN INVESTMENT

American investment in the island's economy resulted in a steady increase in trade between the two countries during the 1880s and 1890s. In the United States, the McKinley Tariff of 1890 had reduced the import tariff on sugar and abolished the tariff on molasses, and this provided a further boost for Cuban exports to that market.

The Spanish-American War of 1898 had left the United States in control of Cuba, and a US military government headed by General Leonard Wood ruled the island from 1 January 1899. One year later, when Cuba became legally independent of Spain, the island was still denied full sovereignty. The provisions of the Platt Amendment of 1902 gave the Americans the right to intervene to protect life and property. Wood noted that the amendment had effectively blocked Cuban independence and prepared the way for US annexation of the island.[6] He regarded Cuba as, "the most desirable acquisition of the United States", prizing it as being "easily worth any two southern states, probably any three with the exception of Texas".[7] The US occupation of Cuba ended on 20 May 1902, and by the following year, the Americans had secured a reciprocal trade agreement with the new Cuban government.

The war had destroyed property and devastated estates, many of which did not recover. At the end of the war, "previously prosperous agricultural regions were now scenes of desolation and depopulation, with nothing to export and barely the means to meet subsistence needs".[8] Louis A. Pérez Jr observes that it was for sugar that the Cuban combatants had reserved the greatest punishment. "And not surprisingly: sugar, the principal subsidy of imperial rule and source of colonial inequity. The destruction of sugar was the cornerstone of Cuban strategy. By 1898 insurgent armies had totally disrupted and all but completely destroyed the foundations of the colonial economy."[9]

César Ayala supports this point made by Pérez, and suggests further that the "struggle against Spanish colonialism was combined with social struggle against the planter class of Cuba".[10] Ayala argues that US control of the government contributed to the displacement of the Cuban planters from the dominant position they enjoyed in the Cuban economy before 1895.[11] He comments that the US occupation "dealt the planter class a second blow by depriving the Cubans of the opportunity to reorder their economy according to national priorities".[12] In effect the war gave rise to social as well as economic disruption.

Pérez notes that while the Cubans saw the destruction of the colonial economy as their means of gaining independence, the Americans viewed the restoration of the sugar system as their means of securing dominance in their relations with Cuba. The strategy pursued by the United States was one which was intended to lead to the integration of the island's principal export crop into the American market system. This would provide the economic base on which to secure entry for American exports to the Cuban market and lead ultimately to political union.

General Wood openly opposed public credit for the Cuban planters. The destitute planters, without access to public credit, "had one of two choices: borrow from American creditors or sell out completely to American buyers".[13] Foreign financial capital controlled bank loans for economic activities on the island, and the first US-owned banking institutions were established in Cuba during the first US intervention, as noted by Jorge Ibarra.[14] Access to credit from these US institutions was restricted to those who could offer the same guarantees as those provided in the United States.

As Pérez indicates, the properties destroyed during the war became easy and cheap acquisitions for American entrepreneurs: "North Americans arrived with capital resources well out of proportion to their numbers, and with equally disproportionate advantages in an impoverished economy. They arrived determined to transform the economic purpose and social function of the land from public domain to private development, from communal to corporate, from the family plot to the commercial plantation."[15] The Americans gained control of vast tracts of land in the province of Oriente. All the factors were favourable for their investment. The Reciprocity Treaty of 1903 reduced the tariff on Cuban products imported into the United States by 20 per cent, and a similar preference was given by Cuba to the importation of American products. The treaty also provided for an extensive free list and other advantages.

The value of this relationship is demonstrated in the figures for 1915, when Cuba sold 81.1 per cent of its total exports to the United States, and bought 67.4 per cent of its imports from the United States. Notably, that the duty paid on these imports amounted to only 54.2 per cent of the total duty paid on all imports. However, the percentage of duty paid on imports from any and all other countries was higher than the percentage of the value of these imports to the total value of all imports. It should be noted though that disruptions caused by World War I would have affected the island's trade with Europe.

For Pérez, the new corporate *latifundia* dramatically signalled the restoration of the colonial economy: "When Chaparra commenced operations in

Table 2.1. Value of Cuba's Imports and Exports for 1915

Countries	Importation	%	Duties	%	Exportation	%
United States	104,723,108	67.4	14,325,214	54.2	206,164,414	81.1
Other Countries of the Americas	8,022,586	5.2	2,408,402	9.1	3,356,875	1.3
Germany	799,903	0.5	197,771	0.7	–	–
Spain	10,817,435	7.0	3,053,513	11.5	8,021,230	3.2
France	5,197,110	3.3	1,215,608	4.6	1,135,404	0.4
Great Britain	15,287,998	9.8	3,218,339	12.2	33,033,016	13.0
Other Countries of Europe	6,203,081	4.0	1,168,293	4.4	1,864,769	0.7
Other Countries	4,397,012	2.8	869,640	3.3	716,048	0.3
Total	155,448,233	100.0	26,446,780	100.0	254,291,756	100.0

Source: Bustamante, *Cuba*, 42.

1900, it was the largest mill ever built in Cuba, the first *central* to employ twelve rollers and boast an initial capacity of 200,000 bags of sugar. Chaparra represented 10 per cent of the 1900 harvest. By 1902, of the 233 *centrales* in operation, Americans owned 55, representing some 40 per cent of the island's total sugar production."[16] Chaparra would become a place of employment for several of the British West Indian migrants, as Cuba became an increasingly important source of supply of sugar on the international market.

Writing in 1915, Albert G. Robinson describes the island of Cuba as "the most important source of commercial cane sugar".[17] He reports on the annual output of over two million tons, which more than doubled the figure for 1903, the first year following the revolution of 1895 that such a large harvest had been realized. Robinson attributed this growth to "the large increase in demand in the United States, and to the advantage given Cuban sugar in this market by the Reciprocity Treaty of 1903".[18]

There had been a precipitous decline in beet sugar production in Europe, as

Table 2.2. Quinquennial Averages for Cuban Sugar Production, 1856–1915

Quinquennial	Tons
1856–1860	414,000
1861–1865	494,600
1866–1870	682,000
1871–1875	682,200
1876–1880	572,600
1881–1885	547,664
1886–1890	645,544
1891–1895	933,470
1896–1900	272,427
1901–1905	943,330
1906–1910	1,396,037
1911–1915	2,215,811

Source: Bustamante, *Cuba*, 59.

a result of the destruction wrought during World War I, and this proved to be a stimulus for the expansion of sugar production in Cuba. In 1917 a Sugar Equalization Board was established in New York to ensure the delivery of supplies to the Allies, and to control prices. The influential sugar lobby in the United States was adamant that the price should be determined by market forces, and the price of sugar rose rapidly because of the strong demand at the time.

Robinson traces the annual cycle of sugar cultivation and harvest in Cuba as he observed it in 1915:

The cane grows throughout the year, but it begins to ripen in December. Then the mills start up and run until the rains of the next May or June suspend further operations. It then becomes impossible to haul the cane over the heavily mired roads from the muddy fields. Usually, only a few mills begin their work in December, and early June usually sees most of them shut down. The beginning of the rainy season is not uniform, and there are mills in Eastern Cuba that sometimes run into July or even into August. But the general grinding season may be given as of about five months duration, and busy months they are. The work goes on night and day.[19]

This production cycle occasioned by the expansion in the cultivation of sugar gave rise to an increased demand for cheap labour, a demand which could not be met from within Cuba. Another factor which no doubt would have contributed to the labour shortage was the genocidal war against the black population that killed some six thousand Afro-Cuban males in 1912. These men were able-bodied workers who had followed Evaristo Estenoz and Pedro Ivonnet in the ill-fated insurrection of the Partido Independiente de Color (PIC), and their absence would have been felt in the labour force during the years following the uprising.

IMPORTATION OF FOREIGN LABOUR

Some observers attributed the growing importance of foreign contract labourers in Cuba to the revolt of 1917, in which Cubans were demanding better working conditions and salaries in order to cope with the inflation created by World War I. However, the practice of importing foreign labourers on a contractual basis had started well before this. There was a precedent in the previous century, when construction work on the first railroad in Cuba began.

Work had commenced in 1834, nine years after the first steam-driven railway began functioning in England. It was the first railroad laid in Latin America and the Caribbean, and proved to be extremely successful. In short order, all the major sugar-producing areas of the island were serviced by railways: "The construction and operation of the railroads increased the demand for an already scarce supply of local labor. The government authorized the railroad companies to import their own labor, in order that they would not compete with the sugar planters who were their best customers. The railroads, therefore, began the system of foreign contract labor in Cuba."[20] Imported white labourers, mainly from Ireland, were used in the initial phase of construction. From England, France, Germany and the United States came engineers and other skilled operators. Asians and Afro-Cuban slaves completed the labour mix.

In relation to sugar cultivation, Knight asserts that, "from its inception, the Cuban plantation agriculture depended upon imported skills, imported capital, and an imported labor force".[21] Later, during the early 1900s, as Pérez observes, the United Fruit Company's operations had experienced labour shortages: "The north coast had lost much of its population during the war, so that when sugar production commenced, United Fruit received government authorization to introduce Canary Islanders as permanent settlers through the port of Gibara. United Fruit abandoned the colonization scheme several years later in favor of short-term contractual arrangements with West Indian workers."[22]

Some observers argue, however, that the foreigners were brought in, not because of a lack of sufficient local labour, but because these people were less demanding than the Cuban workers and were willing to work for less. The *Asociación para el Fomento de la Inmigración* asserted that the power of the Cuban worker was a direct result of a lack of sufficient manual labourers in the country and that this power could be reduced by introducing foreign labour into the Cuban market.

In 1917 the association published a booklet outlining its programme. It relates how a group of *hacendados*, or landowners, had met to formulate a programme. The meeting had taken place upstairs of the National Bank of Cuba, notably with the assistance of Dr Eugenio Sánchez Agramonte, the secretary of agriculture, commerce and labour. The booklet looks at the factors which contributed to what the association described as "a very real crisis for Cuba": "A scarcity of labourers in the fields has always been a problem of extraordinary importance for Cuba. First, the population movement towards the cities in the years following the constitution of the republic; then the tremendous increase in agricultural production, which exceeded all possible expectations in recent times; and more recently the war in Europe closed the doors to migration for those nations."[23] The association asserted that it was an urgent necessity to find labourers to attend to agricultural work. They stated too that the association would not have merit if it were concerned only with meeting a need of the moment and brought immigrants to Cuba, who, because of their race or low physical and moral qualities, would soon have to leave the country or who would notably diminish the efficiency of the native population.

It added that it was casting its eyes only to Europe, and preferably to Spain and the Canary Islands, where lived men of their religion, who would better adapt to their fields and enjoy their way of life, and leave forever among them the sediment which the constant flow of workers deposits, "an injection of good blood into their circulation".[24]

On 3 August 1917, President Mario Menocal approved immigration legislation authorizing the entry of foreign labourers, provided it was guaranteed that they would not become charges on the public purse or threaten the public health of the country. Alejandro de la Fuente cites Cuban fiscal sources as indicating that "between 1917 and 1931 some 300,000 Haitians, Jamaicans, and other workers from the Caribbean region entered the country to work in sugar plantations",[25] and explains that "the Cuban government had sacrificed whitening to sugar production for as a popular saying put it, *sin azúcar no hay país* (without sugar there is no country). According to the sugar barons, without West Indians there was no sugar."[26]

The 1917 law required the immigrants to be registered with the Department of Immigration on arrival in Cuba. It stipulated that any immigrant who committed a crime and was condemned for it would be returned to the country from which he or she came, after having suffered the penalty imposed by the Cuban court. The immigrants were also required by this law to provide proof that they had been engaged in agricultural or industrial labour in their home country or in the country from which they had arrived. In addition, they had to present some person or entity who would assume responsibility for them in case of illness, who would meet the cost of their burial in the event of death, and who would pay to repatriate them if they were found to be unsuitable for the work or would constitute a charge on the public purse because of lack of employment.

Regulations to enable the execution of the 3 August legislation were issued on 29 October 1917. They were published in the form of Decree 1707 in the official gazette of 2 November 1917. The provisions of the decree stipulated that any company or entity which sought to import labourers was required to apply for permission to the secretary of agriculture, commerce and labour, stating the number of labourers, their nationality and the country from which they would arrive.

It was also required to deposit a surety for each immigrant, to guarantee the performance of contractual obligations. This surety could be in the form of cash, Cuban government bonds or certificates of any finance company legally established in Cuba. According to the regulations, immigrants could be no younger than sixteen years of age or older than fifty, except in the case of families immigrating with direct dependants.

The surety for immigrants arriving from North America, Central America, the West Indies and the Bahamas, Europe, and the Canary Islands, or nationals of these countries, was five dollars. For immigrants arriving from Japan or the Pacific islands, or citizens of these countries, it was twenty-five dollars. For Chinese immigrants, or immigrants arriving from China, the surety was fifty dollars.

The decree gave authority to the secretary of agriculture, commerce and labour to fix the surety for immigrants from countries not specifically mentioned in the regulations. Furthermore, any person, company or entity importing labourers intended for hire by another person or entity in Cuba, was required to submit – in addition to the previously stated per person sureties –

another surety of no less than ten thousand pesos for non-Chinese labourers, and twenty-five thousand pesos for Chinese workers. Anyone not authorized to import labourers caught trying to do so would be subject to a fine of fifty pesos per labourer, and five hundred pesos per labourer for a repeat offence.

The regulations stipulated that the workers admitted under the law of 3 August 1917 were required to disembark at the ports of Havana or Santiago de Cuba. Entities bringing the labourers to Cuba could ask permission to have them disembark, and if this were granted they would be required to meet all the associated costs by depositing a surety corresponding to the anticipated amount.

On arrival in Cuba, the immigrants were to be registered and issued with identification passbooks containing the full imprint of both hands on each page. The passbooks were made out in triplicate; one remained in the Department of Immigration, one was sent to the Central Office of Identification, and one given to the person, company or entity importing the immigrant.

Thousands of primarily male Barbadians and other West Indians were among those who made the journey to Cuba. Marc McLeod indicates that "of the 110,450 British West Indians to migrate to Cuba between 1912 and 1927, women accounted for 20,833 of them. Thus less than one in every five immigrants was a woman."[27] The ratios for Jamaican women migrants appear to have been higher than for the regional average. Alistair Hennessy points out that significant numbers of Jamaican women were part of the migratory flow: "There was a striking disparity in sex ratios with women regularly comprising each year 45 per cent of Jamaican immigrants. They were highly prized as cooks and domestics by American employers as well as for their knowledge of English."[28] McLeod notes, however, that "the 'typical' British West Indian immigrant was thus a literate, adult male who came to Cuba to work as an agricultural *bracero* in the eastern provinces of Camagüey and Oriente. Nevertheless, sufficient numbers of women and children settled in Cuba to form families and construct immigrant communities on the island."[29]

THE JOURNEY TO CUBA

A group of about one hundred men, mostly former soldiers, left Barbados at the end of September 1919 to work in the Cuban sugar industry. The men had been recruited by G.S. Archer, who was an agent operating in Barbados on behalf of the Cuban estate owners. He had sought permission from the authorities in

Barbados to recruit two thousand men, and the governor gave his approval on the condition that he give preference to any returned soldier who wished to go.

During World War I, thousands of West Indians had fought for Britain in Europe and the Middle East. When de-mobilization came at the end of the war, the ex-soldiers were sent back home. On 23 May 1919, the first group of 321 Barbadian soldiers had arrived in Barbados, and three other groups soon followed. With their experience of foreign travel and exposure to other ways of life, the returned soldiers might not have easily resumed their former lifestyles and status in the Barbadian society.

It is likely that the authorities regarded them as potential troublemakers, especially since many of them could find no work on their return home. The Returned Soldiers Committee had been established to find some form of employment for the men, and it was to emigration that the committee looked to solve their problem. This was one of the few instances of state-sponsored emigration.

There were no direct shipping links from Barbados to Cuba at that time, and travel between the two islands involved securing US transit visas and going via New York. Therefore, the recruiting agent Archer had to make arrangements for the men he recruited to travel via schooner. Basil Maughan describes the conditions on board ship:

> There were often more than 100 men per trip on board these boats. In those days travelling on deck was quite common on the small inter-island schooners, but this was for short distances with trips averaging about one day. The trip to Cuba lasted 4 to 5 days! By any yardstick these were primitive conditions, and the condition of the passengers by the time they reached Cuba was poor, to say the least.[30]

Thousands of West Indians were, however, prepared to endure the harsh shipboard conditions in order to get to Cuba.

SUGAR BOOM AND BUST

The fortunes of the migrants were intimately tied up with those of Cuba, since their opportunities for employment depended on economic conditions in the country. In 1920 Cuba experienced a crisis in its sugar production. Hugh Thomas describes the dramatic rise in the price of the commodity during this period, which he refers to as "the grand climacteric in the history of Cuban sugar, and a landmark in the history of capitalism".[31]

The sugar harvest began at the usual date, but by 18 February the world price of sugar had already risen to 9⅛ cents. This was well above any previous price ever obtained. Previously in Cuba it had been assumed that 5½ cents was enough to "stimulate the island to extreme prosperity". At this point a mania set in. The rest of 1920 was passed, day by day, in a dream-like atmosphere more reminiscent of a film comedy than real life. Up, up, up, went the prices. On 2 March, sugar sold at 10 cents; on 18 March, at 11 cents; on 27 March, at 12 cents; on 8 April at 15½ cents, and on 15 April, at 18 cents.[32]

This phenomenon, which became known as the Dance of the Millions, continued its trajectory until Cuba's sugar boom reached its climax in the week of 19 to 26 May 1920. Prices rose to above twenty cents per pound, resulting in a reduction in consumption. At the end of May, there was a sharp break in the price of the commodity, followed by a precipitous decline, which was most rapid in August and September. Other sugar-producing nations released their stocks on the world market, with disastrous consequences for Cuba. Panic in October led to a run on Cuban banks, to which the sugar producers were heavily indebted. Hundreds of West Indians who had managed to accumulate savings in the banks there were also among those affected by the crash.

In a comment on the crisis, the author of an article entitled "The Bursting of a Bubble" in a 1921 edition of the *Barbados Herald* writes: "The reasons for the bursting of the Sugar Bubble are not very hard to find. In the first place there are certain fundamental laws governing the value of products, and twenty dollars a hundred pound for low grade sugar was an outrage against these laws."[33] The article goes on to state that the Cuba Cane Sugar Corporation closed the 1921 sugar harvest with a total of four million bags. Sixty per cent of the total was unsold at the time of the article's publication.

STEAMSHIP SERVICE BEGINS

In January 1921, the Xavier Rumeau Line introduced a monthly steamship service between Bridgetown and the port of Santiago de Cuba, an innovation welcomed by the migrant workers whose only method of transport between the two ports had been via the overcrowded schooners. Hanschell and Company, agents for the shipping line, advertised the rates for passages at $110 for first-class accommodation, $75 for second class and $55 for third class.

All passengers had to be in possession of a doctor's certificate when they went to A.J. Hanschell, who was the local consul for Cuba. He posted a consular notice in the *Barbados Herald* of 19 February 1921 notifying passengers intending to travel to the Republic of Cuba that it was necessary for them to have visas stamped in their passports at the consulate before leaving Barbados. The only exceptions were emigrants under contract in accordance with the rules of the Government of Barbados.

No doubt those still considering migration to Cuba would have been encouraged by the headline in the *Barbados Herald*, which proclaimed, "Cuba Rapidly Returning to Prosperity". The newspaper reproduced an item by a Cuban correspondent in the London *Financial News* in support of its headline:

> The crisis brought about in Cuba by the huge surplus of sugar supplies following the boom which ended last year is now likely to pass and it is believed that within three or four months a normal state of affairs will exist. Several banks in the U.S. are prepared to come forward to the assistance of the Cuban Government and it is freely predicted that a loan of 50 million dollars will be raised to assist the sugar planters.[34]

By 1922 at least one other shipping line, the Webster Steamship Company, was offering service between the two countries. George P. Harding was passenger agent for the Webster line, which offered twice-monthly departures for Cuba. His advertisements in the *Herald* promised "low rates; good quarters; each persons has a bath; and 4½ days passage only".[35] Harding also assured the men that they would not be quarantined at Chaparra, and would be sent home at the end of the crop.

The author of an article in the *Barbados Herald* records one departure from Bridgetown:

> The *Wanderer III* of the Webster SS line sailed for Cuba last night with nearly two hundred Barbadians, who go to labour on the plantations. The Cuban crop opened in December and labourers are very much in demand for the reaping season. Prices are good and might improve as prospects of the crop are far brighter than they were last year, and sugar is expected to come back a little into its own.[36]

The article's author expressed the view that, "should the Webster SS Line maintain its service as promised, Chaparra and the other large plantations in Cuba should experience little difficulty in obtaining the labour required", and that Barbados would benefit, "not only from remittances, but also from the direct expenditure of the immigrants who will be constantly on the move".[37]

The movement of labourers between these two Caribbean sugar-producing countries continued unabated. When the SS *Belle Sauvage* arrived at Bridge-town from Cuba via St Vincent on 30 October 1923, there were two hundred returning migrants on board. The *Barbados Herald* of the following day reports, "of Barbadians there were 153; and of the other islands there were 12 for St. Kitts; 14 for St. Lucia; 7 Antigua; 7 St. Thomas; 4 Montserrat; and 3 Dominica".[38]

In December 1925, the British consul in Santiago de Cuba sent a letter to the chargé d'affaires in Havana apprising him that the SS *Vedette* had been wrecked off the coast of the Dominican Republic. According to the consul's letter, the West Indian labourers on board the vessel were coming from St Vincent, Dominica and Grenada to work in Cuba.

His correspondence highlighted the lack of safety precautions on board the *Vedette*. He stated, "I may also mention that this boat is good only for 212 passengers, and not for 650 as they had on board. Besides this she had no wireless nor a graduated Captain."[39] The letter also informed the chargé that, according to a cable received from Santo Domingo, all the labourers were safe and had been taken over by a sugar mill named San Roman.

Lack of public information regarding this incident was of concern to the *Herald*, and the matter was taken up in an article: "We have seen no reference either in the Cablegrams or the local Press to information of the loss of the SS *Vedette*, the Cuban immigrant ship, so well-known at this port, off the coast of the Dominican Republic. As far as we are aware, few, if any, Barbadians were aboard, though there were a large number of passengers."[40]

The chargé received another letter written on 15 July 1926, this one in reference to the *Angelita*. It came from the governor of Barbados. The ship had arrived at Bridgetown on 6 July with 578 persons on board. Of that number, 431 were contracted labourers who were returning home to Barbados. To make matters worse, on the way to Barbados 232 passengers had disembarked at St Vincent. The 280-ton vessel had left Cuba with almost double its registered passenger-carrying capacity.

Conditions on board the ships transporting these labourers to Cuba would eventually become a matter for the attention of the Government of Barbados. On 11 January 1927, the Barbados government passed legislation in an attempt to deal with this problem of overcrowding. The Merchant Shipping (Amendment) Act of 1927 amended the 1898 Merchant Shipping Act. The law restricted the operators of shipping vessels to carrying no more than one statute adult for every ton of the ship's registered tonnage. It also imposed a penalty or fine of a sum not exceeding fifty pounds if found to be transporting more than this proportion and an additional fine not exceeding ten shillings for every individual on board above the number allowed.

While some migrants were leaving their home countries for the cane fields of Cuba, others were returning home, either to resettle permanently or simply to spend the period between harvest seasons there. The *Herald* chronicles one arrival at Bridgetown:

> The Norwegian SS *Gieta* arrived from Cuba on Wednesday morning via Grenada with 252 Barbadian labourers, who have returned home after taking part, under contract, in the reaping season there. There were a few women and children amongst the number. The voyage south occupied 11 days, so the returned immigrants were dispatched to Pelican Island to complete the 14 days' period of isolation which must elapse between departure from a suspected port and the port of arrival. They will be released from the Quarantine Station today.[41]

The article goes on to state that the conveniences on board the ship were superior to those on any ship used in "the immigrant trade between Barbados and Cuba". The "sanitary appointments" and lifeboat accommodation were said to be sufficient, and there was no overcrowding. This was in direct contrast to the call from the *Barbados Advocate* to West Indian governments to "refuse emigration until proper arrangements can be made for transporting immigrants and proper safeguards provided for their health and safety".[42]

The *Advocate* article reports that the SS *Angelita*, registered to carry 450 passengers, had arrived in Bridgetown the previous Tuesday with 518 passengers. It had left the Cuban port of Chaparra with 849 persons on board. The conditions on board ship are described as "culpable indifference to human life and dignity" which could "only be paralleled in the annals of the African Slave Trade":

> There were no sanitary arrangements; there was no provision for cooking and the supply of food was grossly inadequate. Herded together in the narrow space, cleanliness was impossible and larceny was rife. There was absolutely no provision made for a marine mishap. The ship carried three life-boats which are capable of carrying fifty-four persons. These were lying on the deck and were not placed in derricks, so that, if a storm had arisen or any sudden disaster occurred, it would have been impossible to lower them. There was no sleeping accommodation and the men were vigorously kept in order by a number of policemen appointed by the immigration agent.[43]

AMERICAN SUGAR ESTATES

The critical factor which drew British West Indians to Cuba in appreciable numbers was the dramatic expansion of that country's sugar industry, largely as a result of American investment. Mark J. Smith gives the background to the establishment of Manatí, one such large estate which was located in the northwestern corner of Oriente province: "Manatí was established in 1912, at the peak of the period of foreign investment in Cuban sugar properties. The estate was hewn from land on which there had been little cultivation, and none of the commercial, export-oriented variety, then the dominant form of agriculture in Cuba."[44]

A total of thirty thousand acres was put under cultivation within eighteen months, and grinding started less than twenty months after land clearing began. Barry Carr writes of the tremendous amount of labour required to keep these mills functioning.

> At Manatí, for example, 6,600 men were involved in cutting cane at the beginning of the 1927 zafra, while at Chaparra the extraordinary number of 10,000 workers were employed in the zafra. Native-born workers could not or would not meet this increased demand for labor. Instead, the appetite for labor was satisfied largely through immigration, first from Spain and the Canary Islands and then from Jamaica, Barbados and Haiti. By the early 1930s there were between 150,000 and 200,000 Caribbean braceros in Cuba.[45]

The parent company of Central Manatí was the Manatí Sugar Company, which was incorporated in New York on 30 April 1912 and owned by the powerful Rionda family. The company's vast land holdings of over 200,000 acres extended into the neighbouring province of Camagüey.

The Riondas were also principals in the Cuba Cane Sugar Corporation. The establishment of the company was encouraged by the rise in sugar prices resulting from World War I. John Dumoulin states, in *Azúcar y lucha de clases, 1917*, that

> this firm was founded in 1915 by Rionda, and at an opportune time controlled seventeen sugar estates. It had capital of the then fabulous sum of fifty million dollars and made a profit of twelve million in 1916. It was the richest sugar enterprise in the country. Its directors were paid fabulous salaries and travelled like princes in special trains, according to the testimony of sugar workers who are familiar with this period.[46]

The American millionaire chocolate manufacturer Milton S. Hershey was another major investor in the sugar industry in Cuba. Hershey paid his first visit to Cuba in January 1916. According to the Hershey Community Archives, he decided to purchase sugar plantations and mills so that he could mill and refine his own sugar for use in his Hershey chocolate factory:

> The flagship of Hershey's Cuban holdings would be a new mill and town, Central Hershey, located near Santa Cruz. Much like his decision to build his chocolate factory and the town of Hershey, Pennsylvania, local Cuban businessmen cautioned Milton Hershey against his plans. The site chosen for Central Hershey was not close to transportation or a ready supply of workers. However, once again Milton Hershey envisioned the new town that would be constructed along with the sugar mill. His vision and concern for his workers resulted in a loyal workforce. The sugar mill was completed in 1918.[47]

It was there that my mother, Delcina Esperanza Marshall, was born on 12 January 1927. In chapter 13, she recalls her childhood in Central Hershey. Milton Hershey began adding mills to his property between Havana and Matanzas. He is reported to have paid a Señor Pelayo $8 million for his property, Central Rosario. Hershey would later add to his sugar holdings. In 1925 he also bought Central Carmen and Central San Antonio and in 1927, Central Jesus Maria.[48]

Leland Jenks notes, "as profits of the sugar business soared, an active market developed for all kinds of sugar property at fabulous prices".[49] Jenks reveals that nearly fifty mills – approximately one-fourth of the sugar factories in Cuba – had changed hands at the height of the sugar boom in 1919 and 1920.[50]

CUBAN-AMERICAN MARKET DOMINANCE

Not only was American investment in Cuba attracting away the potential labour pool for the sugar industry in the British West Indies, but it was threatening the colonies' preferential market in Britain as well. The American hold on Cuban sugar production was causing some concern for Britain and her possessions in the West Indies.

The British parliamentary undersecretary of state for the colonies, E.F.L. Wood, visited the West Indian sugar-producing islands and British Guiana in 1922. In his report on the visit, Wood reflected on some of the reasons why the West Indies looked to the United Kingdom for help. His comments were reproduced in the *Barbados Herald* of 16 September 1922:

The American preference to Cuba is 4 cents a pound i.e. about £2 per ton, but the production in Cuba amounts to above 3,500,00 tons, of which about 1,300,00 tons is surplus over and above the amount that can be absorbed by the American market. This Cuba production must be sold somewhere, and as Cuba possesses certain natural advantages – unexhausted soil, factories on a large scale – capable of dealing with 50,000 tons of sugar per year instead of the 7,000 tons or less in the British West Indies, and above all very large investments of American capital – the W. Indian producer fears that the Cuban surplus will be dumped, in spite of the British preference, at rates with which he cannot compete in the British market. These fears are at the moment strongly reinforced by a formation in the United States of an organisation called the Sugar Export Corporation, for the express purpose of refining Cuban sugar in bond and of marketing the refined products in Europe.[51]

Again in 1923, concerns were expressed in Barbados about the impact of Cuban sugar production on the island of Barbados. An article entitled "The Past and the Present: A Warning" appeared in the *Barbados Herald*. The author made reference to predictions of a shortage in the Cuban sugar crop, and he called on the governor to ensure that consumers in Barbados would have a sufficient supply of the commodity at a price which bore some relation to the local scale of wages:

Conditions in Cuba, which is the world's largest sugar manufacturer, determine the price at which the article is sold all over the world. Of course the speculator in America has a share in manipulating the prices. The higher these soar, the better is he pleased. To-day the price of sugar had reached a figure which bodes ill for the poor and middle class consumer in the near future. Barbados had a taste three years ago of what high-priced sugar means, and with the remembrance of that awful period still fresh in memory, it is safe to assume that the people here would not submit as tamely as before to a repetition of the unconscionable exploitation.[52]

The author suggested, "If the people of Barbados are wise they will make it plain that a recurrence of the 1920 scandal will not be taken lying down." In the author's view, there was no need to buy sugar to be distributed on the island at inflated market prices. All that was required was for the government to retain a certain amount of locally produced sugar in Barbados, and "compel dealers to retail it at the price which, considering the cost of production, leaves a fair profit".[53]

Barbadian labourers were being enticed to leave home for greener pastures in Cuba. The Cuban Sugar Producers issued glowing descriptions of life on that island's estates, which were included in an editorial published in the *Barbados Advocate*:

> Cuba is the greatest sugar country and the estates of the Cuban-American Company are the largest in the world; they are "Delicias" and "Chaparra", situated on the healthy north coast with hundreds of thousands of acres of canefields, hundreds of miles of railway, two great mills, churches, schools, a town of 10,000 people, electric light plant, bakeries, market places, theatres, clubs, public parks, hospitals, private wharves, a lovely harbour, good restaurants, a large concrete hotel, equal to any in the capital, and in fact every comfort to be found in the largest city.[54]

The article goes on to describe the excellent working conditions and comfortable accommodation which awaited would-be immigrants. The prospect of working in such an ideal environment would no doubt have been enticing to potential migrants. However, the West Indian emigrants would soon experience for themselves the realities of immigrant life in Cuba.

CHAPTER 3

~~~~~~~~~

IMMIGRANT LIFE IN CUBA

ON ARRIVAL IN CUBA, MANY OF THE IMMIGRANTS were subjected to unsanitary conditions at the quarantine station at Santiago de Cuba, a main point of entry.

The secretary of the West Indian Workers Union in Cuba, Henry Shackleton, had written in 1924 to the then governor of Jamaica, Sir Leslie Probyn, to complain about the conditions prevailing in Cuba. Shackleton complained that there were no bath or toilet facilities for the immigrants on arrival at Santiago. Many never received the portion of their deposit which was to have been returned to them if they were released from quarantine before the standard fifteen days had expired. This cause would also be taken up by British diplomats in Cuba.

AMERICAN INFLUENCE

The Spanish-American War of 1898 had left the United States in control of Cuba, the former Spanish possession. Wayne Smith writes that soon after the end of the Spanish-American War, Cubans came to realize that "the United States has simply replaced our old mother country . . . converting Cuba into a mercantile colony and the United States into the mother country".[1]

Smith describes the thirty-one years following the war's end as "the period of the full protectorate", "characterized by corrupt Cuban governments, which did what Washington demanded, and by growing U.S. financial interests in Cuba":

American investments in Cuba increased almost eightfold between the end of U.S. military occupation and the beginning of the world depression. By 1929, the total reached more than $1.5 billion, almost 30% of American investments in all of Latin America. More striking, while American-owned sugar mills accounted for only 15% of Cuban production in 1906, by 1920 they accounted for almost 50%, and by 1929 for a staggering 75%.[2]

It was not just their money which the Americans brought, but their racist manners as well. The American approach to race relations was one which marked their interactions with their Cuban hosts and would have a deep impact on the lives of the new immigrants.

RACE AND IDENTITY

The segregationist policies of the Americans found favour with the host government, as Jorge Ibarra observes:

> From the time of the first U.S. intervention, Cuban authorities sanctioned such old customs and racist practices as not allowing blacks or mulattos to stroll in the parks of some towns and cities, attend certain theaters or artistic performances, enter certain hotels and recreation centers, and so on. It was extremely difficult for black students to enter the University of Havana: In 1899 only 6% of the country's professionals were black; in 1907, 7%; and in 1919, under 12%.[3]

The practice of restricting Afro-Cubans from participating fully in the social and professional spheres and having a say in the major decisions affecting the country was quite evident when a new armed forces was set up to replace the Cuban Liberation Army. This ran counter to aspirations of those citizens of all races who had united to oust the colonial power.

Louis A. Pérez Jr affirms that "the issue of racism had long preoccupied the separatist leadership",[4] and that "a commitment to its elimination in Cuban society had moved into a position of central importance in the insurgent vision of Cuba Libre".[5] He says, "in fact, Afro-Cubans had secured key positions in a variety of separatist organizations, most notably the Liberation Army". He argues that the American intervention arrested and reversed these developments and strengthened the institutional foundations of racism on the island: "The vast preponderance of Cuban officeholders in occupied Cuba were white. In dissolving the Liberation Army, moreover, the United States destroyed the one national institution in which Cubans of color and modest social origins had achieved status and power. Instead of the Liberation Army, a microcosm of the ideological undercurrents and social composition of the revolution, there emerged the rural guard – white, pro-American, devoted to serving property."[6] As they went about their daily life, the West Indians would encounter these rural guards, and on many occasions would be worse off for the experience.

Ibarra outlines the impact which this policy had on the composition of Cuba's disciplined forces:

> As the census of 1899 indicates, of 4,824 soldiers and police, 794 were black. In the 1907 census only 1,178 of the 8,238 members of the armed forces were black. By 1917 the composition of the army varies slightly; of 16,238 soldiers and police, 4,200 were black. Although 60% of the soldiers of the Cuban liberation army were black, they were prevented from taking part in the new republican institutions until 1959.[7]

Vera Kutzinski asserts that "there is no question that racial prejudice was in part fostered by the initial US occupation of the island (1898–1902), a period during which military units were segregated for the first time in Cuban history, and severe restrictions were placed on the immigration of black workers from Haiti and Jamaica".[8] However, Kutzinski does not lay all of the responsibility for racism in Cuba at the feet of the Americans. She admits that

> though it had somewhat different manifestations in the Hispanic Caribbean, racism had not exactly been extinct from the region prior to the North American occupation(s), as is evident, among other things, from the growing disdain with which the socially more "advanced" class of mulatto professionals in Cuba treated the "uncultured" masses of black laborers, augmented by immigrants from Jamaica and Haiti, whom they perceived as an insult to Cuban civilization.[9]

Elizabeth McLean Petras examines how the West Indian immigrants in Cuba were exploited for political ends. She argues that the bloody race war between white and black Cuban workers in 1912 and the existence of a well-organized PIC "motivated the companies to hire black immigrant workers in an effort to divide and undermine the unity of the national black working class".[10]

Kutzinski points out that the PIC was founded in response to the 1908 elections, when, despite campaign promises from both the Moderate and the Liberal parties to end racial inequality, not a single black politician was elected to office. The PIC had been disbanded after the *Ley Morúa* was passed in 1910. This law prohibited the formation of political parties on the basis of race. However, the issue had not been fully resolved and, with the revolt of 1912, there was a demand for the legalization of the PIC. Pérez observes that "political grievances ignited social protest. They were not unrelated, but they were separate. Afro-Cuban politicians demanded a place in the republic, and mobility. Afro-Cuban peasants demanded a place on the land, and permanence."[11]

Kutzinski states that "race riots broke out in Havana and Oriente Province, posing a threat to North American–owned sugar mills and mining companies, particularly in southern Oriente". The province of Oriente was known as the "black belt" in Cuba. The riots had started on 20 May 1912, and the United States had a major role in quelling this conflict:

> Within three days 700 U.S. marines were sent out from Guantánamo, a center of insurrection, into the surrounding hills. The revolt was quickly crushed everywhere but in Oriente. Thus, most of the fighting took place there, where the massacre of Afro-Cubans by the Rural Guards became commonplace. . . . On May 31 a contingent of marines was landed at Daiquirí, the same place they had first landed 14 years earlier. The U.S. forces freed up the Cuban army and Rural Guard to randomly attack the Afro-Cuban population. Thousands were killed, many by decapitation or other forms of grotesque mutilation.[12]

Aline Helg notes that, on the diplomatic front, representatives of foreign governments preferred to observe. Helg makes the charge that, "as for foreign observers in Oriente, they were aware that the truth behind the events was not that independientes had started a 'race war' but that blacks were being killed principally because of their skin color. The US and British consuls informed their superiors of the blunt facts but did nothing to stop the massacre."[13] The uprising came to an end when Lieutenant Pedro Ivonnet – one of the leaders of the *Independientes* – was shot to death in Oriente on 18 July 1912.

Melina Pappademos notes of the PIC that "their egregiously unsuccessful uprising ended in violence: thousands of black men, women, and children were slaughtered, mutilated, hanged. Black efforts to mobilize along racial lines for equality, then, were made both illegal and untenable."[14] Helg contends that the underlying racism against blacks which was unmasked by these events remained long after 1912, and that "it signified the end of black Cuban radicalism even up to the present".[15] As Aviva Chomsky states, the social construction of race was intimately tied to questions of sovereignty and economic development. She argues that the arrival of large numbers of black West Indians added another element to the ongoing debate about the place of Afro-Cubans in their own society: "U.S. domination had cultural effects on understandings of race, not simply by spreading racism, as some have argued. People from across the color spectrum in Cuba debated the issue of race and the nature of 'Cubanness' in the context of a large, ongoing immigration, and of social and economic changes brought about by US investments."[16]

Chomsky concedes that some of their arguments were simply racist, but they also argued that the West Indians were undesirable because they were imported by foreign companies and their presence facilitated foreign profits from Cuban resources.[17] So the reception which the black West Indians received has to be regarded within the context of the Afro-Cubans' own struggles for equality and inclusion and Cuba's efforts to negotiate their national identity in the face of American dominance.

THE UNITED FRUIT COMPANY

The United Fruit Company had been formed in 1899 from a merger of several US-based companies. The transnational firm came to represent the commercial expression of US imperial interests in Latin America, or as Jason Colby describes it, "the intersection of corporate power, U.S. expansion, West Indian migration and local aspirations".[18] He argues that the company's managers and other white Americans carried a complex legacy of race and labour with them. West Indian workers at the company's Guatemala division rose up against their American supervisors in December 1909 in response to an abrupt reduction in wages, racial discrimination and the shooting of a Jamaican. The Americans wanted the revolt crushed, while British diplomats intervened and persuaded the workers to return to work.

United Fruit's treatment of black West Indian workers throughout Latin America was the subject of protests and petitions by Marcus Garvey. The company was given permission by the Cuban government to begin importing West Indian labour in 1912. According to Ramiro Guerra y Sánchez, during the two terms of President Mario Menocal – May 1913 to May 1921 – eighty-one thousand Haitians and seventy-five thousand Jamaicans entered Cuba.[19]

Rolando Alvarez Estévez describes the company as a "trafficker in cheap labour"[20] and notes that many of the Jamaicans who migrated to Cuba did so under the aegis of the United Fruit Company:

In analysing Jamaican migration to Cuba, one must keep very much in mind the role which was played by the transnational United Fruit Company, which years earlier had invested large amounts of economic resources in Cuba as well as Jamaica.

According to the needs of the United Fruit Company or the Nipe Bay Company, the workers travelled on shipping lines owned by the former, after paying a moderate price for their passage. Having maximised its important capital investments in Jamaica, the United Fruit Company facilitated and propelled the migratory flow to Cuba where its economic interests were much stronger.

Oscar Zanetti states, "The West Indian workers constituted, in more than one sense, the optimal solution for the manpower needs of the Company. They were a cheap labour force, highly productive and easy to manage."[21]

The company practised a rigid form of segregation in housing on the estates which it owned and operated. Marcial Ponce was born on a sugar estate called El Cielo near Matanzas city and worked at a number of estates. He recalls the segregated neighbourhoods of Central Preston, which was owned by United Fruit:

> The workers were divided into the poor and the miserable, in blacks and whites and yellows. The people were divided into barrios, one which was called Washington, with comfortable houses, gardens, swimming pools and a club. This was a neighbourhood exclusively for the Americans. There was another neighbourhood called New York, which was for the professional workers, with a club for whites only. The other neighbourhood was Brooklyn, with simple houses and barracks for the black Jamaicans and Haitians. And there was yet another neighbourhood for the Chinese and Spaniards.[22]

Similar housing conditions existed on the company's estates at Banes and Macabí. The houses of the agricultural workers were made of cheap materials and had dirt floors; "in contrast, the houses of the North American employees, and in some exceptional cases, for some Cuban employees, were made of the best materials. . . . Within these housing areas, neighbourhoods were separated according to the category and race of the occupants, and within each of these sections the quality of the houses varied. The barracks for the agricultural labourers were the last rung in this stratification."[23]

The salaries paid to the labourers were generally low during the United Fruit Company's first fifteen years of operation in Cuba. For a twelve-hour day, a factory worker earned $1.00, and a first-class carpenter, $2.25. The United Fruit Company referred to its professional employees of English or North American origin as "first class Anglo-Saxon employees" in order to separate them from the other employees.

CONFRONTING DISCRIMINATION

While they were essential elements in the expanding sugar industry in Cuba, the West Indian immigrants were not welcomed with open arms by the general population. With the collapse of the Cuban sugar industry in 1920, as Leland Jenks indicates, "workers who recently had been actively recruited from abroad suddenly became unwanted surplus labor, and pressures to rid the island of the West Indians began to multiply".[24]

A 1924 editorial in the *Barbados Advocate* reports that Cuban newspapers, in calling for an end to the importation of this foreign labour, described the workers as a "fruitful cause of every kind of disease",[25] and made the assertion that their customs, morality and colour were extremely prejudicial to the progress and morality of the Cuban people.

The *Havana Post* of 2 August 1924 reproduced an item from *El Avisador Comercial* which had the headline "Undesirable Immigration", which called for an end to immigration from the West Indies: "It is a well known fact that the Antillian immigrants in Cuba live in great promiscuity and do not follow even the most elemental mandates of sanitation. It is quite true that the Jamaican and Haitian works [sic] cheaper than the Cuban, but dut [sic] to their customs and peculiarities they are not at all a favorable kind of immigration for our republic."[26] The writer of this article makes a recommendation to the political parties which were then preparing their political platforms for general elections. He recommends that "one of the planks should be the exclusion of Antillian immigration in Cuba and the stimulation of Caucasian immigration from Europe and especially from Spain and the Canary Islands".[27]

Pablo Llaguno de Cárdenas elaborates on these points in a 1924 publication. The publication was dedicated to General Gerardo Machado and his electoral campaign, and urged the government to put curbs on West Indian immigration. His argument was that at the end of the sugar harvest only 20 per cent of the immigrant workers were employed and the other 80 per cent became mercenary vagabonds of sorts because they had nothing with which to occupy themselves.

Llaguno de Cárdenas comments that this situation held no cultural benefits for the country, and in fact did much damage to the native species through mixing with such inferior classes with their congenital defects.[28] He contends that in Haiti and many of the islands of the Lesser Antilles the descendants of tribes from the interior of Africa practised witchcraft and cannibalism, and

these were the immigrants which *centrales* were importing "in their exces-
sive anxiety to enrich themselves, smothering our illusions of improving our
country".[29]

This was the society into which black labourers from Barbados and the other
West Indian territories migrated. While migration to Cuba did enable many of
these migrants to earn much higher wages than they could at home in Barbados
and the other West Indian territories, it also proved to be a testing ground.
Their reception in Cuba was sometimes hostile. That they were foreigners was
a factor which accounted for some of the hostility which was directed towards
them, but that they were *black* foreigners was even more critical.

As the editorial in the *Barbados Herald* of 15 June 1929 remarks, "conditions
in Cuba have never been quite as good as stay at home West Indians could
wish for their more venturesome brothers".[30] However, to suggest that they
suffered only hardship would not be presenting a fair and balanced picture of
the migrant experience in Cuba. The immigrants sought to better their own lot,
and to interact positively with other members of the Cuban society.

SELF-HELP ORGANIZATIONS

The immigrants established a number of self-help organizations in their effort
to create community and confront the circumstances in which they found
themselves. They were the main supporters of Marcus Garvey's Universal
Negro Improvement Association (UNIA). By 1926 there were branches of the
organization in forty-one countries. At that time, UNIA had fifty-two chapters
and divisions in Cuba, the largest number outside the United States. During
this same period, there were only eleven branches in Jamaica, while Barbados
had four.

Marc McLeod asserts, "Garveyism in Cuba was primarily a movement of
British West Indian immigrants. While the development of the UNIA in Cuba
followed from the efforts of top Garveyites in the U.S. to spread their ideology
to other countries, the responses of local leaders to the conditions confronting
British West Indians in Cuba were even more important."[31]

McLeod notes that the emergence of the UNIA in Cuba coincided with
the economic depression of 1920–21, and "the efforts of UNIA organisers to
ameliorate the terrible conditions prevailing in 1921 won them the respect of
numerous British West Indian immigrants in Cuba". He notes that the spread

of Garveyism in Cuba received its strongest push by the arrival of Garvey himself on the island in March 1921.

UNIA would later present a petition to the League of Nations on 11 September 1928, "praying for the League's action in the matter of adjusting the international problem affecting the Negro race as a whole".[32] Among the areas of complaint listed, the petition described the circumstances of British West Indian immigrants in Panama and Cuba:

> In certain countries in the West Indies, like Cuba, our labour is discriminated against, and in little coloured republics like Panama, laws have been made specially discriminating against us. Recent laws have been made in Panama seeking to deny the Negro the right to enter that Republic, even in spite of the fact that the black people of the West Indies made the greatest contribution in helping to erect the Panama Canal, in making the place fit for healthy habitation.
>
> In Cuba, thousands of our people are held there in stranded condition, without any sympathy shown them by anyone nor any sympathy shown them by the respective governments of which they are nationals. Thousands of our people have been murdered in Cuba and in countries of South and Central America, without any interference on their behalf.

Another self-help organization was the British West Indian Centre, which was established in Havana in 1928. The *Barbados Herald* of 12 May of that year reproduced an item from the *Havana Post* which stated that the centre was "composed of a small group of colored men and women, whose object is to unite their fellow men, regardless of class, color or creed, for the purpose of education, religion, business and recreation".[33] The centre said of its education mission, "We shall endeavour to teach English to Cubans and Spanish to English-speaking persons. We believe this will bring about a clearer understanding between both peoples and so create the most harmonious relations among them." A nursery for children six months to two years old, a boys' training school and a branch of the Unity School of Christianity of Kansas City, Missouri, were among the other facilities offered by the centre.

However, it was not just in the capital city of Havana that the British West Indians settled. There were West Indian enclaves in other parts of the country as well. In eastern Cuba, the British West Indian Welfare Centre founded in Guantánamo in 1945 was another organization which was dedicated to looking after the interests of the migrants.

LABOUR AGITATION

Serious workers' movements were emerging in Europe, the United States and Latin America in the first two decades of the twentieth century. This movement regarded revolutionary industrial struggle as a means of destroying capitalism, and this would be achieved primarily through the solidarity of trade unions.

In Cuba, the labour situation was a complex one, in which the importation of West Indian labourers had been used to counter Cubans' demands for better wages and working conditions. West Indians were also used as strike breakers. However, despite the racist and nationalist agendas, some measure of worker solidarity was achieved. It is recorded that it was not only Cubans and Spaniards who participated in the sugar strikes which occurred in 1917, but West Indian workers as well. "One of the leaders of the whole movement was Vicente Martinez, a Spanish anarchist; another according to US authorities, was 'one William Benjamin, a negro, who is believed to be from Barbados'."[34]

The situation in which the immigrants found themselves had given rise to the formation of their own union – the West Indian Workers Union. Henry Shackleton, a Jamaican, was secretary of the union. Shackleton took part in the commission which drafted the charter of the Confederación Nacional de Obreros de Cuba (the National Confederation of Workers of Cuba). West Indian workers were represented in both the Second and Third Labour Congresses, which were held in 1925: "Both events condemned the treatment and exploitation of Antilleans and agreed to address laborers in their countries of origin to tell them the truth about working conditions on the island. Although it is clear that workers wanted to stop immigration, their emphasis was on the 'exploiters' who imported West Indians, rather than on the immigrants themselves, who were referred to as 'comrades'."[35]

While the sugar barons lived like princes, labourers in the industry regarded themselves as paupers and organized to demand better pay and working conditions. At Central Francisco on the south coast of Camagüey, which was also owned by the Riondas, there were three strikes in the month of December 1919 alone. The workers were striking for recognition of the union, an eight-hour workday and a 25 per cent increase in wages, along with some smaller concessions.

General manager Gerard Smith had noticed three men among the Francisco workers whom he judged to be more intelligent than the others: "Rionda was anxious to know if these three were foreigners, for if they were foreign trouble-makers they should be sent away. As it turned out the three men were foreign labor organizers (nationality not recorded) and were deported in December at the beginning of the zafra. Their deportation set off a general strike."[36]

A letter sent in 1924 by the estate manager at Manatí to Manuel Rionda in New York discussed the termination of workers who were involved in a movement to organize labourers at Manatí. They had been asked to vacate the company houses which they occupied. The manager also reported on efforts to organize labourers at Chaparra: "The labor situation at Chaparra has recently taken a turn for the worse. Through Mr. Perez Puelles, Mayor of Puerto Padre, who was here yesterday, I learned that not only the colonos have formed a union but also the factory and railroad laborers of Chaparra, and now it appears that efforts are being made in the direction of also unionizing the cane cutters."[37]

On 23 January 1925, eighteen-year-old Rufus Hoyte left Barbados for Cuba as a stowaway. He arrived at Cayo Juan Claro in Oriente. Even though he had no emigration permit or labour contract, Hoyte found work at Chaparra. His employment there would soon be disrupted by strike action:

> I went out and had about a week cutting cane, then they had a strike. This is 1925. Well we was there during the strike. I believe it was about two weeks the strike was on, no working. Through the strike, the strike going on and men they didn't work-ing and they hear Manatí. They say, "We going down Manatí, man. Cut cane and get money, man." I say, "You all going Manatí?" They say, "Yes." But those men had went to Cuba already and know the place, you know. I said, "Look. I got a brother in Manatí. When you all going you can carry me with you?" They say, "Yes, you can come." But they got to steal away to go, you know, because this is contract. So they get up about two o'clock in the night and come and shake my hammock. "Get up. We going." I get up and put my clothes in the hammock, wrap the hammock, put the hammock over my shoulder and we gone.

With no contract, Hoyte was in a precarious situation. He and his compan-ions appeared to be less concerned about expressing solidarity with the striking workers, and more interested in earning what money they could.

The 1925 strike at Chaparra to which Hoyte referred caused a later-than-usual end to the reaping season, and consequently forced a change in the travel pattern of labourers recruited in the West Indies. The *Herald* reported on the arrival on board the SS *Servette* of "a couple hundred Barbadians" two days ear-lier. The men were said to "have a fairly prosperous appearance, and admitted that whilst agricultural work was hard it was readily obtainable".[38] Recruiting was to have resumed in December, giving labourers who intended to return about three months' rest.

The Communist Party's 1932 political platform devoted a plank to the issue of equality of all workers regardless of race or nationality, which included a denunciation of the exploitation and mistreatment of West Indians. The Communists mobilized dock workers and other categories of workers, but it was in the sugar industry that they ultimately enjoyed the most success:[39] "In 1932 they organized the *Sindicato Nacional de Obreros de la Industria Azucarera*, which led to some of the most important strikes after the fall of President Gerado Machado (1925–1933) with the cooperation of native and West Indian workers."[40]

REMITTANCES

The massive movement of Barbadian workers to Panama and Cuba had significant and far-reaching effects on social and economic development in Barbados. Remittances – the portion of international migrant workers' earnings transferred to the workers' country of origin from abroad – ushered in an era of relative prosperity for many black Barbadians.

Like countless other West Indians who migrated to Cuba, Colbert Belgrave's father felt it important to maintain links with his relatives back home during the fifty years which he spent in Cuba. It was a practice which helped to smooth the transition for the Belgrave family when they returned to settle back in Barbados in 1973:

> I remember my father telling me that how he sent like clothes, sometimes he would send money. And that was true because when I first came here, the first night I got here he took me to look for an aunt which is still alive, we call her Aunt Enid. And that's the only aunt I knew, really by correspondence, because my daddy used to correspond all the time with her. So there was that link, so when I came here I wasn't a total stranger. I knew someone.

Migrants who found work in Cuba's eastern province of Oriente during the rapid expansion of lands dedicated to sugar cultivation would have entered into a labour-scarce market where wages were high. Pérez explains, "the rapid expansion of sugar in the east had the immediate effect of creating a high-cost labor market. Wages began to increase, particularly during 1916 and 1917, as wartime production was gaining momentum."[41] Pérez cites weekly trade publications of this period which gave the wages of "ordinary hoe hands" as three dollars a day and, in some cases, contracted for as much as five dollars a day.

G.W. Roberts explains that, on the basis of information from the harbour master, "it is assumed that during the period 1901–20 money brought into the island by returning emigrants amounted to about £20,000 per year. The value of other transfers in the form of money, such as through banks and in registered letters, as well as in the form of merchandise sent to the island, is difficult to assess."[42] Roberts also notes that it was estimated that these remittances were sufficient to pay for between one-tenth and one-fifth of the annual imports of the island.

The *Barbados Herald* was a firm advocate of migration. The *Herald* spoke out emphatically against suggestions in 1925 that emigration from Barbados should be restricted as long as there was the slightest want of labour for the local cane fields.

An article in the 24 January edition of the newspaper argues that the economic benefits which accrued to the island from the migration of its citizens should be considered in any debate about the connection between emigration and the alleged shortage of agricultural labourers: "The Colonial Secretary in his last report on Barbados writes, 'There are a large number of Barbadians who have emigrated to Panama, Cuba and the United States, and these send very considerable remittances to their relatives here. . . . It would not be surprising to find these [remittances by draft and currency notes] total over £100,000.'"[43]

HARSH TREATMENT IN CUBA

That some of the migrants could accumulate money to send home can only be attributed to their thrift and resilience. At some plantations, workers were paid in *vales*, or vouchers, which were redeemable only at the company store. There were several incidents in which immigrant workers were cheated out of money they had worked for by their employers.

The migrants sent their savings home and they also invested in real estate in Cuba. Some were cheated out of property which they had bought. A letter from the British consulate at Santiago de Cuba to the British legation in Havana outlines a case in which a number of the migrants lost property in the small north coast town of Esmeralda in the province of Camagüey:

A number of Jamaicans bought town lots on the instalment plan, the contracts it would seem were made so that in the event of non-payment for the period of any three consecutive months the vendor has the right to forfeit the agreement and could confiscate the land. Upon the purchase of these lots several British subjects built themselves houses of varying values up to $1,000.00. The vendor of the land then saw a way of making money, and was not to be found when the Instalments fell due, thus making the time of three months lapse. He thereupon applied to the Courts for an injunction to remove these people from their houses. The Municipal Judge it would appear was in the game also and granted the vendor the injunctions asked for. These people have now been ordered to leave their land and houses.[44]

Others were imprisoned, beaten, shot or even killed by rural guards and plantation police who were the law enforcement agents. An unidentified Barbadian man was shot in the face by a Cuban policeman on 22 May 1924. He lost an eye in the process. The man said that he had been stabbed by a Haitian who ran away. When the police came they told the Barbadian to come to the prison. He said that it was while he was picking up a parcel to take with him that the police officer shot him and ran off.[45]

Of all of the reports of the harsh and inhumane treatment of West Indian immigrants in Cuba, the saga of Joe Williams stands out. The Cuban newspaper *La Discusión* reported on 1 July 1919, that the British government intended drawing up a letter of protest, and that the chargé d'affaires in Havana had called on the Cuban government to provide details of the lynching of the Jamaican, since he was a British subject.

That same day's edition of *La Opinión* informed its readers that a delegation from the Radical Reform Party had met with the secretary of the Cuban government, who strongly condemned the deed. He reportedly expressed the view that "everything should be done to bring the guilty ones to justice", since "such expressions of heat and temper ought not to be overlooked".

It was not until the *Barbados Herald* of 6 September 1919 reproduced an item originating in the *Havana Post* that details were made available to readers in Barbados. This item was also carried in the Jamaica *Gleaner* and found its way into the inter-colonial news section of the *Herald*. The headline reads: "Jamaican Murdered by Cuban Mob in a Town near Havana", and the subhead, "Was leading small white child in street in the middle of the day". The text is as follows:

Joe Williams, a Jamaica negro, was recently lynched by a crowd of three thousand citizens at Regla, after he had been captured while attempting to kidnap a little girl seven years of age. The negro was chased and overtaken and after a hearing in the police station, was locked up in jail. That was shortly after midday.

Half an hour afterwards, a throng of Regla citizens attacked the jail simultaneously from front and rear and, disregarding the shots fired by the police and jailers, battered down the front door, seized the negro, and after beating him severely, tied him to the tail of a horse, which was started at a run and kept going by blows from the crowd that followed.

When finally the exhausted horse came to a stop and the negro was cut loose from the animal's tail, he was dead and naked, the clothes having been torn from his body by the rough stony streets.

The people of Regla were maddened to the violent action which they took by the attempted kidnapping coming so close upon the frightful crime of the negro witches in Matanzas who, a few days before, kidnapping a white baby girl, tore the heart out of her living breast and made a meal of it.

No arrests have been made for the lynching of the negro, the population of Regla seemingly being unanimous in their approval of the swift justice dealt.[46]

The *Herald*'s reporting of this incident continues in a different vein. This time from the perspective of the Jamaicans:

A Jamaican residing at Havana declares to the editor of the "Gleaner" that the Jamaican was murdered for no crime whatsoever. He stated that Williams, who was employed in Regla, was in the habit on his way from work in the afternoons, of making presents of sweets to the little child. On the 28th ultimo he had no sweets or small change and when the child, as usual, called to him for the sweets, he told her to follow him to a fruit stand. She did so, and he called for 10 cents worth of mangoes.

Immediately a policeman came up, asked him what he was doing at the fruit stand with the child and, before a reply could be made, started clubbing the Jamaican quickly breaking both arms.

The policeman made a great noise, and a big crowd gathered. The policeman declared that the man was trying to kidnap the child – the police station was only two blocks away – and the injured man was dragged to jail.

In less than half an hour a crowd of three thousand persons gathered, stormed the jail, dragged out the half-dead man, placed a rope around his neck, one end of which was tied to the tail of a horse. The animal was then flogged into a gallop and when it stopped fairly tired out, the unfortunate Jamaican was dead and his body naked.

The Government doctor questioned the child, who said nothing was wrong with her.[47]

Further cases of ill-treatment were to engage the attention of British diplomats in Cuba. Some Cuban citizens were disdainful of this "British" factor in the growing debate about the Caribbean immigrants in their midst. Raoul Piedemonte, whose letter to the editor was published in the *Havana Post*, expressed his views on the West Indians' regard for their British citizenship. "Returning once more to the Jamaicans, who apparently think that their British masters have transferred to them some of their Anglo-Saxon super-humanism, it is most distressing to have them think that for the simple reason that better wages are paid here than in Jamaica, they have a right to come here just because their names are Tom Jones or 'Arry Smith, and not Juan Alvarez or Pepe Fernandez."[48]

The quest by the British West Indians to improve their economic lot in Cuba, and the maltreatment of many of them in their host country would ultimately propel them to the centre of a diplomatic tiff involving Britain, Cuba and the United States.

CHAPTER 4

~~~~~~~~~~

AT THE CENTRE OF A
DIPLOMATIC STORM

WEST INDIANS FROM ALL OF THE VARIOUS TERRITORIES in the region colonized by European powers were attracted to Cuba, but the overwhelming majority arrived from the British West Indies. The premium which the British West Indian immigrants placed on their "Britishness" had practical significance for them because they felt entitled to call on British consular representatives for assistance. It also had the symbolic value of membership in an imperial club, as a counterbalance to the prevailing view of them as a segregated minority.

Table 4.1. West Indian Immigrant Arrivals in Cuba, 1902–1907

	1902–1903	1903–1904	1904–1905	1905–1906	1906–1907	Total
Danish West Indies	5	–	–	6	81	92
French West Indies	–	–	–	23	32	55
Dutch West Indies	–	2	–	–	–	2
British West Indies	848	767	777	2,613	3,647	8,652

Source: *Censo de la República de Cuba 1907,* 64.

A DIPLOMATIC PROTEST

Matters came to a head between Britain and Cuba on 3 January 1924, when the British chargé d'affaires in Havana, Godfrey Haggard, filed a formal protest with the Cuban State Department against the ill-treatment of West Indian labourers.

In his letter to the Cuban secretary of state for foreign affairs, Dr Carlos Manuel de Céspedes, Haggard had indicated that consequent on a Cuban government decree of 24 November 1923, large numbers of "coloured immigrants" were required to be detained in the quarantine station at Santiago. He goes on to describe the "awful conditions" which those persons had been subjected to on arrival, and which had been the subject of representations by the legation:

> In fact, there were neither beds, sanitary accommodation, nor water. The immigrants slept, without distinction of sexes, on the cement floor. This situation, despite my complaints, continued without redress for months, if it does not still exist in its main features. In addition, these persons are the object of exploitation by reason of the difficulty, and sometimes the impossibility, of their reclaiming from the quarantine authorities that portion due to them as refund of the deposits collected from them on arrival.[1]

Haggard's diplomatic note also addressed other areas of concern regarding the ill-treatment of the migrants: "Conditions affecting the coloured British labourer appear to call for consideration, particularly in the Camagüey district. I might site among numerous cases the recent police raid on a Jamaican lodge at Ciego de Avila, when the property of the lodge was stolen and its members arrested and subsequently released without compensation or the explanations for which this Legation had asked."[2] That lodge was Rosa de Ciego de Avila No. 1, of which an H.A.L. Brown was the master. A memorandum enclosed in that same correspondence outlined another incident: "Laban Morgan and Wilfred Dixon, in crossing from one colonia to another near Ciego de Avila, were prevented by the Mayoral, and one of them was shot in the leg, which was broken. He seems to have been attacked merely because he was leaving the estate, and he has now, I understand, been thrown into jail on the accusation of his aggressor."

Haggard also wrote to Céspedes on 22 January 1924, informing him of the cancellation of a courtesy visit by Vice Admiral Sir Michael Culme-Seymour and His Majesty's ships *Calcutta* and *Constance*. He also wrote that if they did not receive a satisfactory response from the Cuban government to their note of 3 January, the British government would publish the note.[3]

More incidents involving the West Indians were reported by chargé d'affaires ad interim, Donald St Clair Gainer, to the Cuban secretary of state on 23 April 1924. They included the case of Edward Robinson and Bernard Hall, who were allegedly arrested on 24 March not far from Baraguá at Gaspar, Camagüey, on a charge of stealing a Cuban child, who was afterwards found to be asleep in its parents' house.

According to Gainer, "they were bound with ropes and ill-treated by the police, are at present in prison and have as yet had no trial".[4] Gainer also reported in that same correspondence on the case of William Hines and four others who were contracted to work on the estate of a Marcelino Gutíerrez at Ciego de Avila. He explains:

> They did work to the value of $1,184.96 and received an order from the contractor to collect at the offices of M. Gutíerrez. Payment was refused, soldiers were sent for, the men were arrested and locked up in the guard-house. On declining to work the next morning they were brutally beaten until the intervention of a non-commissioned officer. They were tried on some count or other and discharged. They have not yet received their wages.

In his response to all these charges, the Cuban secretary of state refuted the allegations of the West Indians and made countercharges, accusing them of being drunken, brawling mischief-makers.

An interesting development is that some of the British West Indians had adopted Cuban or Hispanic names by which they were also known in the community. For example, William Hines, who was involved in the incident on Marcelino Gutíerrez's estate, was also known as Julian Santiago. His four companions also had aliases; Charles Sandiford was known as Carlos Sanfifa, Leaman Higgins as Juan Jaime, Ruben Dailey as José Negro and Simon Wright as Juan Simon.

There was reference to a case involving Albert Barnett, who was known locally as Miguel Torre, and one in which Llewelyn Porter – also known as Francisco Blanco – was involved. This phenomenon of assuming aliases could be viewed in at least two ways. It could be seen as an attempt by the West Indians to facilitate their interaction with members of the Cuban community, who might have had difficulty pronouncing their anglophone names. It might also be seen as an effort to stave off the effects of the growing anti-immigrant sentiment, which would ultimately lead to forced repatriation.

Cuban writer, researcher and social scientist Carlos Moore, describes his own reaction to the psychological bruises inflicted by prejudiced teachers who made him painfully aware that his parents were not Cuban: "My non-Spanish name, Charles Moore Wedderburn, was an obvious indicator of my West Indian heritage. At eight, I repudiated 'Charles' and, despite being whipped by my parents for that affront against them, Cubanized it to 'Carlos'. At twelve I dropped one *o* from Moore to turn it into the perfectly Cuban surname Moré."[5]

CUBA'S RESPONSE

In August 1924, the Cuban government responded to the charges, publishing a "grey book" containing the notes and correspondence exchanged with the British chancery. Haggard had written to governor of Jamaica, Sir Leslie Probyn, in 1924 to inform him that he had sent the note to the Cuban government, "indicating the possibility of stopping all West Indian emigration to this country, and threatening them with publication of the Note unless they begin to behave better at an early date".[6] The British chargé told Sir Leslie that he had no doubt that the note would "come to publication in due course", and that "I have worded it as moderately and convincingly as possible with a view to creating an impression on the Cuban estate owners, from whom alone we can expect for [sic] reforms to come by reason of the pressure which it is hoped that they will bring to bear on their own Government in defence of their interests."

The Cuban secretary of state had shared the diplomatic note from the British legation with Aurelio Portuondo in confidence. Portuondo was a lawyer by profession, and an executive member of the Association of Sugar Planters and the Cuban Chamber of Commerce. He was also a vice president in the Cuban Trading Company and the company's liaison to the Cuban government. He advised the company on matters related to legislation, government regulation and labour disputes.

In a letter to his principal in the Cuban Trading Company, Manuel Rionda, Portuondo described the tone of the note from the British, which its author had described as "moderately and convincingly" worded, as being "harsh, almost aggressive"[7] and the charges as "more or less unjust". He added that in view of the fatal consequences for the company if the migratory current to Cuba were to be restricted or prohibited, he had offered to help Céspedes with the reply to the note.

Portuondo reported that the reply would make minute and well-documented reference to the efforts made by Cuba in favour of the Allies during World War I and to the advantages which they derived from the intense labour of the Cubans. In addition, the response would make very special reference to the benefits which Britain derived from the distribution and price of the sugar which Cuba handed over to the Allies.

Cuban governmental authorities and Cuban-American capitalists were aligned against the British in their representation of the British West Indian labourers. However, in his letter to Sir Leslie, Haggard admitted that in one area of the country the British West Indians were not getting the sort of vigorous representation to which they felt they were entitled as British subjects. This was because of a conflict of interest on the part of the consular representative stationed there: "Mr. Brice our present Consul at Santiago is a useful official, but your Government are no doubt aware that he derives a part at least of his income from the importation of coloured labour into Cuba from various West Indian islands, and he is little inclined to supply reports on the situation, to quarters interested, without instructions from this Legation."[8] He added that Brice was in fact in partnership with Mr Webster of the Webster Line, a fleet of ships which transported the West Indians between their home countries and Cuba, and that they had had "a falling out", with "allegations of dishonesty on either side". Webster sued Brice for damages of breach of contract.

On 29 March 1924, Haggard had ordered Brice to close the consulate and hand over all documents to the manager of the Royal Bank of Canada for safekeeping. Sir Leslie responded to Haggard's letter, conveying the information that Jamaican law contained no power of prohibition, "but, in view of this lack of power, the Privy Council have decided that an amending Law shall be introduced at the next sitting of the Legislative Council, i.e. in April next".[9]

Gainer, in a 25 June 1924 letter to British secretary of state for foreign affairs, Ramsay MacDonald, reported on a meeting with MacDonald's Cuban counterpart, Céspedes, to discuss the matter of the ill-treatment of the West Indians. Céspedes asked if he could call in Aurelio Portuondo. Gainer states,

> On being informed of the matter under discussion Señor Portuondo commenced on a long harangue explaining how beatific was the state of Jamaicans on all the property controlled by his companies or by members of the association, especially in Camaguey Province – a harangue which I interrupted to state that practically

every complaint recently received came from that very district, viz., Ciego de Avila, Moron, Sola, and other towns in the province.[10]

Thomas "T.J." Morris succeeded Haggard as head of the British legation. He had written to London to describe his reception in the new posting. His attitude towards the British West Indians whom he was duty-bound to represent is revealed: "My first few weeks here were far from pleasant. I remember arriving each morning at the office to find it blocked with aggrieved niggers, the local West Indian Societies pillorying me in their publications and *The Negro World* appearing with great headlines, 'Terrible treatment of West Indians in Cuba and British Legation does nothing'."[11]

When he had written to the principal secretary of state for the colonies concerning the status of relations with Cuba, he informed him that "the attitude of the Cuban Government towards us is distinctly unsatisfactory. Unless I misjudge the temper of the people it would require but little to bring about a break in diplomatic relations. The people resent our policy with regard to the West Indian question, and it may seem to them illogical to encourage the representation here of a country engaged in publicly denouncing its administration."[12] In light of this possibility of a break in diplomatic relations, Morris appeared to raise some questions about the advisability of pursuing the policy hitherto adopted by the British government: "We have important interests in Cuba. The British colony engaged in business is considerable: the principal banks are British, and we have over £16,000,000 invested in the railways. Without diplomatic representation these might suffer considerably. With the West Indian question therefore are involved other, and perhaps more important issues."[13]

The officials in London were not unmindful of these considerations. By January of the following year when Robert Vansittart of the Foreign Office wrote to the undersecretary of state at the Colonial Office, his position on the issue was that "it would appear that the policy hitherto pursued by His Majesty's Government has been pushed as far as it is capable of producing good results without risking an increase of Cuban obstinacy and possibly even a rupture of diplomatic relations".[14]

In his 1924 letter, Morris reported that "the total number employed on the sugar estates is estimated at 65,000: they come, for the most part from Jamaica, and include a number of the lowest types".[15] He appeared to be making a case for a more conciliatory attitude towards the Cubans, pointing to improvements at the Santiago quarantine station and a reduction in the use of *vales* (vouchers). Morris added that the police were accustomed "by necessity" to the use of firearms at the slightest provocation and to brutality as a means of repression, therefore, "the treatment of negroes is probably not much worse than that of their own people".

He took his argument further, expressing his feelings, not only about the West Indians, but his Cuban hosts as well:

> Under these conditions, primitive police, corrupt courts and a strong racial preju- dice against all negroes, coupled with the fact that many of those here employed are of the worst type, it would be idle to expect that difficulties from time to time will not occur.
>
> So long as the negroes behave themselves and avoid conflicts with the police they can go their way in peace. The report of the Governor of the Windward Islands, apart from the evidence of many others, goes to show that they are well treated, earn good wages and after going back to their own countries are generally found ready and anxious to return to Cuba.[16]

Morris said the Cuban government was confirmed in the view that "in most cases the negroes have only got what they deserved and the measures taken by the police have been necessary for self defense and the maintenance of law and order".[17]

The British consular official questioned the wisdom of his predecessor, Godfrey Haggard, in publishing the correspondence between Cuba and Britain on the West Indian question, stating that Haggard thought that it would evoke much more public indignation than had been the case. Instead, according to Morris, "a few short references to the White Papers appeared in the London Press at the time of their publication".

Morris wrote that the Cuban government had engaged a lawyer in the Min- istry of Foreign Affairs who was specially employed in answering the British despatches, "and whatever we may write representing a case from our point of view he, with no less perspicacity, will reply representing theirs". In his view, because of this, the value of correspondence and the policy of publicity had, "reached a point of having practically no value". For him, however, it had even more dismal consequences:

> On the other hand, from the West Indian point of view, the publication of the cor- respondence has had a most unfortunate effect in giving the negro an exaggerated notion of his importance and fostering the idea that he has only to complain, no matter what his grievance, for the Legation to support him. In consequence, letters appear here and in Jamaica from negroes and newly formed protection societies

encouraging agitation. Definite warfare is in embryo between the negroes and the Cubans and the position is really becoming a very difficult one.

Not only were the West Indian immigrants at the centre of growing tension between the British and Cuban governments, but the question of their treatment in Cuba exposed some strain in Anglo-American relations as well. In his letter of 23 December, Morris had advised the secretary of state that it would be unwise to continue to rely on the threat of prohibition of emigration from Jamaica as possible leverage in discussions with the Cuban government, since public opinion in Jamaica was averse to halting emigration. Morris pointed to another quarter from which they should not expect any help either: "Nor can we, on the other hand, count on any assistance from the United States. In spite of the predominant position they occupy in Cuba they meet with difficulties no less than ourselves, and realize that nothing short of intervention is likely to bring about any radical improvement."[18]

When Godfrey Haggard was about to end his posting in Cuba, he had written to the secretary of state for the colonies "to place on record a series of conversations with the Secretary of State and the President of Cuba, already reported privately to the American Department",[19] regarding "the suitability of Cuba and Great Britain raising their respective Legations to the status of Embassies". The Cuban officials were said to "have urged" this. However, Haggard did not appear to match their enthusiasm:

> It is difficult to imagine any grounds for acceding to the suggestion of Dr. Cespedes to establish an Embassy in Havana. British interests are small, and, if anything, decreasing: and there is no sign of an intention on the part of the Cuban Government so to direct their policy in the future as to enable them to grow. When Cuba rejected the British Treaty 20 years ago she threw in her lot with the United States and the tendency still further to increase her American connections at the expense of those with Europe, has been noticeable ever since.

The British government had requested its representatives in Cuba to provide comparative figures for British and American exports to Cuba, and the Americans were outperforming them by far.

AN APPOINTMENT FROM JAMAICA

At the height of the diplomatic exchanges between Cuba and Britain over the West Indian immigrants, the Foreign Office sent a telegram to the chargé d'affaires in Havana, Donald St Clair Gainer, informing him that the Jamaican government wished to appoint an official under the authority of the chargé, to assist in dealing with the interests of Jamaicans in Cuba. Gainer was asked to telegraph his observations on the proposal, specifically with reference to what status the official should be given, and whether or not his functions could be confined to Jamaicans.

On the following day the chargé sent a telegram indicating that he would welcome the appointment and recommended that the official be stationed in Santiago, "as two Eastern Provinces of Cuba contain a majority of Jamaicans".[20] He suggested that "his duties could consist in controlling entry of Jamaicans into Santiago, investigating complaints, and keeping in touch with local officials on Jamaican matters. Knowledge of Spanish essential. Would deprecate appoint[ment] of Jamaican as Consular Officer. Despatch follows."

In that promised despatch, Gainer expanded on his views on the matter. He wrote that if an official were to be appointed and paid by the Jamaican government it might be possible to dispense with a member of staff of the legation and so save some expense. The chargé stipulated that the official appointed "would however be required to be a white man, able to speak Spanish fluently and if not decentralized should be permitted to travel freely in the interior".[21] His recommendation was that he be decentralized since the provinces of Oriente and Camagüey contained more Jamaicans than the rest of Cuba. The figures for Camagüey during the 1923–24 sugar crop were roughly thirty-one thousand Jamaicans, so he felt that the natural place for a Jamaican official would be Santiago or Camagüey city.

There was more than a hint of exasperation in Gainer's tone when he explained why he would welcome such an appointment:

> At the present time this Legation and Consulate General is Jamaican rather than Imperial and the amount of work caused by West Indian matters is out of all proportion. This is especially true as regards 1924 where the correspondence received and sent out already exceeds the whole of the 1923 correspondence both inwards and outwards. It is not too much to state that 75% of this correspondence deals with West Indians, chiefly with Jamaicans and much of it has been with the Jamaican Government. Nothing is too trivial for a Jamaican to bring to the notice of the

Legation nor is he even satisfied with a subordinate official, he insists on seeing the head of mission for the time being. Thus other interests must be side tracked for the benefit of Jamaica.[22]

He then addressed the issue of status, expressing confidence in his ability to persuade the Cuban government to accept the official as a member of the staff of the legation, and suggesting several possible titles, among them "Jamaican Secretary", "Jamaican Agent" and "clerk in charge of Jamaican interests". His reasoning was that "if appointed British Consul or Vice Consul at an outlying post he would not expect nor would the Colonial Government expect him to do ordinary consular work – though that of Camagüey is in fact purely Jamaican, except for passport work which means only forwarding applications".

On the matter of duties, the British chargé felt that this official, apart from carefully monitoring the Marcus Garvey movement and similar movements, could well be employed in keeping in touch with government as to immigrants entering the country, since hundreds of letters were received from private individuals and colonial governments enquiring as to the whereabouts of immigrants.

The investigation of alleged cases of ill-treatment, dismissal without wages and similar illegal acts of which the labourers complained, was also given as an area which could occupy him. Gainer felt that "he could handle the corre-spondence covering these matters himself, though under the authority of the head of mission", and he circumscribed the scope of his area of influence by saying "he would have access to local officials only and only for the purpose of acquiring information and assisting Jamaican subjects".[23]

Despite his professed support for the idea of appointing an official, Gainer thought it important to point out that a precedent was being created and that "it is distinctly unusual, perhaps undesirable, for a Crown Colony to appoint an agent of any kind in a foreign country". Then he conceded that "conditions in Cuba are no doubt exceptional, and perhaps exceptional action is required to meet them". He then addressed the question of whether or not it would be desirable for this official to look after the interests of other British West Indians as well:

It should be rembered [sic] that "Jamaican" is a general term in Cuba for a British West Indian, and that thereare [sic] nearly as many natives of Barnados [sic], Grenada, St. Kitts and other Islands together as there are Jamaicans, the Jamaican proper is detested by his brother negroes from other colonies. Would these persons be handled by the Jamaican official or will he only deal with his own country men, and might not other colonies feel called upon to appoint an official too.

British and Jamaican officials continued to struggle to find the appropriate title for this official. The governor of Jamaica suggested "Assistant Secretary for Jamaican Affairs", and this was approved by the secretary of state. However, the British minister at Havana countered with "Inspector of Labour Questions". The Jamaican government proposed a salary of £800, house allowance of £300, travelling at rates allowed to a second secretary at the Havana legation, plus £200–400 a year for clerical assistance. T.J. Morris of the British legation in Havana recommended a slight increase in the clerical assistance allowance.

On 23 September 1924, H. Bryan, the officer administering the Jamaican government sent a confidential letter to J.H. Thomas, secretary of state for the colonies, requesting that a Mr Ian Hamish Campbell be considered as a candidate for the position. However, when Morris went to Jamaica to meet with the governor and interview the candidate, it was found that "he did not possess, on further acquaintance, quite the manner and personality required".

Harry Jocelyn Dignum, a forty-seven-year-old civil engineer and commission land surveyor, applied for the position, which he referred to in his application letter of 28 November 1924 as "Protector of Jamaican Immigrants". He indicated that he had been educated at Jamaica College, had spent three years as superintendent of lines in the Jamaica Government Railway and had also supervised the erection of King's House, the governor's residence.

Dignum also listed among his work experience five years with the United Fruit Company, five with the Punta Alegre Sugar Company and one managing a sugar mill for the Royal Bank of Canada. The Jamaican had been resident in Cuba for the fifteen years prior to his application, and boasted of being able to speak and write fluent Spanish. He also included in his letter that he was the brother of A.R. Dignum of the Colonial Secretary's Office and of C.B. Dignum of the Police Department, and that his father, A.B. Dignum, had been resident magistrate for Trelawny and Hanover at the time of his death.

There had been twenty-five applicants for the position, eleven of them claiming to be able to speak Spanish. With some reluctance, Morris agreed to the appointment of Dignum, who was the only one who seemed at all suitable and in possession of the requisite fluency in Spanish and well acquainted with local conditions in Cuba. Morris had learned on his return to Cuba that at Central Portugalete, the sugar mill Dignum had managed for Royal Bank of Canada, that he had "got into trouble with a married woman, and let her down rather badly".

In his report to the Colonial Office, Morris stated plainly that he would have preferred to find someone else, and that it would probably have been easy to find someone better from elsewhere. However, since the Jamaican government, in sanctioning the money for the appointment, had more or less stipulated that it should be given to a local man, he recommended to the secretary of state the appointment of Dignum as inspector for labour questions. Morris and the governor had discussed the title "at some length" and had agreed that "the title of 'Assistant Secretary of State for West Indian Affairs' is one that would hardly be suitable for the particular man in question".

Dignum's appointment letter of 23 December 1924, stated that he would be headquartered in Santiago de Cuba, his travel expenses would be reimbursed, the travelling allowance would be one pound per night for each night's absence, there would be no rights to pension, the position was subject to termination by a month's notice on either side, and he was expected to sail for Havana on 7 January 1925.

An item in the *Annual General Report of Jamaica* for 1924 stated that Dignum had been appointed under the title of "secretary of immigration", and, "as far as can be judged at the time of writing, the arrangement is working to the benefit of all concerned".[24]

Morris, then British consul in Havana, sent a telegram to the Foreign Office at the beginning of 1925, reporting that the Cuban government had appointed a staff officer of the rank of major, Major Lorenzo del Portillo, to accompany the secretary for immigration on a tour of the country. He stated that Major Portillo had specific instructions to cooperate with the secretary for immigration, and to: "use all possible influence with Governors and others to bring about settlement locally of outstanding cases to secure wherever suitable and possible release of prisoners awaiting trial and to devise means, probably by recommending deportation, of dealing with remainder".[25]

He added that he had received great courtesy and assistance from the government, and that if the new officials should prove efficient, "there now seems a chance that within a few months the problem may be solved and normal friendly relations with Cuba restored".

In March 1925, Morris wrote to Secretary of State Austin Chamberlain to report that a significant number of cases had been settled in a short period, and that "I should like to think that within a short time no British subject will be found in prison here". Morris's despatch of 6 May of that year to the Foreign Office stated: "I am glad to report that West Indian question is now entirely cleared up. . . . Have not had a single complaint of ill treatment for last three months, great number of prisoners have been released, better conditions prevail everywhere and relations with the Cuban Government are now most cordial and friendly."[26] Morris's optimistic assurance that the West Indian question had been "entirely cleared up" proved to be somewhat premature. Twenty-five years later British officials in Cuba would still be dealing with West Indian complaints of serious abuse by Cuban officials.

Dignum served for less than a year, giving notice on 30 September 1925, to take effect 31 October 1925. His successor was W.S. Ewen. He took up his appointment in March 1926 and served until the first quarter of 1931, when the affairs of the office were turned over to the British vice consul.

An article dealing with "West Indians in Cuba" in the *Barbados Herald* of 3 January 1925 reports that news recently received from Jamaica gave the information that that government had appointed an official to go to Cuba to watch over the interests of Jamaican labourers. The author of the article supposed that the action had been taken because of publicity given by the British government to cases of ill-treatment of West Indians in Cuba and raised questions about the role of British representatives there:

> The powers possessed by the British Consul in Cuba did not apparently extend to the protection of West Indians. It is inconceivable that West Indians would have suffered to such an extent, without the intervention of His Majesty's representative, if the British Consul were empowered to intervene. Jamaica has, with a high sense of duty and responsibility, decided that the care of her people in foreign lands deserves her most careful attention. And the appointment of a Protector of Emigrants is good evidence of that fact.[27]

The *Herald* article goes on to suggest that the Barbados government should take a leaf out of the book of the Jamaicans. It did not advocate appointing a protector of Barbados emigrants, but recommended that the Barbados government contact its Jamaican counterpart "and make some arrangement for their official to take some notice of the Barbados emigrants".

The author reasoned that since the sum of £2,000 had been voted for the newly created post, and it was estimated that about twenty thousand Jamaicans were employed in Cuba each year, the Barbados government could offer to pay the official the sum of £200 to £300, since it was "safe to place the number of

Barbadians in Cuba during the season at considerably over a thousand and perhaps two thousand". He acknowledged that of course everything depended on whether Jamaica would be willing to accept this arrangement, but felt that the idea should be pursued, "inasmuch as it is impossible for us to provide a whole time official".

Under the headline "The Problem of Migration", the *Barbados Herald* reproduced an item from the *Port of Spain Gazette* which stated:

> It may be that the decision reached as to the conferring upon the Jamaican Commissioner in Cuba a West Indian status will have some beneficial effects in enabling him to look after the interests of all West Indians seeking employment there; and while it has been urged as a sign that the W.I., as a whole, has thereby shown its recognition of the principle that every state is bound to look after its own subjects in foreign countries still, we venture to point out that it would be better by far if the people of the British West Indies were not compelled to seek foreign residence as a condition of earning a livelihood.[28]

This issue of wider West Indian representation had also been raised in the form of a question in the Jamaica Legislative Council in 1926, at the time of the appointment of Ewen to succeed Dignum. The response came that "no communication has as yet been addressed to the Governments of other West India Colonies as information in regard to the number of West Indians in Cuba is not yet available. I have reason to believe, however, that Jamaicans number only five per cent of the whole. The newly-appointed secretary will be instructed to obtain the exact details as soon as possible."[29] There is no indication of whether or not this question was ever raised with other British West Indian governments, however, the problems of the immigrants continued well after the 1920s.

PERSISTENT PROBLEMS

When the consular agent in Camagüey wrote to Havana in August 1951, he stated that cases of ill treatment of British West Indians were becoming "all too frequent" and unfortunately it was impossible to do anything about them locally: "Both Camaguey and Santiago, over the last eight years have had many of these cases of assault on British West Indians and even cases of murder and *in not one single instance* has any satisfaction been given. The local authorities stick together and when the case comes to trial, everything is against the B.W.I. and witnesses are afraid to declare against the Rural Guard or Police."[30]

AN APPEAL TO EMPIRE

Cornelius Brown, a Jamaican labourer from the district of Dover in the parish of St James, died on 6 May 1951, in what his fellow West Indians in the community of Elia viewed as suspicious circumstances. They wrote on 15 May 1951 to the British consular agent in Camagüey, J.B. Hall, concerning Brown's death. These concerned citizens stated in their letter that Brown had left home around 6:00 p.m. on Sunday, 6 May, and had not been seen the Monday morning. His disappearance had been reported to the police at about 6:00 or 7:00 p.m. that day. On Tuesday, 8 May, his body was found in a sewage pit near the homes of two rural guards.

According to the authors of the letter, the doctor who performed the post-mortem examination stated that Brown "died from homerage [*sic*] caused from blows in his face which knocked out some of his teeth".[31] The British West Indians were concerned about Brown's demise, but they were also anxious for their own safety as well if Cubans could ill-treat and murder them with impunity. They beseeched Hall to pay a visit to Central Elia to investigate the case. In their words, "We the undersigned as British West Indians and apart [*sic*] of the common Wealth [*sic*] of His Majesty The King, are earnestly making an appeal to you through His Royal Majesty the King."

Hall did make an effort to follow up the matter with the Cuban authorities, writing three letters to the police chief of the district. After he received no response, the consul then wrote to the police chief's superior, who informed him that their investigations revealed that Brown fell as a result of being drunk and suffered head injuries. In his report to Havana, Hall expressed the view that there was no more to be done regarding the case, and revealed that he had been informed that Brown was "a very heavy drinker".

In his 10 August 1951 letter, the British consular agent wrote to acquaint his principals in Havana with a case involving another Jamaican labourer, John Allen. However, he also made specific reference to the case of Cornelius Brown: "If I take up this case with the Officer in charge of the Rural Guard in the Province of Las Villas, nothing will be done. I already have a case very much like murder of a B.W.I. in Central Elia some months ago and can get nothing out of it, not even a reply from the Lieutenant of the District."

According to John Allen's brother Daril, his brother had rented land at Central Nasabal in Las Villas province from one Armando Franjul to plant rice. After the land was prepared and planted, Franjul demanded the land by force, saying that he wanted it to plant cane. Allen said that he would have to wait until he could harvest his rice, but the landowner insisted that he vacate the property right away. Franjul went away and brought back a lieutenant of the rural guard, who also demanded that Allen move. The guard struck Allen, who tried to defend himself. The men "sprang on him",[32] beat him "like a wild animal", tied him up and threw him in jail. The incident took place on 4 August 1951.

Daril Allen recounted all this to the British consular agent. He stated, "after finding that they cannot defraud him of his right concerning the land, now the Lieutenant and the guards them [sic] form a plot" to prosecute the Jamaican. They charged him with beating the lieutenant and threatening to kill him. He was not granted bail, and was apparently being denied food. Daril Allen sought the intervention of the consular agent, making an appeal on behalf of his brother as a subject of the British Empire: "You will have to take a drastick [sic] step so as to defend him in all cases so that the Cuban may know that Britain rules the waves and she cannot be slain." No doubt these sentiments would have been echoed by his Barbadian counterparts who had arrived in Cuba from Little England.

Allen's letter was supported by one from a Marcus Francis, another West Indian immigrant who described himself as "a Brittisher [sic] and a soldier of the first World War".[33] He corroborated Daril Allen's version of the events of 4 August. Francis signed his letter "Soldier and Brittisher [sic] for ever".

Thomas Aiken, a Jamaican friend of the victim, took up the correspondence to the consular agent in Camagüey two weeks later. He testified to Allen's poor physical condition: "According to his explanation to me and what I have observed when he had taken off his clothe [sic] and showed me his body, he was totally illbused [sic] like a wild animal. The blows which he had received by the Officerers [sic] of the Cuban Government which is seen and his body its [sic] beyond measure."[34]

This concerned member of the West Indian community was growing anxious because, thus far, no satisfactory response to the original appeal to the British officials had been forthcoming: "He told me that he wrote you a letter some two weeks ago informing you have [sic] the troubles and trials which he had past [sic] and you answered him stating that you have sent the letter to the Consular [sic] in Havana and at this present moment he as [sic] not got no answer from him nor from you, so he his [sic] very much troubled because at any moment he may be called in court." Aiken closed his letter with a plea:

"Please Sir I sincere [*sic*] implore your aid asking you to send something for him so that he may not have to be a trouble to each and every one, trusting you will oblige." The consular agent replied to Aiken, sending ten dollars. He later visited Allen in jail and found him to be a mild-mannered man who did not appear to be capable of the acts of which he was accused. The consular agent asked the chargé to "consider the advisability of taking up this case with the higher Cuban authorities in Havana". There is no indication of such action by the chargé in the records.

CHAPTER 5

〜〜〜〜

BARAGUÁ

THE MUNICIPALITY OF BARAGUÁ IS A LOCATION IN which significant numbers of British West Indians settled. It would appear to have been an oasis of peace and security for British West Indians residing there, while others located in that very province were subjected to extremely harsh treatment. Even though this isolated community was located in Camagüey, home of the Cuban Ku Klux Klan, it appears that West Indians there escaped the harsh racism experienced by their compatriots elsewhere in Cuba.

Baraguá is located approximately three hundred miles east of Havana, and approximately two hundred and seventy-five miles west of Santiago de Cuba. Baraguá lies forty-eight miles to the southeast of the city of Ciego de Avila, now the capital of the province of Ciego de Avila. However, when the municipality was established, Ciego de Avila did not exist as a province, and the area formed part of the province of Camagüey.

AMERICAN INVESTMENT

It was the enterprise of American investors which created the conditions for West Indians to migrate to Baraguá. In 1916 the American-owned Baraguá Sugar Company leased land in an area which was then in the southern part of the central province of Camagüey from a Domingo Dones to begin its operations in Cuba. Successor companies to the Baraguá Sugar Company were Baraguá Sugar Estates and Baraguá Industrial Corporation of New York.

When construction of the factory started, immigrants from the West Indies began arriving in Baraguá. It is estimated that more than 500 of them helped in the construction of the factory. Many of them came directly from Panama, where they had worked with Americans on the construction of the Panama Canal, to work in the American-owned sugar-producing operations in Central Baraguá.

The first *zafra* began on 31 January 1917 and ended on 11 June 1917 – a total of 130 days. That first harvest, with one mill in operation, yielded 17,262 tonnes of sugar. The following year a second mill was added. While the majority of the field labourers were Haitian, the British West Indians dominated the workforce in the factory.

Teófilo Gay recalls that at one point there were Barbadians in charge of the three shifts at the sugar factory. The three were Mr Lowe, Mr Maloney and Mr Roach, all members of the Christian Mission Church. The contributions of other West Indian workers were recognized when the factory celebrated its fiftieth anniversary in 1966. The records indicate that Messrs Stewart, Wellington and Charlemagne were present to receive their long-service awards.

In 1899 census figures put the population of the municipality of Ciego de Avila at 2,919,[1] and by 1907 it had reached only 4,242. There was a significant increase by 1919 to 16,408 during the period when the sugar estates were being established and immigrants were arriving to take advantage of the employment opportunities which they offered. This figure grew only marginally to the 17,849 recorded in 1931.

In 1907 there were 118,269 inhabitants in Camagüey and 455,086 in Oriente.[2] Five years later, there was a reported increase of 37,746 in Camagüey and 54,594 in Oriente. The largest proportion of British West Indian immigrants settled in these two provinces.

RECREATING HOME

The tall chimneys of the *central* in Baraguá dominate the town, and mature breadfruit trees and Jamaican ackee trees are among those that mark the areas where the British West Indian migrants settled.

Joseph Atwell says his parents never forgot their homeland, even though they never achieved their dream of returning home after settling in Baraguá:

> My mother and father were Barbadians, and we went to English school here in
> Cuba. My father came in 1917, and my mother came in 1920, and I was born in

1921. The first thing that my father always tell me is that Barbados is a very small country, but big in culture. And they have some of everything there, because they have tea meetings and various societies. And they always have some function to elevate the people over there.

Some of the other West Indian territories represented in Baraguá include Jamaica, Antigua, Grenada and Trinidad. Ruby Hunte reveals: "I was born in Jamaica, but leave from Jamaica small. My mother died when I was two years old, so I raise without a mother, with my aunt. My aunt brought me here to Cuba in 1918. Went back to Jamaica and come back [in] 1925, so from '25 I'm right here." Another member of the community Teófilo Gay explains his ancestry: "I born in Cuba. My father was a Grenadian, my mother was a Panamanian. They came here and they knew one another and they got married, and I am just a fruit from those countries."

Lilian Elcock was born in Baraguá in 1929 to Barbadian parents Millicent (née Weekes) and Charles Theophilus Elcock. Mrs Elcock was from Oldbury, St Philip, while her husband was from St Thomas. At the age of twenty, he had gone to Panama, and then from there to Cuba. In Cuba, he worked repairing the cars for the train which carried the cane to the *central*. She was a housewife who raised five children. Lilian Elcock recollects: "Our life was very nice. We was poor, but we could handle it. We had good teachers. My teacher was from Barbados, which his name was Fred Parris; a very nice teacher. He was very strict, but he was a very nice teacher." Elcock remarks that her mother wanted to take her and her sister to Barbados, but Mr Elcock did not allow it.

Gloria Nelson was born into this West Indian community in Baraguá in 1948 to Barbadian parents who met each other there. Her father, Oliver Nelson, had left his homeland at the age of twenty-two. She relates their story:

My father went to Cuba in 1920. My mother went to Cuba about 1917. My mother when she left Barbados was three years old. My grandmother took her to Panama. My grandmother's husband, he worked on the Panama Canal and when the work ended, there were three sisters – my grandmother and two other sisters. When the work was ended, two went to New York and my grandmother went on to Cuba, so my mother was raised in Cuba.

My father left from Barbados and went direct to Cuba, because they were recruiting people to go to work in sugar cane factory and things like that. So he went down there. But when he got there, instead of staying in Oriente where they landed, he went directly to Baraguá.

Resident in Barbados since 1970 until the time of her death in 2006, Nelson had fond memories of her childhood years in Cuba: "Growing up in Baraguá was fun. When we were young, we were a family of eight children. And it was a community like... mostly Barbadians, Antiguans, Jamaicans; we had one or two Trinidadians living there, but there were more Barbadians. And we were divided into Jamaica Town and Bajan Town, and we lived in Bajan Town. It was like a community, close community. Everybody knew everybody." Her father was a building contractor, constructing houses and boats, while her mother was a housewife. He was an influential member of the community and became Grand Master of Cuba District Grand Lodge No. 1 of the Masonic Lodge.

One of Gloria Nelson's childhood friends and neighbours was Colbert Belgrave. His father, Cleophas Belgrave, had travelled from Bridgetown to Baraguá in 1923, while his mother, Monica Gill-Belgrave, had migrated from Panama, where she was born of a Barbadian father and Jamaican mother. His father worked initially as a tractor driver in the sugar industry, while his mother was a housewife. Belgrave now resides in Barbados.

Another neighbour was Ethelbert Scantlebury, who had been born there in 1925. He was one of five boys, and they had one sister. Both of their parents were Barbadian. His father had gone over to Cuba after working in the Canal Zone of Panama. He worked in the sugar industry, first in the fields, then in the factory and finally in transport. The elder Scantlebury was also a member of the Masonic Lodge, and the Episcopal church committee. Ethelbert Scantlebury expresses his views on the labour and race-relations situation which pertained at the *central*:

> The coloured race didn't have no position inside there, [that is] to say, a good job. It wasn't easy because the work were scarce in Cuba. Let us speak about that, because the work were scarce in Cuba. Then many of the bosses, which you call the foremans [sic], which were Gallegos and other Cuban natives, they looked for the positions for their people, the white folks. We, the coloured race, really had was to seek a day's work, either on the sugar floor or on the dump.

PLACES OF WORSHIP

Religion was an important element in the life of the West Indian community. Colbert Belgrave lists the Christian denominations which were represented: "I remember that we had the Christian Mission, the Salvation Army, the

Episcopal – which you would call it the Anglican Church now – and the Seventh Day Adventist Church, as well as the [Roman] Catholic."

Gloria Nelson also remembers:

> We used to go to all. We had to go to all. Our parents forced . . . first and foremost we used to go to the Christian Mission, because we grew up in the Christian Mission Church. We had to go to Sunday school [there] on most Sunday mornings. Sunday evenings we go to Sunday school at the Episcopal, and then at night-time we go to church at the Christian Mission. And Saturdays we had to go to the Seventh Day Adventists. When the Salvation Army having their programmes, we used to sing and recite there. When the Christian Mission having their programmes, we used to sing and recite there. When they having a programme at the Episcopal, we do the same thing.

THE IMPORTANCE OF EDUCATION

Education was also very important to the West Indian migrants, and they ensured that their children received some level of instruction. The first public school was opened in 1920. One outstanding teacher there was William Preston Stoute. Stoute was from the Barbadian parish of St Philip. At the age of twenty-three, he had left Barbados for Panama, where he began his career as a schoolteacher. He achieved some measure of fame when he became chairman of the United Brotherhood of Railway Shop Laborers of Panama. In 1920 the Barbadian led nineteen hundred workers there in a two-week strike, and was held in jail for six months. After thus running afoul of the Panamanian authorities, Stoute left for Cuba. His son, William V. Stoute, who was still resident in Baraguá in 1997, tells part of his father's story:

> He was in Panama during the period of the construction of the canal. He started out as a teacher for the children of the West Indian and Latin American workers. He was also a trade union leader. The lives of the immigrants in Panama were not easy. The conditions of work were unfavourable. Housing and medical care were poor. Things were very hard. They decided to rebel and call a strike for recognition of their rights. My father played a very important role in this demand of the workers. My father came to Baraguá after 1920 because he had called the strike and submitted the strikers' 14-point demands and failed. He couldn't obtain the recognition which the workers were demanding, and he had to leave Panama and come to Cuba, because the first thing they did was to fire him from his teaching post. Then all doors were closed so he had to travel to Cuba.

On Stoute's death in Cuba in 1923, his obituary notice in the 31 March edition of the *Barbados Herald* stated: "He was noted for his vigorous advocacy of the rights of the Negro. Departing from the Zone to Havana, Cuba, to retire and live a private life, . . . he performed some very benevolent work for his race on behalf of the UNIA. He lectured on many occasions and caused thousands of members to enrol and live up to the redemption of Africa. He lauded Garvey."[3]

Because many of the West Indian migrants held the view that their stay in Cuba would be for a limited period, and that they would eventually return to their home countries, they made every effort to ensure that their children were taught English.

Teófilo Gay was a beneficiary of this education: "We had English schools over here. I reached sixth grade in English. Their way of thinking was very strong, because most of them believed, always studied, to go back home, so we studied English. The *Royal Star Reader*. Our school, everything in English. That's how we learn English, read and write, and that's how we speak English." Gay acknowledges that the curriculum of the West Indian students in Baraguá had much in common with others throughout the British Empire: "Our education system was based on the one which Great Britain established in all of her colonies. We learned the monetary system – pounds, shillings and pence. In Geography we knew the location of Nova Scotia, but didn't know where Venezuela was. We knew more British history than our own."

Colbert Belgrave also describes the kind of education he received in Cuba during his formative years:

> I went to school in Baraguá, the only difference was that it was mainly Spanish. We did the same things like what you do here [in Barbados], from primary to secondary level, then you go on either to college or university. And school, as here, it was only like forty-five minutes English. But my daddy, being that he was a true Bajan, and he always intended of coming back home to Barbados, he insisted that I would get private tuition. So he would send me to classes on evenings, which I did not enjoy at the time. So this old gentleman was a Jamaican teacher, and he would drill us with English until about six in the evening. So that was every day, from Monday to Thursday. Friday we would not go to classes because my parents were all Adventists.

Gloria Nelson also had her own experiences with the bilingual education on which the migrants insisted for their children:

> English was spoken in the community, and as a matter of fact, we used to go to school when we were children, we were small like four/five years old, before we go

to public school we used to go to the English school. And we used to learn English. Then after we go to public school, you start with your Spanish. But some parents used to maintain that their children go to private English schools up until sixth standard. And I remember clearly that there was a headmaster from the school, the private English school that they used to go to by the name of Santiago from Antigua. And he used to make sure that most of the West Indian parents send their children to learn English first, and then Spanish.

COMMUNITY RELATIONS WITH THE AMERICANS

Lilian Elcock remembers the Americans who owned and operated the sugar factory:

> They used to give us plenty help when we having any sport. They used to give us the bag of sugar. They send and make the buns to give us free, and when the cricketers coming in from outside, they used to give us an amount of goods to help feed the cricketers, and the fans that come along with them. They wasn't bad to us. It wasn't such a big pay our parents used to get, but they wasn't bad to us in those days.

Gloria Nelson also has similarly positive memories of the American presence in her childhood hometown:

> Where we lived in Baraguá they had . . . we called it the Spaniards' quarters . . . up the road. They used to have the Americans living in that area. Most Americans that owned the *central* and the sugar factories and what's not, they used to be living in those quarters. And I can remember vaguely . . . not the names or anything like that . . . around Christmas time they used to bring . . . they used to call them *aguinaldos* . . . gifts and fruits and apples to the people that work in the sugar factory, and bonus.

This benign relationship between the Americans and the immigrant community in Baraguá appears to have endured for a number of years. When the British vice consul in Camagüey, G.B. James, was looking for financial assistance for the repatriation effort in 1949, he also turned to the Americans there, specifically to T. Walter Killilea. He wrote to the consul in Havana stating: "I am hoping to obtain from the Baragua Industrial Corporation, a payment towards the cost of repatriating some of their former Barbadian workmen. This matter is having the attention of Mr. T.W. Killilea, Manager of Central Baragua, and I hope to get about $50.00 per head. Mr. Killilea is a good friend of mine, and will do his best for us with his Directors."[4] There is no indication in the records of the response to this request which James had made for funding for about twenty former workers at the sugar factory.

Even though Baraguá seems to have escaped the hostile confrontations experienced by West Indians elsewhere, it should nevertheless be noted that Baraguá was a society stratified by race and class. Colbert Belgrave does not hold the view that this constituted racial segregation: "I wouldn't say it was really racial division because I think that we knew exactly where we belonged. And there were a number of people, like all over, that they would kind of show you some kind of discrimination. Like they would say, well, 'We live here, and down there is what they call the *barrio*', which was the West Indian community, were mainly black people." Despite this stratification, Belgrave remembers that there was still "a lot of mixture of black and white in that area". According to him, "the Cubans would come down mainly to the West Indian club because it was always, I guess, the dancing was different and the music was different likewise".

Gloria Nelson's recollections of race relations in the community differ somewhat:

> Yes. There was racism and it still exists. I was kind of young then, but I found out then that my father, he was a man respected in the community, and a lot of white people used to come at my house and he used to visit a lot of white people. And my mother used to exchange gifts with some of them. We used to live good with the white people, but they still had people that showed their racism towards blacks and so on.

One of her older sisters, Olivia, won a beauty contest in 1953, an achievement which Basil Maughan regards as "not a mean feat in racially conscious Camagüey".[5] Nelson recalls that although her own parents enjoyed good social relations with the white citizens of the community, it was still a very racially stratified society: "They used to have two sets of people living in Baraguá – black and white. And they used to have . . . climbing the social ladder. They had people up there and down there. And they had a black society and a white society, with two clubs. The black people could not go into the white people club, the white people could not come into our club." The West Indians' club where they held their dances and other social activities was located in Bajan Town. It was called the Imperial Club.

Elsewhere in Cuba, the separation of the races was more strictly enforced. For example, at Central Conchita, which now has the new revolutionary name of Central Puerto Rico Libre, segregation existed at dances and other social events, and union meetings. These events were usually unmixed, or if black and whites came to the same official celebration a ribbon divided the dance floor, a demarcation which even mixed marriages had to respect.[6]

CELEBRATING EMANCIPATION DAY

From the time of their arrival in Baraguá, the West Indian immigrants displayed the culture of the countries from which they came on every first of August, which is celebrated as Emancipation Day. It is a tradition which remains alive to this day. Joseph Atwell remembers the sugar factory administration being an integral part of the celebrations:

> That is an old tradition. In times before the triumph of the revolution, the sugar company always give us a treat for the children. And they invite the children and explain to the children about emancipation, how there came to be freedom and so forth. Well after that and the new government took over, they called and a commissioner asked why it is that we don't celebrate First of August again. So we say those people used to sponsor it, the administration always sponsor it. Well the Party said, "No. We will sponsor it too. Make a list of all that you all need." And that's the way we do it. So every year it become stronger and stronger.

According to Gloria Nelson, the Episcopal Church used to be responsible for the Emancipation Day, but would have an ecumenical committee to help plan the celebrations. Dancers would plait the maypole; groups would sing songs such as "Sly Mongoose", "Millie Gone to Brazil", "Day O", "Hold Him Joe", "Da Cocoa Tea" and "Brown Skin Girl", and the donkey and shaggy bear would also entertain the audience. Nelson remembers that while it was a day for the entire community, it was one which the children in particular enjoyed:

> They used to play rounders on that day, and they used to have great cake, and they have the sweet bun and sugar water, lemonade. Everybody used to come, and they used to give out these things to the people and they used to come and eat and have fun, like a big picnic. . . . And they used to have maypole dancing on that day. They used to have a cricket match on that day, playing games and what's not.

Figure 5.1. Descendants of British West Indian migrants parade through the streets of Baraguá on the First of August. In the background is a wooden house with its slanted roof, typical of the West Indian section of the municipality.

Today, the First of August celebrations are still important to the community. For community leader Teófilo Gay, it is a way of preserving the West Indian culture in Baraguá:

> To preserve a thing you have to help it go on . . . and our First of August is one thing that we preserve over here to maintain our culture. We have small children that dance the *cinta* [maypole] every first of August. Now in our community, if you don't celebrate the first of August it's problems, because it's something, very strong in our community now. And you could see, not only black, white . . . not only descendants of English people . . . you can see Cubans, everybody. And the government, the [Communist] Party support it.

CRICKET CULTURE

The game of cricket has been another passion for West Indians for many years. Cricket was also an important element of the community's sporting and social life in Baraguá, as well as in the other West Indian immigrant communities in Cuba. Lilian Elcock remembers, "In our day it used to be plenty because it was

Bajan Town and Jamaica Town. And they always had fans for the two sides. But it was very nice in our days. They used to go and play in Havana; they used to play in Central Hershey."

Colbert Belgrave also remembers the cricket matches in Baraguá: "If we look at it from the West Indian point of view, I can't play cricket. I never liked cricket, but in Baraguá they used to play a lot of cricket. They even played, I remember I was small at the time, a team from Jamaica came and they played cricket."

In a chapter on the "Psycho-Social Aspects of Migration" in *Economics of International Migration*, Alfred Sauvy writes that assimilation is attained "when a former immigrant or his descendants can no longer be distinguished from nationals and are no longer conscious of their original characteristics".[7] Viewed from this perspective, Baraguá can be regarded as a bastion of British West Indian ethnic resilience in Cuba.

CHAPTER 6

～～～

RELIEF AND REPATRIATION

THE CUBAN BANK CRASH OF 1920 HAD HAD a severely adverse effect on the efforts of some of the West Indians to accumulate savings. Thousands of immigrants, particularly in Camagüey and Oriente, had been left destitute. For some, there was no option but to return home.

REPATRIATION

When the SS *Guantanamo* – a freighter – arrived in Barbados in early October of 1921 in the wake of the Cuban sugar crisis and bank crash, the 604 British West Indian passengers on board had been repatriated from Cuba at the expense of the Cuban government. Of the number, 328 were Barbadians. The others were from Nevis, St Kitts, Antigua, Suriname, Saba, Barbuda, Grenada, St Vincent, Dominica, Montserrat, St Lucia, Trinidad and Demerara. Almost two hundred other West Indians who were desperate to return home had been left behind.

Newspaper reports of the day indicated that the men had arrived from the port of Santiago de Cuba:

> Many of these men had accumulated at this shipping port since April and May, their numbers increased by immigrants who daily come in from the interior at their own expense, and who intended paying their passage home out of modest accumulations. Later, the wreck of the schrs. "Ada Ruba" and "Exploit" added considerably to the number and Santiago was soon the location of homeless men, broken in spirit and pocket.[1]

The Cuban government had at first not accepted responsibility for the men, and they had spent many months homeless and destitute on the streets of Santiago. The residents of that city, however, are said to have been "not lacking in hospitality. They issued food and permitted liberties of an unusual social nature. Hammocks were allowed to be strung in verandahs, and accommodation, as far as convenient, was permitted in outhouses &c."[2]

Eventually, the Cuban government made arrangements with the steamship company to transport the West Indians only as far as Barbados. While the Barbadians were landed at Pelican Island and quarantine arrangements put in place, the migrants from the other colonies were not to be similarly accommodated. The *Herald* states that "the local government was evidently not prepared to house them without first communicating with their respective Governments". The Barbados government deemed the replies from those governments to be unsatisfactory and refused permission for the other West Indian citizens to land. The ship returned to Cuba with them on board.

The country to which the Barbadian migrants had returned was not one which offered bright prospects. The editorial in the *Barbados Herald* of 15 October 1921 paints a gloomy picture: "Whilst the humanitarian will be pleased to welcome home again those hundreds of persons who emigrated to Cuba in search of employment and in the hope of bettering the unattractive conditions under which necessity forced them and theirs to eke out an existence, it is to be regretted that their island home can offer them nothing of any greater substantialness than sympathy."[3] The *Herald* editorial continues that emigration, which had proven so often to be the solution to labour problems in Barbados, was hardly possible, since there appeared to be no likely place to emigrate: "Cuba, the land of apparent possibilities, has failed us. Panama, once God's gift, is now barren of opportunities, and has been closed to us. British Guiana, which offered even at its best but little, has stilled her call; and look around us as we may there is not one single prospect that is pleasing."[4]

According to the *Herald* of 11 November 1922, the SS *Remelik* of the Webster Line had made three trips from Cuba to Barbados since September of that year, transporting 563 Barbadians who had been under contract with Chaparra Estates Limited. The last batch of 110 had arrived just the previous Sunday, and "evidently closed the list of contracted labourers for which Chaparra is responsible".[5] The newspaper reported in the article headlined "Repatriates from Cuba" that the *Remelik* would not be returning to the island to continue her fortnightly service between the two countries until December, but in the interim would ply between Cuba and Jamaica.

Around this same time, labourers were also being sent back to Barbados from Panama. On 6 September 1922, the SS *Albaro* arrived at the Bridgetown port from Colón with eighty-two Barbadians on board. They had been repatriated as destitutes by the Panamanian government.

CUBAN CONDITIONS IMPROVE

In a comment on the establishment of a fortnightly steamer service between Barbados and Cuba by the Webster Line, an article in the *Barbados Herald* of 21 October 1922, stated,

> Many Barbadians have, in the past, tried Cuba with benefit to themselves financially. Others who were unfortunate enough to be at work there during the 1920 crash in sugar prices and the ruination of the sugar trade, have suffered considerably. Could the latter have got out with their savings at the time of the trade slump suffering would not have been so great. But lack of steamship opportunity and the sudden restriction of employment completely eat up their capital gain and reduced them practically to a state of pauperism and semi-starvation. Conditions are now much improved. The sugar situation is being restored to normality, money is again being freely circulated and labour conditions are consequently seeming attractive.[6]

For those Barbadians willing to venture out to Cuba again, the government of the day made its position clear. The Colonial Secretary's Office issued a notice on 10 February 1923 informing would-be emigrants to Cuba that on arrival they would be subjected to a period of quarantine lasting fifteen days or more, and that conditions in some of the quarantine stations were "far from satisfactory".

In the notice, which was published in the *Barbados Herald* of 17 February, the Barbados government also clearly stated its position on the question of repatriation. Prospective migrants were warned that the government could accept no responsibility for securing their repatriation to Barbados should they desire to return, and that they were going at their own risk. They were advised "to satisfy themselves that they will be able to ensure repatriation either at their own expense or at the cost of their employers' as may be arranged".[7]

However, the Barbados government eventually assumed responsibility for the repatriation of some individuals. For example, the *Barbados Blue Book* of 1930 lists expenditure of twenty pounds for the repatriation of a J. Cox from

Cuba, and the Legislative Council subsequently voted an annual sum for the express purpose of bringing home returning nationals from that country.

HURRICANE RELIEF

It would not be their economic circumstances relating to the lack of employment from which the British West Indians would require further relief in 1926, but from the work of nature.

When a devastating hurricane hit Cuba on 20 October 1926, Havana province and portions of the provinces of Pinar del Rio and Matanzas suffered severe damage. A cable from Manuel Rasco-Portuondo, vice president of the Cuban Trading Company, to company president Higinio Fanjul indicated that the affected area stretched from San Cristóbal in Pinar del Rio to Jovellanos in Matanzas.[8]

The cable included press reports that wind speeds reached 150 miles per hour, and that ten-and-a-half inches of rain had fallen between 11:00 p.m. of Monday, 17 October and 3:00 p.m. of Tuesday, 18 October. Newspapers also put the number of dead at two hundred, the injured at more than three thousand, and the number of houses destroyed at four hundred.

Salvador C. Rionda's letter to his uncle in New York after a tour of the affected areas stated, "The countryside in general offers an aspect of desolation, as if a wave of fire had passed over it. The apparent cause is that the wind with its intensive velocity carried the water from the sea in waterspouts, inundating the pulverised countryside."[9] With regard to the hurricane's impact on the housing stock, Rionda added: "I can assure you, without exaggeration, that if this hurricane had passed over Miami or any other city in Florida, today nothing would remain of them but a memory. The modern buildings in Havana are the ones which have suffered the most, demonstrating that the Spanish colonists had the right concept of housing adequate for tropical conditions."

British West Indians were also among the property owners affected by the devastation caused by the hurricane. A list compiled by the British consulate in Havana contained the information given in table 6.1 on British West Indian house- and landowners whose properties had sustained severe damage or were destroyed.

Immediate relief efforts were undertaken in the wake of this hurricane to provide food, clothing and bedding for the displaced immigrants. British chargé d'affaires L.C. Hughes-Hallett had written to the American Chamber

Table 6.1. British West Indian Property Owners Affected by 1926 Hurricane

	Land		House
	Total Price	**Owing**	
Mullings, J.A. Jamaica	$480.00		$1,529.99 paid for
Powell, A. Jamaica			$200
Staples, Maud Jamaica	$750.00	$447.00	$650 paid on house $50 owing
Blair, Septimus Jamaica	$1,600.00	$260.00	$500 paid on house
Wood, Arnold Barbados	$800.00	$500.00	$900 paid for
Smith, Nathaniel Barbados	$1,000.00	$828.00	$1,000 paid for
Chance St Vincent	$3,128.00	$2,771.00	$1,800 paid for
Lowe, Aubrey Barbados	This man has paid for his land. House was a wooden structure on masonry piles, and was blown over. Can be reconstructed, but will require considerable expenditure.		

Source: Report from British Chargé d'Affaires, Havana, October 1926. FO 277/203.

of Commerce of Cuba concerning employment for Jamaicans out of work as a result of the hurricane.

Hughes-Hallett reported the deaths of seven Jamaicans, and estimated the number of destitute Jamaicans at between three thousand to four thousand who required food, clothing and bedding. He sent a telegram to the governor of Jamaica requesting permission for expenditure of five hundred dollars in relief for the most urgent cases, and a further two hundred pounds if necessary.

The branch of the UNIA and African Communities' League operating in Havana wrote to Hughes-Hallett to report that in their geographical area of responsibility, "We believe that after a careful study that there are about 1,500 British West Indian families that have suffered during the recent hurricane, comprising about 2,500 persons."[10]

The letter, signed by secretary Wilbert Barnes and chairman C.E. Arnold, recommended the setting up of three distributing stations to serve surrounding districts. The UNIA officials felt that this step was necessary in order to eliminate some of the infelicities of the existing relief effort which they had observed while conducting their study. First and foremost, they were of the view that British West Indians were not accustomed to meals handed out by Cubans, and preferred to "do their little bit at their homes irrespective of the amount given". In addition, they reported that "we have also been informed that British West Indians have been grossly insulted at some of these places where food is served, and on some occasions were told to go to the British Consulate where things would be provided for them. The next point is that the Natives would be served first in all cases, when as a matter of fact that was not done at the British Legation."[11] There is no indication in the records on whether or not the British legation acted on the suggestions of the UNIA officials.

Again in 1932, there was another call on British West Indian governments to provide relief for their citizens in Cuba affected by the passage of yet another hurricane. On 5 December 1932, the governor of Jamaica wrote to members of the Legislative Council with the news that the British minister at Havana had advised him that "about 4,000 Jamaicans have been rendered completely destitute as a result of the recent hurricane which struck Cuba and wrought extensive damage in the province of Camaguey".[12]

Governor Slater also informed them that the minister had indicated that a sum of one thousand pounds was needed for the relief of the most urgent cases of distress, and he requested the council to make a grant of this sum. When the matter was put to the vote, there were twelve nays and one aye. This decision was communicated to Havana, prompting a telegram to Governor Slater from the British minister shortly thereafter, asking if there was any information he could supply or anything he could do to induce a reconsideration. The minister asked: "Is there no prospect of even a sum smaller than £1,000, or must I accept negative decision as final and leave unfortunate people without any relief at all? Situation will be all the more difficult in that case because Barbados Government have cabled me £1,200 for their distressed natives. Please reply by telegram urgently!"[13] The Standing Orders were suspended to allow for a question which had been proposed, debated and disposed of to be proposed again in the same session of the council. This time, the vote was seventeen ayes and eight nays.

This initial reluctance on the part of the Jamaican government to assist takes on a new significance some years later when viewed in the context of a note in the minutes of a meeting of the British West Indian Welfare Centre in Guantánamo. Even though there had been reluctance to provide hurricane relief for British West Indians in Cuba, the migrants would later send such relief to their home countries affected by hurricane. The minutes recorded the acknowledgement of receipt of hurricane relief donations from members of the centre by two British West Indian territories – Barbados and Grenada.

MIGRATION PROSPECTS DIM

The Jamaican secretary for immigration in Cuba, W.S. Ewen, had shared his views on the labour situation there with the *Gleaner* newspaper of Jamaica in 1929. The report was reproduced in the *Barbados Herald*:

> In an interview which a representative of the "Gleaner" had with Mr. Ewen a few days ago he mentioned that there was still difficulty experienced by Jamaicans in finding employment in Cuba. The labour market was positively glutted and although warnings had been issued to labourers in this colony as to the difficulty of obtaining work, nevertheless, they continued to flock there. Mr. Ewen did not say so but from other sources a reporter of the "Gleaner" learnt that it is more than probable that in the near future the Government will have to repatriate many Jamaican labourers in Cuba who are out of work and who are experiencing the greatest difficulty to exist.[14]

In October 1929, the Barbados government amended the Emigration Act to require persons desirous of emigrating to foreign countries, other than under a contract of service, to obtain a permit from the harbour and shipping master or the chief clerk of the Shipping Office. They were also required to pay a fee of four shillings and two pence – approximately four times the average daily wage of the male Barbadian agricultural labourer – or else satisfy the permit officer that they possessed independent means to support themselves while abroad. A proclamation dated 4 October 1929 declared Cuba to be a country to which the provisions of the act applied.

There were also developments in Cuba at this same time that would have a direct effect on the prospects of the aspiring migrants. The Great Depression had created further havoc in an economy that was already ailing, and Cuba took steps to protect its labour market. The Cuban secretary of state wrote to inform the British minister at Havana that every potential immigrant would be required to appear before the Cuban consul with an application, which would have to be approved by the immigration department. According to the letter – reproduced in the 23 November 1929 edition of the *Barbados Herald* – this new rule had been instituted, "with a view to avoiding the entry into the territory of the Republic of undesirable persons", and also to "obviate financial difficulties for the immigrants and for the shipping company which brings them to Cuba".[15]

While these new rules designed to control immigration were being implemented, some British West Indians were also looking to return home from Cuba. In *Population Movements in the Caribbean*, Malcolm J. Proudfoot points to increasing return migration to Jamaica during this period: "From 1926 to 1929 an increasing movement of return was recorded. This movement reached its peak in 1931, when net inward migration was 9,400. After 1929, recorded departures of labourers to Cuba never exceeded 200, whereas repatriation continued at a heavy rate, and in the six years, 1930–1935, the recorded inward balance was 20,500."[16] This phenomenon was also noted in the *Jamaica Annual Report* for 1929, in which it was observed that conditions in Cuba and the neighbouring Central American republics continued to diminish:

> Conditions in Cuba were such that many Jamaicans who had established temporary homes in the Republic were unable to earn a livelihood there, and were forced to apply to the Secretary for Immigration at Santiago to be repatriated to Jamaica. This was especially so towards the end of the year, and the following figures are illuminating. In 1928, 156 Jamaicans were repatriated by the Secretary for Immigration; in 1929, no less than 840 were repatriated. Of these 122 were repatriated between January and June, and 718 between July and December.[17]

The negative trend continued, and the report for 1930 painted no less gloomy a picture about the situation in Cuba: "Conditions in Cuba during the year went from bad to worse. Unemployment was rife and numbers of Jamaicans who had settled in Cuba became destitute and had to be repatriated by the Government of Jamaica. During the year a total of 2,049 persons were repatriated at a cost of £5,462."[18]

Overproduction by the world's sugar-producing countries had led to another crisis in the industry at this time. At a conference in Paris in November 1927, the Cuban government had reached agreement with the main European sugar-producing countries – Czechoslovakia, Poland and Germany – to restrict crops. Cuba's 1927–28 crop was reduced to four million tons. However, it became evident in the spring of 1928 that Czechoslovakia was the only one of the three other parties to the agreement which had actually restricted their crops, while Germany and Poland had extended theirs. Cuba immediately dropped the restriction policy, and its 1928–29 crop was increased to five million tons, a figure which was matched by Java.

This overproduction of sugar lowered the price of the commodity in the open market to such a level that in most countries the cost for both beet and cane sugar was below the cost of production. This situation obtained even though, since the end of World War I, consumption had been rising at the rate of 4 per cent per year.

An article by Francis Maxwell on the sugar crisis was published in the 11 January 1930 edition of the *Barbados Herald*. He states that, "besides being the largest producer in the world, Cuba is offering on the open market an amount of sugar that is roughly equal to the total offered by all the other exporting countries put together, hence it is only natural that the island forms the focus of the present sugar crisis".[19]

In mid-1930 the United States increased the duty on Cuban sugar when it passed the Smoot-Hawley Tariff Act. This was another blow to the Cuban economy. Cuba's share of the US market declined precipitously. Louis A. Pérez Jr describes the impact of this development.

> The cumulative effect of this tariff policy was devastating. Sugar production, the fulcrum upon which the entire economy balanced, dropped 60 percent. Cuban exports declined by 80 percent, while the price of the island's principal export, sugar, fell over 60 percent. Sugar producers struggled to remain solvent by lowering wages and cutting production by laying off workers. The *zafra* was reduced again, this time to a sixty-two-day harvest – only two months' work for tens of thousands of sugar workers.[20]

Alan Dye comments, "It is difficult to overstate the severity of the consequences of the loss of market share and export revenue on the Cuban economy, since 80 per cent or more of Cuba's exports consisted of sugar, and more than half of it was exported to the United States."[21] He indicates that "the collapse threw the working population into destitution and the nation into a social and political crisis".[22] This development would spell trouble for the foreign labourers in Cuba.

ANTI-IMMIGRATION LEGISLATION ENACTED

By 1931 the Cuban government introduced legislation to curtail altogether the immigration of foreigners, including the West Indian labourers. It absolutely prohibited the importation of labour. The decree fixed a penalty of five hundred dollars and a six-month detention for those who broke the law.

A draft immigration bill was introduced in the Cuban senate by Dr Francisco Maria Fernández in January 1932, which sought to prohibit the entry into Cuba of all classes of immigrants, regardless of their gender, occupation, character or nationality. This prohibition was to be effective for a two-year period. The penalty for infraction was given as one thousand dollars or six months' imprisonment, or both. The immigrants involved in the infraction of the law were to be returned to the country from which they came, at the expense of the company which had taken them to Cuba.

With Decree 2232, published in the official gazette of 19 October 1933, the Cuban government initiated the first measure towards obligatory repatriation. The decree authorized the forced repatriation of foreigners found to be without work or any kind of resources. The government undertook to pay the passages of the repatriated immigrants and to provide ships at the country's principal ports to transport them to their respective countries of origin. A donation of two dollars was to be given to each returned migrant. The president of the republic had set up a special fund for the execution of this repatriation programme.

On 8 November of that year, *La ley de cincuenta porciento*, or the Nationalization of Labour Decree, was signed into effect. This and other measures were introduced by the Provisional Revolutionary Government of Ramón Grau San Martín, which as Pérez observes enacted reform laws at a dizzying pace, under the injunction "Cuba for Cubans": "In labor matters, government reforms included minimum wages for sugarcane cutters, compulsory labor arbitration, an eight-hour day, workers' compensation, the establishment of a Ministry of Labor, a Nationalization of Labor decree requiring Cuban nationality for 50 percent of all employees in industry, commerce, and agriculture, and the cancellation of existing contract labor arrangements with Haiti and Jamaica."[23] Pérez opines that perhaps under normal circumstances, these reforms might have met many long-standing worker demands, but they did not mean much when there were no jobs to be had.

St Lucian Charles Ray was one of the migrants who felt the impact of the new law. He had been working at the sugar factory at Chaparra:

Then afterwards a chemist came from the United States, American fellow. He was a good chemist, good chemist, nice guy. Then he wanted to open, apart from the factory, a laboratory. He call it *laboratorio de control* to control all the factories that belong to the Americans in Cuba. We had Chaparra, had Delicias, Tijuaron, Mercedita, Constancia *y la refinería de Cárdenas*, all these were American-controlled. So he wanted two guys to work with him, outside from the factory. Like this is the factory here, and that house over there is a big, big place. So he take that place and make a laboratory in that place. So I went to work with him, because the other guy that he took with him was a Cuban and don't speak English, so I used to translate the English into Spanish for the guy. I was a young little boy.

Ray's job was "picking up sugar, picking up molasses to carry to the laboratory for the chemists to test". With the passage of the new law, his job in the laboratory was in jeopardy.

I work at the factory until 1937. They throw me out from the factory, because they didn't want no more English persons to work. *La ley de cinquenta porciento.* They had to be Cubans. From 1936 they was behind me, but I still was working. Then the chemist told me, "They going to fire you, because they don't want West Indians to work in the factory." I say, "O.K." Then my friend who was a chemist, the Cuban guy, he told me, "Let's go to Puerto Padre. With ten dollars, I'll make you a Cuban citizen. And when they come behind you, they can't do nothing, because you'll be a Cuban citizen." I told him, "I don't care what the hell they want to do. Let them do what they like." [I was a] young boy; didn't care.

However, it was not only Ray who was affected by the changing labour conditions, but other members of his family as well, including his father, James Henry Ray.

But then my father was working in the factory and they kick him out. My brother was working in the hostel *como cocinero*, the cook; they kick him out. I say, "I don't care." In 1937 when the crop finish, then the American guy told me, "I can't keep you no more, because they behind you, so I have to let you go." I say, "O.K. Good. Let me go." I went and do my shoemaker work in Chaparra.

By 1935 organized British West Indian emigration to Cuba had effectively come to an end.

Basil Maughan concludes: "The tradition of emigration and the opportunity for it merely served to postpone the day of reckoning."[24] He argues that when large numbers of Barbadians could no longer find work in Cuba after 1935, and many of them were forced to return home, this helped to ignite the social unrest which soon followed:

> The emigrants returned to an unchanged plantation system and a lack of agricultural diversification, as well as high unemployment and very low wages. The rigid social system in Barbados had not changed in any way since the war. These factors, exacerbated by the Great Depression, contributed greatly to the disturbances of 1937. Had there been no large-scale emigration from Barbados during the early years of this century, the above factors, coupled with an exceedingly high population density, might have combined to create a massive social upheaval long before 1937.[25]

BRITISH WEST INDIAN RELIEF FUND

For the Barbadians and other British West Indians who remained in Cuba, the British government established the British West Indian Relief Fund in 1944 with a sum of twenty thousand pounds per year for the relief of these citizens of the empire, in order to cope with the worst cases of sickness and destitution.

The establishment of the relief fund was "contrary to the normal policy of not maintaining British subjects abroad except on a limited and temporary basis",[26] according to a letter from Thomas Brimelow, British consul in Havana, to the acting colonial secretary in Belize, British Honduras. Brimelow explained in his letter that, "owing to the Cuban Labour Laws which discriminate against all foreigners, many of these British West Indians are seriously affected and there is considerable distress among them".

Brimelow also informed the Belizean official that the Foreign Office had issued a notice in April 1945 indicating that from the first of that month the relief expense would be borne by the Foreign Office. However, the notice was careful to state that the Foreign Office wished "to maintain the principle that responsibility for distressed British West Indians is that of the Colonies of origin, while recognising that in the present instance the Colonies would not be able to bear the full expenditure involved".

While the British consul had some difficulty collecting from other governments, the response from the Colonial Secretary's Office in Barbados indicated that "it was agreed in 1944 that the annual liability of this Colony for the relief of Barbadians in Cuba should not exceed £1,200",[27] and that arrangements were being made for this amount to be paid to the Foreign Office through the Crown agents for the colonies. Then on 30 November 1949, the governor informed the secretary of state for the colonies that the Barbados legislature had agreed that Barbados would accept liability for the cost of passages of aged and infirm Barbadians repatriated from Cuba.

Because of a scarcity of US dollars, it was decided to reduce the British West Indian Relief Fund administered by British colonial officials in Cuba by 50 per cent for the fiscal year beginning 1 April 1948 and by 20 per cent each year thereafter until its final abolishment. In 1948 a total of $71,730.43 was spent on relief. Of that amount, $44,089.61 was disbursed to Jamaican nationals, $10,715.21 to Barbadians and $8,443.05 to citizens of the Leeward Islands.

The following year, the total was reduced to $41,479.16. The sum of $16,848.83 was spent on Jamaicans, $9,178.00 on Barbadians, and $8,775.91 on immigrants from the Leeward Islands. The question of a further cut of 20 per cent for the financial year 1949–50 was reconsidered, because of the adverse effects which the first measure of halving the relief fund had had on those who depended on it.

Repatriation, rather than relief, then became the focus of the efforts of the British officials. The consular official in Camagüey, G.B. James, had written to the consulate in Havana on 16 May 1949 indicating that Bona and Company, agents for the Italian line, were expecting the SS *Lugano* in Havana around 20 June. However, the ship's owners were insisting on a guarantee of about one hundred passengers, but the vice consul considered this figure out of the question for two main reasons: "(1) the small-islanders are very scattered and hard to get at, except in Central Baragua, (2) on several occasions they have 'backed out' at the last minute, and refused to go, thus making any 'guarantee' on our part a total loss".[28]

He estimated that a fairly accurate number of "certainties" for repatriation would be around thirty-two persons, "consisting of 21 Barbadians 4 Antiguans 1 British Guiana 1 Dominica 1 Grenada 2 Montserrat 1 St Vincent 1 Trinidad". The rate of passage quoted by Bona and Company was $80.52 per person. However, there were other costs associated with the repatriation exercise which had to be factored in. The British vice consul added that "to the above figure of $80.52 must be added at least an average of $23.00 for Barbadians for rail fare, food, and other expenses in Cuba, and $35 for other small-islanders, to take care of their transportation to Barbados, and their expenses in Cuba".

REPATRIATION BY AIR

The British vice consul suggested to the consul that as an alternative to the *Lugano*, that His Majesty's minister in Havana or the consul himself write to the general manager, British West Indian Airways (BWIA), Abercrombie Street, Trinidad, "asking that they grant us a rebate of – say – 25% for our Repatriate fares". This would not have been the first attempt to secure a rebate, since the British vice consul added, "I enclose copies of correspondence which may prove of interest. You will note that the matter of the 'Rebate' has been 'side-stepped' by the B.W.I.A., and nothing has resulted so far." Earlier that same year, he had written to the airline's Jamaica branch office on the matter.

James included in his letter a list of the prevailing airfares from Camagüey to the West Indies: To Barbados, Grenada or Trinidad the fare was $162.19; to St Kitts, $131.37; Antigua, $136.50; St Lucia, $159.62; and to Demerara (British Guiana), $211.60. There was no airfield at St Vincent, so passengers had to go to Barbados first and then by sailing boat (one day). Similarly, those wishing to go to Montserrat were obliged to go to St Kitts first, and then home by sailing boat. Dominicans also had to go to St Kitts, and then onward by boat on a journey which lasted two days. The airfare to Jamaica was $33.73, but there was a monthly boat service from Santiago for about $17.00.

The British colonial officials in Cuba had turned their attention to repatriating the West Indians by air because, in the words of the British vice consul in Camagüey, "The boat service, at present, is very irregular and uncertain. Therefore airplane transportation is the only answer."[29] This information was given in the vice consul's 26 January 1949 letter to Hugh Coxe, the branch manager of BWIA, stationed in Kingston, Jamaica. It was also stated in the letter that there was an urgent need to repatriate to "the lesser Islands several dozen (probably over 100 eventually) destitue [sic] British West Indians".

The letter sought to secure concessionary fares from BWIA for repatriates whose passages were being paid for from funds provided by the British government. It stated clearly, "Native passengers paying their own way and therefore not repatriates would of course pay full rates as per your 'General Tariff Schedule'." The colonial official was not subtle in his attempt to secure a positive response by introducing the question of the American competition, when he wrote, "in order to conserve hard-to-come-by U.S. dollars, we would like to send these repatriates via Jamaica and so give you the business. But, there is the competition of the Pan American Airways to be considered."

The British vice consul stated that it was not possible to get away from the Pan Am fares from Camagüey to Kingston, but suggested that a cut of 25 per cent by BWIA in the onward fare from Kingston would make their rates compare favourably with Pan Am's. BWIA was slow to respond, and another letter on this subject was sent to Coxe on 18 February. Ten days later he replied, indicating that the request had been forwarded to the airline's general manager in Trinidad. The British vice consul followed up with further correspondence on 8 March, restating his case. Again his appeal was to British imperial solidarity, with a not-too-veiled reference to the American competition: "The general idea of the preferential rates is twofold: (a) to conserve American dollars which otherwise would go to P.A. Airways, (b) to keep the business 'in the family' [so]-to-speak. Of course the 'Preferential' rates would only apply to Repatriate cases. Any British West Indian paying his, or her, own way would be charged the regular full tariff rate".[30]

BWIA finally replied on 27 December 1950. The letter from the airline's Trinidad headquarters was signed by the assistant general manager, John H. Rahr, and stated that it was "regretted that we are unable to grant the discount suggested, but we shall be prepared to accept payment in sterling through our Kingston Branch on cheques drawn by your Embassy on a bank in Jamaica".[31]

There is evidence to suggest that even though BWIA did not grant the concessionary fares requested, the British colonial officials proceeded with their programme of repatriation by air. The vice consul in Santiago de Cuba reported to the consul in Havana that since the beginning of 1950, there had been no ships running from Santiago to Jamaica willing to take passengers, which meant that the only way to repatriate was by air.

The Government of Jamaica paid the cost of transport from the Cuban interior to the point of embarkation and the cost of maintenance while awaiting passage for citizens of Jamaica, in addition to what was the cost of the sea passage when ships were sailing. The difference between the cost of the air passages and that of the sea passage was borne by the British West Indian Relief Fund.

The vice consul wrote too that, although in some cases the other British West Indian governments had agreed in principle to defray the cost of repatriating their nationals, none of them was willing to pay the cost of travel by air, and since at that time there was no other way of getting the people home, the whole cost of repatriation by air fell to the British West Indian Relief Fund. This meant that the fund paid for repatriation to the Leeward and Windward Islands, Trinidad, Barbados, and British Guiana.

His counterpart in Camagüey had written to the consul in Havana on 30 June 1949 stating, "unfortunately, the idea of sending 'Repatriates' by sea from Jamaica to the Lesser Islands was found to be impossible, owing to the non-existence of any regular – or even 'half' regular – line of inter-coastal steamers or sailing craft".[32]

In August of that year, Jeffrey Jackson of the Foreign Office sent a memo to Havana outlining his views on what the British government's long-term policy on repatriation should be. He first suggested that, in the short term, attention should be diverted to the possibility of using charter planes to transport the West Indians: "A shuttle-service, lasting several weeks, by some economical plane (Bristol Freighter, Cargo Dakota etc.) should cost far less per capita fare X number of repatriates."[33] Jackson then enumerated his recommendations for "the course which our long-term policy must inevitably follow":

1. An early exodus of most present relief cases, preferably by some not too protracted method, e.g. a sort of air-lift.
2. Thereafter, <u>cessation of all relief</u>.
3. Promptest repatriation of subsequent relief cases by normal procedure as and when they occur. <u>No relief to be granted pending repatriation</u>. Provision for repatriation in Cuba, etc. at a fairly high and steady figure for some years.
4. An eventual situation by which relief cases will cease to be our concern being either dependent on children of local nationality and associations, or, in the final event, local nationals themselves.

The Foreign Office official expressed the view that "anything else would imply either an eventual recrudescence of the relief problem, or abandonment of our humanitarian attitude."

By 11 October 1949, G.B. James, the British consular agent in Camagüey, had prepared a draft circular which he submitted to Thomas Brimelow in Havana for his approval or alterations. He proposed circularizing the twenty-seven British West Indian centres in Camagüey and Las Villas provinces, "provided that the Relief Fund is not too drastically cut".[34]

The circular, addressed to "British West Indians in Cuba", began by stating, "the relief fund for destitute, sick and aged British West Indians may be closed at any time now".[35] It advised anyone in the condition mentioned above, and who had not so far applied for repatriation, that they would be given a final chance of being sent back to his or her home if they registered with the vice consulate immediately, to take advantage of the offer before the fund was completely exhausted. They were also advised to give full details of what papers they held, "to prove that they are natives of the Island they claim as their home."

The immigrants were told that every effort would be made to repatriate as many of them as possible, that those who registered first would be given first consideration, but that no guarantee whatsoever could be given that everyone who applied would be sent back home. They were warned in the circular that, "when the Relief Money is quite exhausted, those British West Indians left in Cuba will have to fend for themselves . . . as no further Repatriation can possibly be undertaken".

In an attempt to "cover all bases", a footnote urged all British West Indians to make the information contained in the circular "generally known to everyone, so that no British West Indian can have the excuse later on of saying that he (or she) did not know of the above Repatriation offer".

Jeffrey Jackson at the Foreign Office had sent a note to Brimelow in Havana indicating that the Treasury had just telephoned to say that they had approved the request to maintain the relief budget at $40,000, and that their formal approval would follow in a few days. The consul replied to James on 19 October, confirming that the relief fund would not be cut, but would remain at $40,000. In his follow-up letter to the consul on 27 October, James states, "Your draft notice appears to me to fully meet the case for B.W.I. relief and repatriation."[36] It is not clear whether this refers to an amended version of the draft circular he had sent earlier, or whether in fact the consul had composed his own.

In any event, James indicated to the consul that about four out of seven immigrants had no papers whatsoever, since they had been either stolen or destroyed by fire or cyclones. He suggested, therefore, that a paragraph be added stating: "Those who have lost all their papers, should say how they were lost, where and when, and give every bit of information they can about themselves at once so that their statements can be checked with their Islands. No one will be repatriated who cannot prove that he or she, comes from the particular Island they claim as their home."[37]

The British consular agent noted that the consul had not touched on the matter of illegitimate children born in Cuba, "who, up to the age of 16 are accepted by Jamaica, if their mother goes with them". He ventured, "we will probably hear of such cases soon enough anyhow". James requested three hundred of the notices, which he planned to ask almoners and other British West Indian helpers to display in prominent places, and he also proposed sending copies to individual cases. He told the consul that he was making out lists of prospective repatriates for the information of the various colonial governments, and would be copying to him whatever information he was able to gather.

Despite the news that the relief budget for that year would be maintained at $40,000, there was another concern occupying the British officials. The pound sterling had been devalued in relation to the US dollar, and was now worth $2.80. While it was not clear initially exactly how the relief budget would be affected by the devaluation, the officials felt it prudent to act provisionally on the assumption that the sterling commitment would remain unchanged, and the dollar equivalent be proportionately reduced. In view of this, the order went out to take steps to reduce relief expenditure by one-third. James wrote to the consul stating: "We are carefully carrying out this reduced relief policy, and are refusing aid to most British West Indian [sic] except in urgent operational and serious cases. Prospective long distance flights for Barbadians and other small Islanders have been cancelled for the present, although I have some rather tragic cases I would like to dispose of."[38]

Barbadians were among the British West Indians who appealed to His Majesty's representatives in Cuba for assistance in repatriation to their homeland

Table 6.2. Barbadians under Sixty Asking for Repatriation to Barbados

McCollin Family (6)		Sons aged 23. 21. 18 Daughters 15. 13. 11
Joseph Shorey	58	Has Birth Certificate. Anxious to go
Fitz Brewster	55	Has Ctf. Baptism. do. do. (Ex WWI soldier)
Edward Freeman	55	do. do. do. do.
Cyril A. Rowe	39	do. do. and B/C Son of Martha Hunte (above)
Albert Catlin	51	Passport here. Anxious to go. No work.
Robert Barrow	55	Ctf. Baptsm. ex-soldier WWI do. do.
Elfrida Ford	?	Legally married to Beresford Ford
Joseph Harewood	54	Ctf. Baptsm. and Passport
George Colleymore	53	Ctf. Baptsm. Willing pay part passage
Walter Codrington	51	Ctf. Baptsm. do. do. do. do.
Enid do.	41	Legally married to Walter Codrington
Codrington Family (6)		Sons 18½. 16½. 12. 10. 5. One daughter 1 year
Joseph Brathwaite	51	No papers but genuine Barbadian. Willing pay part of his passage

Source: FO 277/255/66, PRO.

Table 6.3. Barbadians over Sixty Willing to Be Repatriated to Barbados

Benjamin Chase	68	Papers stolen, but definitely a Barbadian
Rosalie Chase	60	Papers stolen, but definitely a Barbadian
Clifton Clement	65	Papers stolen, but definitely a Barbadian
James Burgess	64	Written Nuevitas again 10th June re papers
Alexander Jones	71	Written again re papers. 10th June
John R. McCollin	63	Has B/Ctfcte. issued by Havana Consulate
Maud McCollin (wife)	58	Has marriage ctfcte. 6 children in Baraguá Ages 23. 21. 18. and 11. 15. 13
T. Ann Fornum	70	Has certificate of Baptism
Josephine Worral	73	No documents but genuine Barbadian
Adriana Mapp	63	Says she has a Birth Ctfcate
Joseph Thomas	63	Has birth and Baptism Cetfcate
Edward F. Kings	69	Has passport
Clifford Graham	72	Says he has Birth Ctfcate
Charles Wilkingson	67	He has a passport
Martin Luther Hunte	69	Has Ctfcate Baptism
Martha Hunte	76	Has a passport
Arnold Harper	70	Has passport and birth ctfcate
Wilred Bellamy	61	Has passport

Source: FO 277/255/66, PRO.

for themselves and their family members. This is reflected in the official notes regarding those under sixty years of age who were asking to be returned to Barbados. Those over sixty years of age who were willing to be sent back also got the attention of the British consular authorities.

On 29 November 1951, the consular agent in Camagüey wrote to the consul in Havana, J.W. Pethybridge, stating that "repatriation is slack at the moment, some expecting to get their 'Retiro' and others hanging on, almost starving, waiting for the Crop to start in January. Many will find that they cannot get work then and others will find that they are too far gone to work and then I expect many applications for repatriation."[39]

When G.B. James had written to the British consul in Havana in 1949 suggesting that he write to BWIA requesting the 25 per cent rebate, he had also noted in his letter that it should be remembered that the British West Indian native is very reluctant to go back home with no money whatsoever, and no matter how destitute he – or she – is, they prefer just "existing" in Cuba. The only way therefore to "persuade" them to go, is by withholding all relief of any kind. If we did not do this, we would have them on our books as "sick" and "hand-outs" for years – in fact as long as Relief Funds lasted.[40]

Another significant aspect of James's letter was his reference to the attitude of the Barbados government on the question of repatriation of natives of that country. His final paragraph states: "One factor I would like to mention is that the Government of Barbados has already shown strong disinclination to a large batch of repatriates being dumped on their shores *all at one time*. You have correspondence confirming this."

Thomas Brimelow, British consul in Havana, summed up the British perspective on the question of West Indian migrants in Cuba when he wrote:

The difficulty hitherto has been that their native Islands have not yet wanted them back. Nor have the Islands agreed yet either to pay for their repatriation, or even to accept them in large numbers if they are sent back at someone else's expense. It was this reluctance on the part of the Islands to accept their own people that forced us in the first place to institute the relief scheme in Cuba. Had the Islands been willing, the correct policy to have followed from the start would have been repatriation rather than relief. So long as the Islands remain firm in their opposition to repatriation, we are likely to find ourselves eventually reduced to a position in which we have no funds for relief purposes and no permission to repatriate needy British West Indians.[41]

The British West Indian question had been a matter for concern for British officials in Cuba for almost half a century, and was still engaging their attention just a decade before Fidel Castro's revolution triumphed in January 1959. As late as the financial year 1952–53, representatives of His Majesty's Government in Cuba were still providing poor and sick relief to British West Indians there. In 1951 total expenditure to the tune of $27,700 was recorded for that financial year.

The British officials were assisted in their efforts to provide relief by the Anglo-American Association, which was based in Havana. The association reported in 1951 that it had disbursed a total of $400 per month for the relief of British West Indians who called at its offices at San Juan de Dios. Of this monthly sum, $200 came in the form of a subvention from the consulate to the association. This money was used for repatriation, for funerals and for

Table 6.4. Poor and Sick Relief (Havana Province) for Quarter Ended 31 December 1951

Recipient	Poor Relief	Sick Relief	Total
Joseph Bailey	$2.30		$2.30
Rose Chase	0.50	0.48	0.98
Dora Clarke	1.00		1.00
Alfonso Cook		5.06	5.06
J. Jordan	3.00		3.00
E. Hope	3.00		3.00
George Malone	3.00		3.00
Charles Belgrave	3.00		3.00
Rufus Prescott	3.00		3.00
Ivan Clark	3.00		3.00
O. Cadogan	3.00		3.00
Angelina Ford	3.00		3.00
Roy Hurdle		5.30	5.30
Alonso Simmons		1.56	1.56
Elena Braffit [sic]		2.29	2.29
Eustace Jones	0.62	3.89	4.51
H. Phillips	3.60	1.00	4.60
William Hoyt		3.56	3.56
Hortensia Brown		5.60	5.60
Maybelle Liven	0.49		0.49
Total	**$32.51**	**$28.74**	**$61.25**

Source: Report of British Consul, FO 277/261, PRO.

providing assistance to hospital cases for the purchase of necessities such as medicines, transfusions and abdominal belts.

When Raoul Piedemonte had written his letter to the editor of the *Havana Post* in 1924, one of his objections to the West Indian immigration was the superiority which they allegedly assumed because they were "British". Another difficulty which Piedemonte identified was the transitory nature of their sojourn in Cuba, which he believed was detrimental to that country's economy: "If Jamaicans were to make their residence here more permanent and gave their children a chance of becoming Cuban citizens, as well as British subjects,

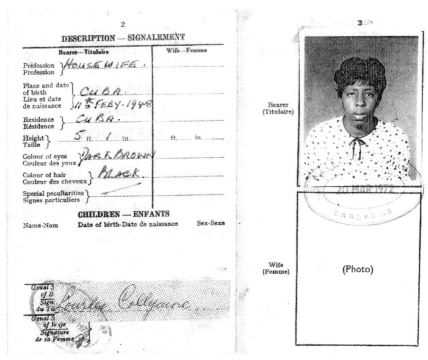

Figure 6.1. Barbados passport issued to Lourdes Collymore on 20 March 1972

public opinion towards them would undergo a more favorable change; all to their benefit."[42]

The fact is that some of the migrants were there for a season, while others remained permanently. Remaining brought with it the need for the migrants to examine their sense of national identity in the face of economic and political changes in Cuba. While the migrants would have gone to Cuba with one notion of their place within the British Empire, their interaction with British government representatives would have challenged those ideas. Nevertheless, the West Indians would have to rely on British diplomats there for consular representation for some time to come.

The Collymore family of Guantánamo was among those who remained. However, the dream of returning to Barbados endured for them, even up until 1973. After the patriarch, Adolphus, had been repatriated in 1971, the rest of the family had acquired Barbados passports in March 1972. The British embassy in Havana was instrumental in attempting to facilitate this return, as is evidenced by a letter to matriarch, Dolores Collymore. Writing on behalf of the consul, L.E. Gill stated in correspondence dated 6 September 1973:

> I am to inform you that the Government of Barbados has been approached for assistance in getting you and your daughters, Lourdes and Isabel Collymore, to Barbados. Please let me know if you wish to emigrate to that country.
>
> I must warn you, however, that in case you do, local emigration regulations in force may prevent you from leaving Cuba and although you and your daughters have Barbadian citizenship and are holders of Barbados passports, your Cuban nationality must prevail while you are in Cuba.
>
> This Embassy, nevertheless, will be glad to assist you if you intend to seek permission to leave but we cannot guarantee your departure.
>
> In the event that you are allowed to leave Cuba you may be required to travel with Cuban passports and it is therefore advisable to apply for these now if you have not yet done so.[43]

The youngest member of the Collymore family, son Adolfo, was reportedly not granted permission to leave Cuba. Not wanting to leave him behind, these family members who had managed to secure Barbadian passports remained in Guantánamo.

CHAPTER 7

GUANTÁNAMO

GUANTÁNAMO IN EASTERN CUBA IS ANOTHER PART OF the island in which British West Indian culture has flourished. The immigrants founded fraternal mutual aid and protection organizations as a means of coping in their new environment.

The Catalina Lodge, established in 1906, was the first organization founded by West Indians in Guantánamo. Barbadians there joined the lodge. Among its members was the Jamaican Edmund Skelton, also a founding member of the British West Indian Welfare Centre.

The Mechanics Lodge located at Los Maceo 24 was another fraternal organization to which the British West Indians belonged. It was established on 10 November 1928. Barbadians were also to be found on the lodge's list of members.

But perhaps the most important organization which looked after the interests of the migrants was the British West Indian Welfare Centre. It was founded on 11 November 1945, with the specific mandate, "to preserve and develop British West Indian cultural heritage; to provide legal assistance to the British West Indian community; to create a strong social and welfare program; and to identify, organize and link with other British West Indian communities".[1]

The centre had been established with assistance from the British government, and with the blessing of the British vice consul for Oriente, Niel Hone, who attended the foundation meeting and took the chair for election of officers to the executive committee.

Skelton was elected the centre's first president. He had been a journalist in New York, and founded a newspaper in Guantánamo. Like other West Indians there, he would also find employment at the US Naval Base.

Table 7.1. Selected Members of the Catalina (Oddfellows) Lodge in Guantánamo

Name	Date of Birth	Place of Birth	Next of Kin
Edmund Artemus Skelton (Clerk, Naval Base – initiated 20 May 1944)	15 August 1897	Bruce Hall, St James, Jamaica	Amybell Skelton (wife) Children: Myrtle, Roy, Ernest, Ethel, Julia and Leonard
Robert Brathwaite (Carpenter, retired from Naval Base)	27 January 1895	St Philip, Barbados	Albertha Brathwaite (sister), Julia Haywood (niece)
William Stay	27 July 1909	Georgetown, St Vincent	Gloria Estel Stay (daughter)
Charles Jeffers deceased 8-3-63 (Thrombosis cerebral haemorrhage)	28 October 1894	St James, Nevis	Children: Pelaf (6), Aaron (4), Carlos (2)
Moses R. Moore	3 January 1898	Market Hill, St George, Barbados	Joseph Moore (father), Eleen Moore (mother)
Charles Brathwaite (Cook at public school in Santiago de Cuba)	4 July 1913	Barbados	

Source: British West Indian Welfare Centre.

The centre became a pivotal location in the lives of the members of the West Indian community, offering social, educational, legal and welfare assistance to its members. General meetings were held on the second and fourth Sunday of each month, except the month of December, in which elections were held. Meetings of the executive committee were held the Saturday before general meetings. It boasted of more than two hundred members in December 1945, when Dr Alberto Martínez Mejías was elected lawyer for the centre.

Article 14 of the centre's by-laws relates to the death grant which would be paid on the demise of a financial member. Section 2 states that each adult member would be taxed one dollar while members paying half contribution would be taxed fifty cents. The beneficiary of the deceased would receive sixty dollars, and any surplus would be passed to the maintenance fund.

Table 7.2. Selected Members of the Mechanics Lodge in Guantánamo

Name	Date of Birth	Place of Birth	Next of Kin
Alfred D. Hinds (died 14 June 1967; buried 15 June 1967)	14 April 1890		Muriel Hinds (wife), Ernesto and Alfredo (sons)
George P. Tennant	25 March 1897	Mountainside, St Elizabeth, Jamaica	
Victor Westerman	1 January 1902	Charlestown, Nevis	Emily (daughter), Fred (son)
Charles Linton	10 January 1895	Christ Church, Barbados	Michaela Linton (wife)
John T. Pell	9 January 1896	St John's, Antigua	
James Matthews (died 10-9-55)	21 September 1896	Parham, St Peter's, Antigua	Clarisse Matthews (wife)
Arnold R. Hynds	10 June 1903	Grenville, Grenada	Bertha Palmer Hynds (wife), Samuel Courtney Hynds (son)
Simon Lewis (died 20 August 1964; buried 22 August 1964)	26 March 1903	Dennery, St Lucia	
Cyril Howell	23 February 1897	Clifton Hall, St John, Barbados	Ina Howell (wife), Rebecca Howell (mother)

Source: British West Indian Welfare Centre.

Article 12 dealt with exceptions to the sick benefit and death grant. Interestingly, section 1 stipulates that children of British West Indians who indulge in political affairs that were not British would not be accepted in the sick benefit and burial schemes.

However, the members of the centre were concerned not only with their own welfare, but that of their countrymen back home. At a meeting on 27 February 1955, they took the decision to make a contribution to the construction of the University of the West Indies hospital at Mona, Jamaica. They agreed, "through the initiative of Rev. Derrick, to have a mass meeting on 27 March at 4:00 p.m. to loose a fund scheme to make a donation to the building of a hospital for the Jamaican university".[2]

The minutes of the general meeting of 12 February 1956 recorded the acknowledgement of receipt of hurricane relief donations from members of the centre by Barbados and Grenada. The entries state that "Barbadoes [sic] received money for hurricane relief, very greatfull [sic]"[3] and similarly, "Greenada [sic] receive money for hurricane relief, very greatful [sic]".

While addressing a general meeting of the centre in 1945, Vice Consul Hone reviewed the situation of the British West Indian immigrants. He pointed out that the visit of Sir Frank Stockdale KCMG and Sir George Forbes, then British minister, in 1942 to different parts of Cuba, including Oriente, made it possible by their report to the British government that a grant was made to alleviate the most distressing cases of want and sickness among the British in Cuba.[4]

Hone added that in Oriente alone, there were about forty thousand British West Indians, and that the money which came to the fund for assistance from Britain only (none from the islands of the British West Indies) was not sufficient to give to any and every one – only those who were in dire necessity and were very sick could be attended to. He said too that there were 163 cases of operation in the clinic at Santiago in the previous year, and one cost more than $300. But anyone who was really sick and could not afford treatment would receive immediate help.

In a further endorsement of the work of the centre, Hone told the gathering that all cases of labourers' compensation should be handed to the officers of the centre, that no documents involving contracts for agricultural purposes should be made without consulting the centre for advice by its lawyers and that no one was entitled to any help from the funds of the centre as a matter of course, nor was the British government obligated to provide legal assistance for any of its people anywhere.

In contrast to some of the other British officials whom the immigrants encountered in Cuba, Hone appeared to have a genuine respect for the West Indians, and that high regard was reciprocated. He told members of the centre at a well-attended mass meeting held at the Fausto Theater that he was born in London, but that since coming to the West Indies, "he had a special feeling" for them, and his effort to get them together was genuine. He said he knew that if he succeeded, he would get very little praise, but that if it failed, he would get much blame.[5]

Skelton "pointed out that in the B.V. Consul, all British West Indians had a genuine friend, witnessing his all around interest in B.W. Indians".[6]

At a general meeting early the following year, it was noted that a Mr Clarke commented on Hone's letter offering bail to the poor as "love in the highest", and a Mr Burke joined and said, "Best white man I have met in our interest", and the House murmured assent to both expressions.[7] In adding his contribution to the discussion, a Mr Steele said, "It must not be forgotten that Mr. Hone has been the best man for us, seeing how intensely genuine was his interest."

At a special meeting on 28 July 1946, Hone told the members that, "as the sole British Representative in Oriente, his duties were increased, but that did not mean that his interest in the cause was less".[8]

When the second anniversary of the centre was marked, Vice Consul Hone said in his remarks that, although all that was expected was not achieved, he felt satisfied that much had been done, and that in his recent report to London, he was glad to have been able to say that "the Centre was worthwhile, and much invisible outside was accomplished".[9] Hone, however, regretted "to find a lack of cooperation, and he hoped that should the 'dollar crisis'. . . affect the Centre, the B.W. Indians would join together and keep the Centre going for their own welfare, especially if England should find it necessary to stop the grant".[10]

The day of reckoning soon came, as indicated in a letter from Hone read at a meeting on 23 November 1947. The letter stated that the centre would be closed, since the British government could not continue to sponsor it. There had been a 10 per cent increase in rent.

However, the members were determined to keep their centre going, and in April of the following year, Father Derrick said "we should let Mr. Hone Vice Consul know that we'll keep up the Centre, and since the furnitures were bought for the Centre, we have a right to it".[11] At that meeting, they also acknowledged correspondence from a Mr Williamson regarding his arrival in Jamaica, in which he "expressed gratitude to members of the Centre for the financial aid given him".

The centre was still going strong in July 1950, when the members took up the case of a Mr Adams who had been hospitalized after being beaten by two rural guards. The minutes noted: "Fr. Derrick said that the Centre should take up all cases of B.W. Indians, whether certain parties desire or no, for the Centre stands for all and should be the source of bringing solution to our needs whether some desire or no."[12]

Father Derrick got the support of a Mr Linton, and "after full comment of the mis-representation of B.W. Indians in this Town", it was agreed that "a letter be drawn up and sent to Mr. Hone showing him the necessity of an appointed representative in our community".[13] However, by the next meeting on 23 July, in response to a question from a Mr Cobham, the general secretary reported that the letter had not been sent.

It would appear that the general secretary had a long-standing difference of opinion with the enthusiastic Father Derrick regarding the representations that were appropriate for the centre to make. In July 1947, Dean Derrick had "asked about the dole to the indigent from the British Sick Relief Fund, and asked that a letter be sent to the British Vice-Consul demanding that the system of giving *vales* be stopped, and that the amount be given in cash, to avoid hardships and inconveniences to the people concerned".[14]

The general secretary said that "he would not send such a letter, because he thought the Centre had nothing to do with that – it was the expressed business of the Vice-Consul".[15] The president said that he had brought up the matter more than once, to no avail. A heated discussion ensued. Paradoxically, the president had remarked at that same meeting that "he was glad to note the wonderful improvement of the people, so far as protection from abuse by local authorities was concerned". But he had cautioned "that can be off-set by the lot of evil that is being said by members themselves".[16]

Hone was awarded the Order of the British Empire in 1953, and remained as vice consul at Santiago up until the 1959 revolution, as a listing in the 1960 Anglo-American Directory of Cuba confirms.

St Lucian Charles Ray had gone to Cuba in 1924 with his parents as a young boy. He moved from Chaparra to Guantánamo when he got married in 1949. "Oh they had plenty West Indians", Ray recalls. "The Welfare Centre was all West Indians; down there was all strangers. I belong to the Welfare Centre. That was important in Guantánamo, the Centre."

Apart from the centre and the fraternal lodges, the church was another important institution which served to provide the British West Indians with spiritual support. St Thomas Catholic Church, located at 752 Serafin Sánchez, and All Saints Episcopal Church, situated on the corner of José Martí and Aguilera streets, were two such religious institutions. Ray remembers that the services were held in English:

And, ah, English church, and English ministers speak English. Because when the English people speak Spanish you can't understand them. Down there was English

ministers – Mr Derrick, Mr Piggott, used to come to Guantánamo. And everybody used to run go to the church to hear Piggott speak. He was a Barbadian from
Barbados. Good minister. Yeah, I used to go to Piggott church from the time I was
a boy in Chaparra. When Piggott come to Guantánamo to preach, all the English
people would go to church to hear him preach.

A prominent member of the Guantánamo West Indian community, who no
doubt would have been in the congregation, was Edmund Lee Hope, a tailor
who had migrated from the district of Warners in the parish of Christ Church,
Barbados. He had been baptized at the nearby St David's Chapel in 1868. His
foreigner's identification passbook, which was required of immigrants to Cuba,
is pictured here (figure 7.1). He is recorded in the passbook as being a native of
England and his citizenship as "English".

After sojourns in Canada and Haiti, Mr Hope settled in Guantánamo, where
his tailoring establishment catered to the sartorial needs of the local community. In Haiti, Mr Hope met Lidiere Gleamaud. They were married in Haiti on
26 April 1916. Their son, Herbert, was born in Haiti in 1918; William was born in
Guantánamo in 1920; and Theodore was born in Guantánamo in 1922. Mr Hope
died at his home in Guantánamo on 17 September 1946, at the age of sixty-nine.

Figure 7.1. Foreigner's identification passbook of Barbadian immigrant Edmund Lee
Hope

Figure 7.2. Edmund Lee Hope with his Haitian wife, Lidiere Glemaud

Figure 7.3. Mr Hope stands outside his business premises, which advertises "British-American Designer and Cutter – E.L. Hope"; with him are his wife, Lidiere, and their sons (*from left to right*) Herbert, William and Theodore

American involvement in the construction of the Panama Canal had led to work for the migrants, and again the US investment in Cuba's sugar plantations in the eastern provinces created employment for the Barbadians and other West Indians. Yet again, there was another instance of Americans being a source of employment for the immigrants.

The US Naval Base at Guantánamo Bay had been established in 1903 with the signing of the Platt Amendment. It had been expanded considerably during World War II. As the United States was preparing to enter World War II in 1941, there was a significant increase in the demand for workers to recondition the base. There was an appreciable internal migration, when labourers employed as day workers on sugar plantations moved to the city. At the height of its operations in the early 1940s, the base employed thirteen thousand people and, after the war, had a workforce of approximately thirty-five hundred. "West Indians were often preferred workers to Cubans and held a disproportionate number of jobs at the naval base, a fact that was the source of discontent amongst non-West Indian Cubans who wanted equal access to the more stable employment that the base offered."[17]

Cold War politics would intervene. In 1964, when the United States detained Cuban fishermen found fishing in US territorial waters, Cuba temporarily cut off the naval base's water supply in retaliation. In turn, the United States gave an ultimatum to some 2,000 base workers. They could choose to be exiled on the base or continue living in Cuba, losing their jobs and pension as a consequence. Fifteen hundred opted to remain in Cuba and 445 chose the base, while 750 workers were allowed to go back and forth, undergoing extensive security checks each time.

Charles Ray was one who had found work on the base, but who chose to remain in Cuba when the ultimatum was given.

> In 1942, my sister [Virginia] . . . this one coming there . . . she, ah, she come to Guantánamo. In 1943, my brother was working in the factory, my oldest brother, was working in the factory and he sent for me. He say if I want to work, Guantánamo have work. And I came to Guantánamo in February. And after about a week or two, I get a job at the base. And I've been working on the base until 1964. Yeah, I work on the base from '43 to '64.
>
> Then in 1964, when they started taking out the people from work, who want to remain can remain, who want to go can go, well I say, "I'm going." And I came out from the base retired. Those days I had [was] about 51 years already. I came out from the base and up to now I'm in Guantánamo.

Edmund Lee Hope's son, William, was also among those employed at the naval base. He was hired on 30 December 1941 as a general helper at the rate of $2.32 per day. On 1 July 1942, he was transferred to the position of mimeograph operator for an annual salary of $1,200. Subsequent transfers and promotions took him to the position of clerk typist, earning $2,912 a year. His employment ended on 12 February 1964, when he opted to continue living in Cuba. He then began teaching physics and English, as well as working as a musician.

Hope had designated his wife, Irene Jústiz de Hope, as his beneficiary to receive his federal death benefit and pension. When he died in 1969, because of the state of relations between Cuba and the United States, the latter prohibited such payments to residents of Cuba. As a consequence, she did not receive the payments then, nor before her own death in 2010.

Membership Certificate
DEATH BENEFIT ASSOCIATION
Naval Base - Guantanamo Bay, Cuba

Name William HOPE
Pay Number 32-9204
Beneficiary Irene Justiz de Hope
SERIAL Collection No.
Nº 32503 X 21

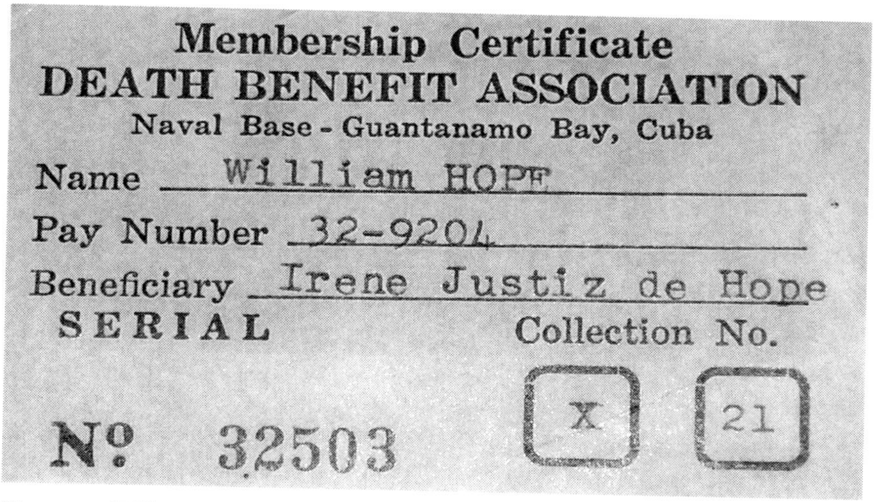

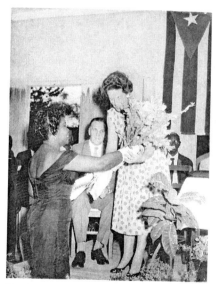

Figure 7.4. William Hope's Guantánamo Bay Naval Base Death Benefit Association membership certificate

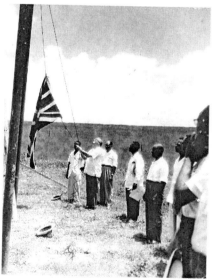

Figure 7.5. Gwendolyn James, a member of the British West Indian Welfare Centre, making a presentation in 1951 to the wife of the British vice consul Niel Hone, as he looks on. *Courtesy of the British West Indian Welfare Centre, Guantánamo, Cuba.*

Figure 7.6. The Union Jack is hoisted in Guantánamo. *Courtesy of the British West Indian Welfare Centre, Guantánamo, Cuba.*

Figure 7.7. All Saints Episcopal Church, Guantánamo, has long been a centre of worship for British West Indian immigrants. Services are now conducted in English and Spanish. *Courtesy of the British West Indian Welfare Centre, Guantánamo, Cuba.*

Figure 7.8. An early executive committee of the British West Indian Welfare Centre, Guantánamo. Standing second from left is Edmund Skelton, the founding president of the centre. *Courtesy of the British West Indian Welfare Centre, Guantánamo, Cuba.*

Figure 7.9. Female members of the British West Indian Welfare Centre. The Cuban flag and the Union Jack form part of the backdrop for the photograph. The centre was an important source of social, legal, educational and moral support for the immigrant community. *Courtesy of the British West Indian Welfare Centre, Guantánamo, Cuba.*

CHAPTER 8

~~~~~~~~~

EYEWITNESS-PARTICIPANTS
IN HISTORY

THE NARRATIVE OF BRITISH WEST INDIAN MIGRATION TO Cuba is one which is located within the changing global landscape of the twentieth century. The West Indians in Cuba would have been witness to, and participants in, significant social, political and economic developments which took place in the country during the period. During the course of the turbulent century, social mobilization gave rise to a series of strikes, conspiracies and coups, revolts and revolutions. They would be affected by local, regional and global changes.

LOCAL CHANGES

British West Indians had started arriving in Cuba in search of work during the very early years of the twentieth century, though not yet in the appreciable numbers of later years. They would have been present when the Liberal revolt erupted in 1906. It prompted the Second US Occupation (1906–1909) to pacify the situation and protect American interests. A front-page article in the *Los Angeles Herald* of 1 October 1907 declared "Cuban Revolt Is Spreading". It gave some insight into the nature and impact of the disturbances.

Charles Edward Magoon, the military governor appointed by the United States, was mentioned in the *Herald*'s account: "Governor Magoon has determined to deal with outlaws and insurrectionists with a strong hand. The orders of the rurales, it is stated, are to capture, kill or drive them into the ocean."[1] Military repression would be a common response to rebellion.

In the period of the Second Occupation, the PIC had been formed in 1908. As Jorge Domínguez asserts, "legal discrimination against nonwhites had intensified during the two United States occupations".[2] In response to the passage of the *Ley Morúa*, prohibiting political parties or movements made up exclusively of members of any single category or race, the *Independientes* rebelled in 1912: "Although much of the party's national leadership was in Havana, the actual insurrection occurred mainly in southeastern Oriente province, with a secondary focus in Las Villas."[3]

Rupert Mullings recalls his father relating that when he made his first trip from Jamaica to Cuba, that the situation there was quite tense. From his account, it might have been during the period of this particular uprising:

> It was somewhat a difficult time because they had come out of a serious revolution in the early teens – 1912, '13, '14. It's an interesting story because he said they were still lining up people and shooting them. And my mother's older cousin who was also there as early as 1912 told me of a case where they were being lined up. And he was very light skinned, and looked Cuban, straight hair, straight nose, white looking. And when his group was being lined up he told them that they were British citizens and they left them. My father concurred that this was happening. So the British citizenship was critical to them at the time when they had the revolution.

When, in February 1917, the Liberal Party rose in revolt in reaction to the re-election of President Mario Menocal through what it considered electoral fraud, the result was an upsurge in banditry and local insurgency primarily in the eastern part of the country. Ultimately, it would usher in another period of American military presence in Cuba, which would come to be known as the Sugar Intervention. This time it was facilitated by the Cuban government to protect the sugar crops. Domínguez argues that the dominant strategic question for President Woodrow Wilson at that time was World War I rather than Cuba. However, American businesses and the US Navy had a different set of interests: "Some of the largest U.S.-owned sugar plantations and mills were in Oriente, Cuba's easternmost province. The United States naval base at Guantánamo was also in Oriente, and the navy believed the area strategically important for the defense of the southern United States, the Caribbean and the Panama Canal in case of war."[4]

Towards the end of March, rebels had partially destroyed sugar mills and raided villages in and around the Jobobo sugar mill in Oriente which was owned by the Cuba Company (an early railroad company). Official reaction to suppress the uprising was brutal. "Government troops shot some twenty black residents, including several British subjects, at Jobobo without trial and barbarously killed two Jamaicans at the nearby Elia sugarmill. Despite the lack of evidence that British West Indians were joining the Cuban rebellion, it seemed government troops felt that 'black outsiders' were to blame for the ills of the island."[5]

While Gillian McGillivray includes the West Indians among the twenty persons killed at Jobobo, Jorge Giovannetti describes them all as being black British West Indians. He states that the immigrants were lined up to be photographed and were machine-gunned instead; that they were robbed and pulled out of their houses at sunrise, forced to dig their own graves, killed in cold blood and buried by their kin.[6]

There was West Indian involvement in the sugar strikes which erupted in 1917. Some of them were leaders of the workers' movement, including one William Benjamin, who was believed to be from Barbados. Rufus Hoyte related his experience of a 1925 strike at Chaparra, which occurred one week after his arrival from Barbados.

The political life of the country engaged the interest of the West Indians. The Sargeants' Revolt which was organized by a group including Fulgencio Batista toppled the government of Gerardo Machado on 4 September 1933. On 14 January 1934, Batista forced provisional president Ramón Grau San Martín to resign, ushering in a period where for almost a decade he controlled the country's affairs from behind the scenes with a series of puppet presidents. Batista was elected Cuba's first mulatto president in 1940 and held office until 1944, when his party was voted out of office. Batista's ascension to power would further divide the country along racial and class lines.

He became the butt of jokes by some white Cubans, who referred to him as a *negro mono*, a "nigger monkey". Carlos Moore was prohibited by his parents from repeating these jokes in their Jamaican household in Central Lugareño, where Moore grew up.

The Moore household was sympathetic to Eduardo Chibás, leader of the Ortodoxo party, who was regarded as embodying "the hopes and aspirations of all segments of the disgruntled Cuban population, from poor white peasants and victimized blacks to upper-class intellectuals".[7] His weekly radio programme held the full attention of the household. Neighbours would gather on the Moores' veranda "waiting in silence to hear the distinctive tones of the man everyone said would be Cuba's next president".[8] When Chibás committed suicide on live radio on 15 May 1951, Moore says, "Our home was in mourning. A black cloth hung around the picture of Chibás in our living room. The radio was turned low. At our little cemetery people placed flowers."[9]

Nearly twenty years after the Sargeants' Revolt, Batista staged a second coup on 10 March 1952. This time, it was against elected Cuban president Carlos Prío Socorras. He had returned from exile in the United States. Moore states that "blacks constituted about 40 percent of the population and greeted the general's return to power with undisguised satisfaction. They defended him against racial mockery, which they took personally."[10] He describes the reaction in his home and neighbourhood to the general's reappearance. "I rushed home from school to find my family and neighbors huddled around the radio, a mixture of contained joy and fear in their faces. My father shook his head in wonderment, cautiously refraining from any opinion that might later be attributed to him."[11]

In November 1954, Batista dissolved parliament and was elected constitutional president without opposition. By late 1955, student riots and anti-Batista demonstrations had become frequent. These transitions taking place in Cuba would lead ultimately to the major political change which occurred in 1959. The stage was set for confrontation with the July 26 Movement guerrillas.

"At the beginning of the 1950s", assert Oscar Zanetti and Alejandro García, "Cuba entered a new (and violent) upsurge of the national crisis. Faced with the uncertain prospects of the sugar market, the country displayed all of the fragility of its traditional single-crop economy."[12] The sugar industry remained the country's most important productive activity, and the 1958–59 harvest was a prime target of the guerrillas, as they sought to overthrow Batista. In the lead-up to a general strike which began on 9 April, "Between March and April 1958, revolutionary activities reached a high level. The guerrillas spread beyond the area of the Sierra Maestra, and acts of sabotage by the underground movement were stepped up."[13]

This increase in sabotage paralysed railroad transportation, critical to the sugar industry. It was reported that since the end of October fifty-two bridges and culverts had been destroyed and more than seven kilometres of track had been bulldozed. In short, 75 per cent of the system was unusable: "The complicated links between the plantations, the sugar mills, the warehouses, and the ports, which the railroad provided, had been broken in several regions. Not only the appropriate materials but also the use of armed force was required to restore them."[14]

Jorge Ibarra opines, "In general, in the 1950s, blacks participated in the revolutionary movement not as blacks or as workers but as part of the humblest strata of the revolutionary masses. Rather than making special class or racial claims, they joined the popular movement inspired by the revolutionary program of the July 26 Movement and of the Revolutionary Directorate that promised economic benefits to the lower strata of the population."[15] And Andrea Queeley makes the claim that, "during the Cuban revolution, base workers smuggled supplies to the rebels in the Sierra Maestra".[16]

However, Carlos Moore argues, "The Cuban revolution was essentially a victory of the anti-imperialist segment of the white Cuban middle class", and that "the Afro-Cuban population, having suffered far deeper frustration – even betrayal – throughout its history, had essentially abrogated its role in domestic power politics".[17] The situation would have been complicated further for black Cubans by the fact that the movement sought to overthrow a mulatto president. Samuel Furber contends, "There is no hard evidence to support the notion of black support for Batista. However, the alternative proposition that blacks were underrepresented in the ranks and particularly in the leadership of the opposition to Batista has a more solid foundation."[18] He concedes though that "like everyone else, blacks celebrated the revolutionary victory and lined up to meet the procession of the rebel soldiers led by Fidel Castro that for a whole week traversed the island from east to west".[19] Moore also admits that, "in the first months of 1959, Castro's popularity and multi-class appeal were overwhelming. He appeared as the conciliator between conflicting classes, ethnic communities, and interest groups."[20]

GLOBAL AND REGIONAL CHANGES

As Cuba refashioned itself as a nation from Spanish colony, US protectorate and to republic, sugar remained at the heart of the country's export economy, making it vulnerable to fluctuations in commodity prices in the external market. As Zanetti and García describe the post–World War II era, "the fleeting respite that World War II gave the Cuban economy began to fizzle out in the late 1940s as the world economy returned to normal. A slight drop in the price of sugar in 1948 and 1949 was the first indication that the good years for the country were drawing to an end. . . . The collapse finally came in 1953, when the price of sugar dropped to an average of slightly under 4 cents a pound."[21]

Developments in Europe also had a profound impact on Caribbean politics. There was a post-war push to end imperialism and create new, independent countries responsible for their own governance. Jeffrey Sachs remarks, "The Second World War finished the European conflagration started in the First World War, again with profound consequences for the global economy. This time the destruction in Europe was so profound that the European imperial powers were too exhausted and discredited to maintain their hold on their empires."[22]

Harvey Neptune describes the period between the onset of World War II and the triumph of the Cuban Revolution as marking "the high age of decolonization for the Caribbean". "In these two decades the issues that inspired the region's people to collective public action were framed as part of the larger struggle over their subjection to imperialism."[23]

The migrants in Cuba had experienced the ambiguities of imperialism in their dealings with British consular representatives and American employers there, as they sought to "face life" in a complex and often hostile environment. Elsewhere in the Hispanic Caribbean, other British West Indians faced similar circumstances working for US multinationals, within the context of capitalism and modernization. These interactions would have influenced the attitudes of those who remained as well as those who returned home, as the former colonies from which they came evolved into nation states.

PART 2

~~~~~~

ORAL TESTIMONIES OF THE MIGRATION EXPERIENCE

CHAPTER 9

〰〰〰

CELIA LEONORA CAMPBELL JONES

"When I came here all here was cane field. Down in Bajan Town was tree stump. The Barbadian, Jamaican, plenty other nations came here and all those stump they cut down. . . . And after that, poco, poco, *everything begin to build up and come better."*

I WAS BORN ON THE THIRTEENTH OF FEBRUARY, 1906. Well, I have so much names it's a shame. Home, they call me Dorrie; they call me Lilian. And my right name is Celia Leonora Campbell. They would like to study how I get that name now. Because, here, I had to send to the Public Buildings in Barbados to get my birth certificate.

I used to live in Reece Hill, St Thomas, with my grandmother. I left Barbados on 8 August 1920 and arrived in Cuba after eleven days. There was nobody to receive me.

My mother send for me, but she had a young baby and she couldn't receive me so she sent me to Havana, and then afterwards she send for me here in Baraguá. And I came here fourteen years of age. I was seasick on the boat. I spent eleven days. I wasn't happy. I came in the boat that call the *Ada Ruba*. That boat I believe it sink on the way back.

When I came here all here was cane field. Down in Bajan Town was tree stump. The Barbadian, Jamaican, plenty other nations came here and all those stump they cut down. And when I came here, I tell you the truth, when my mother brought me up here, and I was coming through Colorado I cried, because I believed it was so pretty. I come in on a jeep, and the morning was cold, and nothing but bush you just see the car coming through. And when I came in here and see where I had to stop, I cried. Cried, cried, cried, because it was a pretty place, and it was so nice and everything. And after that, *poco, poco*, everything begin to build up and come better.

Who ain't work in the *central*, they cut cane, weed grass and anything like that. In those days we had little thatch-roofed shacks that they pick up lumber and knock up. The early days wasn't as bad as these days. At that time the West Indians really used to get treat good, but now everybody is Cuban and get treat the same way. Not good, nor not bad. Hard and rough. The goodness we get now is good houses. These days now are better when you talk about the homes, but days gone by was better than now. Because we could go to the shop and we could buy one-cent biscuit, one-cent bread.

Now we can't get no more than one bread, a little something when you squeeze it, it go in like a windball. And on Sunday, don't have mouth to eat bread. A little bread Monday, Tuesday, Wednesday, Thursday, Friday, Saturday. Sunday we don't have no belly for bread. And now I have sugar, and Sunday I can't drink milk. Diabetes; can't drink milk now. I really did like the days gone better than these days when it comes to eating time, because now we have to cook without oil, we have to cook without *manteca*. Sometimes we don't get sufficient salt. We get five pounds of rice, no more, for a month. Five pounds of rice for one month, for one person. Sometimes they give you two, and owe you three.

My father was in Barbados. And my mother was in Panama with her husband, and he came over here to work. My mother was Rosalie Keziah Campbell. The most of the work at that time was washing dirty clothes, cleaning house and cooking for the men. But she never clean, she wash and cook. She died young at thirty-nine, and I had to take care of my two younger brothers.

My mother was a Salvationist. I brought up in the church from Barbados, and when I came here she was in the Salvation Army and I brought up there. And from there, I join the Episcopal Church in 1938. And all of my family is church members. All, down to the little tiny one now, she coming up in the church.

We used to plait the maypole and sing songs like "Sly Mongoose" and "Millie Gone to Brazil". Myself and a lady by the name of Audrey plait the pole right there at the corner yonder. But I can't dance the pole now. I can't make it, my knees are weak.

I remember plenty things. I remember when the folks was going over to the war they sing:

Goodbye Broadway; hello France.
We are ten million strong.
Goodbye sweethearts, wives and mothers.

It won't take us long.
Don't you worry, I'll be there.
It's you I'm fighting for.
So goodbye Broadway; hello France,
We hope to help you win this war.

I can't remember now the song they sing when the war over.

The family that my mother used to write was Eliza Gilkes. Eliza Gilkes was her mother. Her sister died and leave a son by the name of Harold DaCosta Gilkes. She died six years ago and the son one year, two, now; and leave a boy by the name of . . . well he take the same name, Harold Gilkes. I write to him and this boy received the letter, and told me that he died. The son married last year.

I get a little bit of education, not much, because my head was hard. After my mother died, I do washing. I work hard. Is only now I am not working. I wash plenty dirty clothes. I wash, I starch, I iron.

I have five children. Along with the father, I school them, bring them up in school. He was from Barbados too. He died. Well now I can't do nothing more. All of my children speak English. They went to English school; the church had a school. I bring them up in school and in church, four girls and one boy. I had a girl in the States and she died; it was six children I had. And all of the grandchildren speak English too.

Once I made an effort to go back to Barbados. When I got to the consul, they tell me that one of the children couldn't go, that I couldn't leave with him, so I finished with it. But I would love to go to Barbados right now. I am the only Barbadian left here now. They have five Jamaicans, but I am the only Barbadian, and the only woman. I am ninety-one years old. Ninety-one years is a long time. My feelings at times is very poor. The way I feel on mornings when I wake up, I don't think I'll live to see many more years. I may live to see a few, but not many.

This interview with Mrs Jones was conducted at her home in Baraguá, Cuba, on 19 October 1997. Mrs Jones did get her wish to visit Barbados again at Christmas 1998, at the invitation of the Cuban-Barbadian Friendship Association. She was accompanied by one of her daughters, Winifred. As she told a journalist, "I was always Barbadian, I didn't change. If I did change I won't be here quisas." "I just want to sit down and eat and listen to the carols. I heard carols this morning. I love them. I like to sit down, eat and drink sorrel and love Barbados." She returned to Baraguá, where she lived with her daughter. Mrs Jones died in 2009.

~~~~~~~~

CHAPTER 10

MARADELL ATWELL GREENE

"Bajans live together when they outside. Nobody would tell on the other who do this, or who do that. Man got beaten up . . . and although the man woman curse all night – she was living in Bajan Town – she still can't find out who beat the man so. And he had looked like a package that come from far when he come from the doctor, with a lot of different bandages stuck all over him like stamps."

I WAS BORN ON CANAL ZONE IN A place they call the Cow Pen. I don't know why they called it that, but I personally feel good because I say I born in a manger like Jesus. So I used to fuss on the other children. It was really a place called Pedro Miguel, but the English people called it Petro Miguel. Bajan people spoil Spanish very bad. The Jamaicans speak a better Spanish, but somehow the Bajans like to humbug the Spanish. We used to live in Churríllo [choo-REE-yo] and they call it "Chuhrilluh" [chuh-RILL-uh].

My other two sisters born in Santo Tomás hospital in Panama City. They are Panamanians straight, but I'm American in a way. I went to school at the Webster School. We had a teacher from Barbados who had this school. He was a fair-skinned man. But he used to beat me too much, and my mother asked him at a funeral why he beat me so. He said he liked to beat. So she took me from that school and sent me to the seaside school, the Baptist school, and they had a woman down there teaching. She was an organist. She was a woman who could sew good. So she taught us to drill good and that sort of thing.

My father always did two jobs. He was a shoemaker and he was a seaman. In Panama, he was working on the canal. Although he came from St George, he was a very good diver. But he always travel with his shoemaker tools. His name was Joseph Nathaniel Atwell. My father went to Panama in 1904. He went to Panama twice, because he didn't like it at first, but he went and come back again.

My mother's name was Ethel Louise Chandler, and that was the regular Chandler name from St James. She was a dressmaker from Barbados. Whenever they were having a wedding, they would invite her to come up and sew for this wedding. But they could not pay in cash. They would give her a kid, or something like that. She was working very hard at that, and that's what caused her to go to Panama, because in Barbados you never used to make money, but people would treat others very kind. She went to Panama in 1908, and she went to Cuba with us in 1920.

My father was up there. Most of the Bajans went to Baraguá. My mother left with two friends – one was Barbadian and the other was Jamaican. We left and went to Colón and then headed over to Cuba. My father didn't want us to come to Cuba, but my mother wanted to come to Cuba with us three, because he was out there three years. I was six years old when he left Panama.

When we went to Baraguá, we had to travel on a train sleeping there all night. In those days we didn't have this big road. We had to pass a lot of cane fields and so on, when you went by car. The company had a kind of gasoline car running on the track line. So we used to be able to go as far as Colorado by the train, and get off the train and get on this company car running on the track line.

So when my mother got on this train there was a man driving on this train who asked my mother, "Madam, where are you going with these children?" We occupied two seats on the train facing one another and we were talking all the time. She said, "To Baraguá." He asked, "To who?" And she said, "To Atwell." "That blowhard?!" Who tell him to say that, 'cause I don't like anybody saying anything bad about my father, so I didn't like him at all. But he sat down on the handle of the seat, chatting to us all the time.

My husband that I married to, he was on the same train too but he didn't come near us. And he knew us very good, but he said he didn't say nothing to notice us because we were children dress up in long nightgowns. And I didn't know that until I got to Baraguá and knew him for a time. His brother, as soon as we got in now, he was at my father and somebody went and tell my father that we come. These boys were always round my father because their mother had a house next door to him. He then said that he would go outside and meet us and brought us in.

When I left Panama I was nine years old. I was good at arithmetic and so. I wanted to join the Red Cross, but I don't know why my mother wouldn't let me join. Everything I wanted to be in. But she let me join the Christian Endeavour, where they had a band of little children who used to go and pray for people.

In Cuba, my mother send me to pray for a man dying in hospital. That hospital in Baraguá was only a kind of a rest house. And he naked. When I got at the door with my sister – my mother always send out two, not one – and when I go with the prayer book, a man saw us with the book and told another man go and cover the man. When we got there, this man there trembling. That was a man who went to Cuba to try and make a little living. He left his wife here in Barbados, and the wife had another friend and tell the friend to take care of him. She out there laughing at him, take his flannel pants that he used to play cricket in and starch it, blue it and all that kind of thing. She laughing and telling my mother the jokes, and I hearing as a little girl.

We didn't have any school except the Spanish school. Very few people wanted to send their children to Spanish school because the Spanish children used to beat the English children if you meet there at the big store. Because we very much liked to wear hats, and they would knock off your hat. So we would clash. One Salvation Army captain came in. He had a four-octave organ and he started keeping school and people glad to get a little school to send their children to. He gave us some long division – pounds, shilling and pence. After he went out from there, there was another man, Conrad Smith, he was a Combermere boy. He came in and he was at the Christian Mission and he started keeping school.

Then teacher Stoute came in – William Preston Stoute from St Philip. He was a teacher in Barbados. He left Barbados and went to Panama. He used to work at a hospital and led a strike there. After he got into trouble, I understand that he put in the newspapers that he was dead, and left for Cuba.

Well everybody glad that a man like that was coming to keep school. The company, which was American – the Baraguá Sugar Company – had two mills on that factory. They built a school out of wood and told him that they would pay him a salary and still let the schoolchildren parents give him something. So to start this school, he held this exam and separated the children. We had some big, tall ABC children, and we had some small children who knew something. He taught us some of everything – Spanish, he taught us about the clouds. He taught us dancing. At that time it was Arthur Murray steps. Well you know boys are very shy; they didn't want to dance with the girls and all that sort of thing. Teacher himself would dance with us and show us those steps. And he loved to play his guitar.

I remember one Christmas we put on a play about how Santa Claus suffered before radio came up. Santa Claus heard about this thing and then he couldn't be in peace until he understand it. He just saw it in the papers and he heard about it. So he put all the toys away, and the toys had nothing to do, just wondering. The reindeer not coming, nothing not happening because Santa Claus is worried with this thing. So the song went:

> Papers, papers, daily papers, which one will you choose?
> From Detroit or Chicago, from New York or San Francisco,
> Right here for the latest news.

The children, we start singing now:

> I wish I knew where Santa lived, I'd tell him a thing or two.
> Perhaps he'd help us out if he just only knew.
> Papers, papers, daily papers which one will you choose?
> Right here for the latest news.

So he read the papers to get the news, and we heard that he was coming out after all. I was a doll at the time, one of them that could just say, "Mama", and clap hands and walking very stiff saying, "Mama". And a boy next to me, he would clang two cymbals together, you know, and I would "Mama" right across the stage. And some of us dolls would be performing.

> Santa Claus is truly coming; this is what he said.
> He is coming down the chimney while we are in bed.
> Christmas trees are ready, but we dare not peep.
> Christmas secrets, how much longer can we keep?
> Now the greatest thing of all, ere the sleep upon us falls,
> is hanging up our stockings by the fireside.
> Christmas stockings, Christmas stockings,
> Christmas fireside bright,
> Holly twining, candles shining,
> windows glow with light.
> Santa's coming, Santa's coming in his reindeer sleigh.
> Listen, listen, soon we'll hear him on his way.

At last Santa come out now, and he sing:

I am feeling better now.

The wife come in and sing:

Signs of care have left his brow.
Since he bought a radio fine,
he's a wiser, happier man.
You'll surely doubt, but Santa Claus will never fail the children.
Of that there is no doubt.
He's been a little blue,
yet his heart is warm and true.
He's the same jolly, good old scout.

So that's how we ended up.

In our schooldays now, when we have holiday, we would put on the oldest clothes we have and pass around and invite other children to go to the nearest farm to us to look for mangoes. When you go down there you wouldn't find mangoes alone. You would find pears and different sorts of fruit. If we get down there and find that another gang got there before us, you go by another farm. A man would open the gate and tell you come in and pick what you want. Because Cuba was a place in the early days where Cubans used to say that they plant and they don't mind who eat, because when they come, they find something to eat.

I used to post the registered letters to my mother's father, Mr Edward Thomas Chandler. That was her father's name. I used to post the letters myself, and post to her sister, Grahamie. She was a hawker. I came here to Barbados and sew for her. My mother used to always send money.

After my mother got expecting with my brother, she took me to the bank with her and put my name down, and she done travelling. When he born, I wasn't eleven yet, but I was responsible. All that business I had. My father, sitting down doing his shoemaker work, used to send me to buy his shoemaker leather and the bristles and everything. There had a place with a horse in Ciego de Avila, and at this place I would stop and buy leather for him. I know about the top leather, the sole leather and the inner soles, and all the lasts, and I was a little girl. And when it come to buying shoes, I buying shoes for everybody. I had a length of twine with a knot and I measuring. I worked very hard when I was a child.

Where the Americans were living, I used to mind a little girl. She used to call the place where we were living "t'other side of the mill". The breeze blowing a certain way, and they had the town built so that most of the ashes down on the other side of the mill. The Americans in those days were one standard up, and they were above the Cubans themselves. And the white Cubans had their own quarters in those days. They had a theatre and a dancehall.

The sugar mill business. Nobody came up there to cut cane. Very few people came up there to cut cane. They would do their own trade. They would take one house and divide it in two, to make less space, and you live on one side and I live on one side. And everybody putting up a signboard. This body is a tailor; the next person is a shoemaker. So the Cubans came down one day and said, "*Mira este plan.*" "Look at this plan. The people come from China and all about and putting up these signboards." This man started, and his brother – Marcelino – was a kind of a warder about the place, but he was a very peaceful man. But when it come to Marcelino brother, he say that all these signboards have to take down. Everybody had to take down their signboards and hide them.

Anyhow, the Cubans started saying that they want 40 per cent of whatever money they make. Then they cry out that they want the whole 100 per cent. So you would stay home and see a bunch of people going up to work, and then see them coming back down. They lost their work. My husband turn and say that he going to his own country where he was born, because Barbados should do the same and give the Barbadians the same work.

A lady named Miss Pelley that I used to work for – she was married to an American man – she would stay in her window and call to them and say, "You working? Why you not working?" She would give them her husband's name, and he would pull out whoever was working and put that person to work.

All nations mix up together, although we had Bajan Town, we had Jamaica Town, and we had another place called Williamson Town. A lot of Jamaicans still live in Bajan Town. In Williamson Town, that was a kind of town following the train line, you know. It was mostly Jamaicans, but the Bajans very aggressive. They wouldn't let the Jamaicans have a picnic in peace, unless they asked the Bajans' permission. They say, "They asked your permission?" "No." "Well go down there and pull down their tent. Neither *fi* nor *fa* playing on that violin."

Bajans live together when they outside. Nobody would tell on the other who do this, or who do that. Man got beaten up and that sort of thing, and although the man woman curse all night – she was living in Bajan Town – she still can't find out who beat the man so. And he had looked like a package that come from far when he come from the doctor, with a lot of different bandages stuck all over him like stamps, like he come from a distance. But nobody would tell on the other, and that poor woman curse all night. Bajan people live together well when they outside . . . better than here. They wouldn't tell on one another.

People used to walk from Oriente to Baraguá. They were generally men. When people hear that men come in, everybody would push open their window to see the new men. They come up tired and hungry and so on, and Bajan people love to entertain. Everybody take in a few. People didn't rob and steal then. People used to try to accommodate people.

The people would walk from distant places when they seeing hardship in the other places. Or they hear about Baraguá and they hear about these people up there, they will walk all night and they find something to eat along the road. And we hear a band of men coming and we get up.

The only church that Cuba acknowledge at the time was the Roman Catholic. And after the Roman Catholic, then the Salvation Army. But the Salvation Army came in late. I can remember when they even lock up the flag. The people saw this flag marked "blood and fire", and the Cubans are very smart people; they understand English and you wouldn't know. But after they found out that it was a good thing, they liked the Army. The Saturday before Easter they would christen children, and sometimes, if they missed one baptism, you would see big children walking up to their own baptism.

We had the cricket club, and we had all sorts of things happening. They wanted to raise money for the cricket because we wanted to buy gear, because everybody poor and couldn't afford to buy gear. They wanted to send away for gear. So we girls go out on the pasture and play we cutting down the grass and so, you know, because we know the men going to come and help. They cut it down.

I made a lot of buttons and sold to help out with the Abyssinian war. Everything we got into. They had a man named Edghill – he died here in Barbados – belonged to the Christian Mission. He had a very strong voice. He used to say that if he saw Mussolini, he would do this, that and the other with Mussolini. As soon as we hear now that they really had a representative come to Havana and picking up money and we getting money to send, he said, "Here in this factory, this American mill, we only hanging here by a leather strap – we don't have any good hinge – so this man going to come up here to pull them off of us." All this strong talk about Mussolini finish. He frighten enough because this man coming in the place.

They decided they want to make a contest, blue against white, two girls against each other. They say, "Well we will give these girls fifteen dollars each to buy a kind of paper dress or something like that, nothing expensive." But don't trust Bajans. Night-time you see a bunch of Bajan women come down to my mother, they ask me to be the white queen. The brown girl with long hair all the way down, she was the blue queen.

Well everybody say she going to win, 'cause she have the hair and the colour. They say the only difference between us is that I can sew and do different things, and this girl couldn't manage herself. But I still foolish to go and put myself against a brown-skin girl. I not afraid of nothing; never was, I don't care what colour you are. The fairer they are, the better. The whiter they are, the better they like me. We used to go out and give speeches. This poor girl, wouldn't go out in the sun. She not going to get her complexion spoiled, I could go along with mine. So I had a little four-octave organ, and I pick up that – I could fold it like a valise – and I gone outside and set it down, and we start now the crowd come.

Then a man named Curtis Lashley, he was a good actor, and he was my kind of secretary like. And he wrote a letter and gave me to take to the sugar company people. The administrator there just like the governor here or something, you know. And the men read it and so, and they said yes, they would come and see this thing. The night of the contest they came and said, "Yes, we know this girl. She came to our office." So I got their vote.

The man pretending to be her father was a very popular man, Barbadian you can bet, and he would be the man to give away all the brides. Anytime you having a wedding, you got to invite him. And when you having a concert at the schoolhouse, he waiting until fairly late, and you see him stepping going in with a scroll of paper like a student, and we laughing because in those days we can't find nothing to laugh at, so we young and we laughing at everything. He stepping right around the town, he not taking no shortcuts. So he was chosen father for this brown-skin queen.

Poor me now, being the dry-head organist as they used to call me, a Grenadian man was acting as my father. We had another Bajan man too, Conrad Smith. Conrad Smith was a Combermere boy. When you come out there and you hear Combermere boy, they used to worship you. We had a band playing for each one. Her band would play, then my band would play. The Grenadian hall where they kept this thing was to the back of our house, so I went out from high evening time with my clothes, so nobody saw me go in. But she was very, very late. Everybody want to know why this queen can't come. She was in the town, Ciego de Avila, trying to fix up something to come in. So the people said.

She had a bouquet of white ginger lilies. I had a bouquet of paper roses, but that wouldn't do for her. As soon as she come in now, a Grenadian man that didn't like her – because she was married to a Grenadian man too and never used to treat him right, and the Grenadians didn't like her – the man just took it out of her hand and put it in my hand. And he took my white paper flowers in a vase on the table beside me to decorate the place. I'm sitting there posing sitting sideways with my shoe buckles all asparkle, and a dress from Delong. I copied it out of the *Havana Post*, short to the front and long to the back, and I had it beaded the same way, and nothing but roses. White crepe-back satin, beaded. I band my hair with beaded black net.

My brother-in-law, he was a man from Cayman Islands. He went and got a guard, a policeman, to be at this board. Every now and then, they get a certain amount of votes, and they would write them down. Every now and then, they would check to see who got the most votes. They gave a time now for it to be up. Anyhow, I did my best, and I won it.

Well I took the queen's crown, because the man to crown me, he didn't crown me. He said he made the crown for this other blue queen, he didn't make it for me. Another Grenadian man had to come and put it on. We come now to marching out. The same time that is where my husband came in now. He never got up to me, but in marching out he came and hook onto me and we all marching out. Nobody invited him, but he come and hook onto my hand. That's the way we ended the contest. So I took the crown now, when I got home, and put it in the centre of the table and make it into a vase and put flowers down in it, and opened back the door so everybody could see what happened to the crown. I was terrible. That's what I did.

I got married in 1935. My husband was from St Peter – Whittington St Clair Greene. His father's name was Adams, and he should name Adams, but he choose his mother's married name, Greene. He was such a rude boy, he used to call the teacher "Trumpeter Gadfly" behind his back. In those days he gave his name as Adams. His father was a very ambitious man, but like ambitious men who were very often led off with sexy-looking women. And that's what his mother was. That's how he come to name St Clair Whittington, see. The father said he was Whittington, Lord Mayor of London. Yes, the father used to read a lot, so he gave his son that kind of name. The father died early in his young days.

When he was over there in Cuba, he was a mechanic. He was working up Santa Clara. He said he had place with tub, and this, that and the other. But whatever he had there, I didn't want it. So he came down to Baraguá to get close to me, and he had no work at all. He had to turn around then and sell [lottery] tickets.

I came to Barbados just before the riot in 1937, the seventeenth of February. I was married one year. My mother didn't want me to come. She said she know Barbados and she tell me to carry the machine, carry the organ. Everything she had clean out the house and give me. Of course, both of them belonged to me, as the oldest and working. But I was a very unselfish person, always ready to give up. So I told her, "No. The others in the house, what they going to live on?" "Well if you don't carry the machine, what you going to do?" she asked me. "You can't sell, put things on your head. You wouldn't be able to put any flying fish on your head. You would have to sell frays."

My husband said, "All over the world got machines." She said, "All over the world got machines, but you don't have the money to buy when you get there." So she insist that I must carry the machine. So to bring the machine, he unpick it and put it in a box. Then he start looking around then picking, and brought rocking chairs and put them in a box.

When we came to Barbados, we lived at the Smiths for nine months. I had brought a parcel for Daddy Smith from someone who had known him here in Barbados. The signboard had been taken down, so we couldn't find Buckingham Road. We saw a little girl at the standpipe, and she turned around then and asked us who we were looking for and we said, "Daddy Smith." She said she going up there too, and she took us straight to the house.

My husband wanted to carry me to his family in St Peter, but Mother Smith said we should wait until her husband came in, so we waited. But by then it was after three o'clock and the last bus used to run at three. So we had to borrow the cart from the neighbour next door and went to collect our luggage that we had left with somebody that came from Cuba before. Then Mother Smith said, "You can't take a girl like this to the country." Thank God I was something then. So they wouldn't let me go to the country, and we stayed there for nine months.

Daddy Smith say it's a good thing that we there, that we were an example. He said I do everything; I could wash, and wash good, and know about the cooking. I know a little bit about everything. I turn around and work, and I'm not lazy.

He [Mr Greene] was very good at gambling. When they had races he would be on the pasture playing tiki tiki, which Daddy Smith didn't like because he said it was against his religious principles. But my husband was a very stubborn man. He would talk to you very nice and so, but he would do what he wanted to.

I do this lot of embroidery and things that they never see before. I telling them how women things are lapped right over left. They thought everything lap left over right, but no, a woman is right over left. I knew all those things. In those days, all the flare dresses was fitted from the waist and as far out as you could. But I brought in a fashion now that they fitting at the hips, a different style altogether. And this girl who come at Mother Smith see it and like it, and I made a dress like it for her to wear to a wedding. I turn round now and trim her hat, you know, I had a different taste.

So a woman name Elsie came in the next day and pick up the dress and ask, "Who did this dress?" Mother Smith said, "It was done at Smithville." There was a little jealousy, you know, but I play I didn't notice. I can't afford to notice things. I don't notice a lot of things. But I start sewing for Elsie right off. She wanted me to make her clothes, and I start making for her.

The interview with Maradell Greene was recorded at my home in Barbados on 8 December 1996, her birthday. Mrs Greene enjoyed a long and distinguished career as a seamstress in Barbados, outfitting many brides. She was also an ardent admirer of Grantley Adams, and was very active in the Women's League of the Barbados Labour Party. Her brother, Joseph Atwell, was my first interview subject while on assignment for the Caribbean Broadcasting Union in Baraguá. She returned to Cuba to visit her brother on at least one occasion, and he was able to visit her in Barbados once. Mrs Greene died in 2009.

CHAPTER 11

~~~~~~~~~

EARL ALONZO "PANAMA" GREAVES

"And a gentleman say, 'I going to look for Mr Greaves.' And then they find Mr Greaves. And when Mr Greaves was coming to us Mama says, 'Look your father coming there.' And he says, 'Oh Lord, look at my children. Look at my children.' And he start to cry."

I WAS BORN IN PANAMA THE SECOND DAY of September 1913, and my mother brought me here from Panama with my father to Barbados. He was from St George, Bridgecot, and my mother, Ida Alleyne Belgrave, was from St Philip. I was six months old when I came here. When I came here, they were established in St George, Bridgecot, and from there I went to school.

My schooldays were very drastic to learn and so forth. I remember the name of the school was St Augustine School. The master of the school was Mr Bert Moore. The church was beside the school there, and the reverend was Mr Joseph Sisnett. I raise up here in the school days, you know, rolling roller and pitching marbles and so forth.

Well my papa, here in Barbados when he was a small boy, he was working at a sugar cane factory, a windmill, oiling the machinery and so forth. Because in those days it was wind, windmill, you know. The machinery and cogs and so forth needed grease, and he was working as a young boy there before he go to Panama. But Mama, she used to work with her mother, my grandmother, in St Philip. Until a uncle that we had who was a carpenter take she, as a small, little girl to Panama and there she met Mr Greaves, my father, and they married.

In those days in Panama there wasn't no tractor or anything to blow up anything, and they used to use dynamite. And he was in charge of a team to blow up the dynamite to break up the hills. So on that day he had an order that at twelve o'clock everybody supposed to leave the field and go away far, far, a mile from there before they blow up. And he had received the order, but Papa was a man he liked to do and overdo and overdo, and he stayed back. And when they BOOM!, he get wounded. He could have killed himself. But on that day there were two or more Barbadians get killed, and he get wounded in his legs.

And Mama she was home doing washing to get by, and both of them get together, and they was a couple, married people. And with what they earned down there – working, working as youngsters – they came back to Barbados with what little they had, and with a little boy named Earl Alonzo Greaves.

In 1922 Papa decided to go to Cuba. He went to Cuba and was established in a place named Ciego de Avila, Baraguá. In 1925, after he went there, he sent for us to visit Cuba.

That was something terrible, terrible, terrible. I remember good, good, good, good when Mama decided that morning, "We are preparing to go down tomorrow to go out to Cuba." We start from St Phillip. Family come down to greet us you know, and take us down to the wharf. Up to now anytime I pass there and see it, I want to cry to see that in those days the ship was not like the modern ships today. In those days, the ships were steamships and so forth and they was way out in the water out yonder, and you had to go out in a rowboat and step in the ship.

When we get down there now, it was a morning when we going to depart to go to Cuba, and I hear the people saying, "St Lucia over there; St Lucia over there." They discussing, you know, and the ship going and going and I don't see no land. I only see the sky and water, the ship pull out, pull out. It was a steamship and in those days it worked with coals, and it was a Norwegian ship, but I don't remember the name of the ship. But I do remember, and I'll never forget as long as I live, when they get in the water and going down to Haiti; that was a half past four in the evening when they reached there and we stay there for a couple of hours.

The next morning, we pull out now to go down to Cuba. That was terrible, terrible, terrible. They got the four winds they call it there . . . the water . . . one come from the east, north and south and they all mix together, and I remember the captain of the ship telling everybody, "Go down below; go down below. Cover up."

Next morning when we wake up, on top of the ship was cleaner than this place here. The wave going down, you know, and come up. And when you look over yonder, you see the oceans just like a mountain coming and you have to meet that and go up top that. You go up, go up, and then you come down. You must imagine when it receive the lash at bottom everybody with their Bible praying and saying, "Oh Lord, forgive us", and this and that and the other. And my mama says, "Well, Mrs Haynes." "Yes, Mrs Greaves." "Mrs Gaskin." "Hello Ida, what happen to you now?" "I here with my three children. If we go down, well, we have to give our souls to God." I remember all of that.

Next morning early, they says, "Hey, we see something over yonder like Cuba!" "Look over yonder." "I ain't see nothing." "I ain't see nothing." "I ain't …" "Look over yonder." "Look now." "Look now." When the waves go down you don't see anything, but when it come up you see over yonder. And my dear friend, when I look up I see something like a long piece of stick on the wharf. They say, "Look it there. Look it there." "That is Cuba." "You telling lies, man." "I know it. I know it. I know it." That was in the morning about half past nine, ten o'clock. And we draw more nearer and nearer. Three o'clock the evening, we going into Punta Maisí. We safe now, and everybody happy and glad. But you have to go round the curve now to go down to Central Delicia. Delicia is a place also plenty of Barbadians there, and I remember when we reach there, all the Barbadians come out to receive us, you know. But we cannot come off the ship now until we get a order, because we have to vaccinate.

They vaccinate us, you know. And then we go off after ten o'clock the morning, Mrs Greaves and her three children, and Mrs Gaskin and all the families together. And the first lady that visit us, it was her sister and her brother-in-law was there at Central Delicia waiting for us. And from Delicia, we depart to a place called San Germán. And we going down now, you know, my mama and me, and her two children, girls, and a lady that came down with us that she going to stay in Baraguá now. Now, when we get to Baraguá she say, "Mrs Greaves, you going to receive four more stations. Descend to Gaspar and all the way going down. Do not get out until you reach Ciego de Avila." Because we had the big Everlasting trunk full of things and so forth. And so said, so did.

And the Lord always provide. The Lord always helps people, especially those who believe in Him. Little as you expect help, is help right there. A man by the name of Mr Hinds was sitting down in the same … behind the same seat where my mother sitting down. He says, "Good day. You all are Barbadians?" "Yes." "I know you all are Bajans. I hear you talk, so I know you all are Bajans. Where you come from?" We say, "From St George, and we going now to Ciego de Avila." "Ah, I going to help you." And he help us to Ciego de Avila. And we get off at Ciego de Avila now. Listen now to the surprise. My papa was waiting for us in July, and we advance and come in May. So when we was there at the train station standing up, my mama don't see nobody that she know, except Mr Hinds. "Mrs Greaves, I gone because I got to go to Central Stewart." He used to work in a Central Stewart. "Anyway, you'll meet somebody 'round here."

And after that, a few minutes after, a gentleman passed by and my ma says, "Joseph Goodridge, that's you? Joseph. Joseph. Joseph." "Ms Greaves? Wait, what you doing here?" "No man, I just come down." "Lord, Ms Greaves." They had meet from Panama . . . in those days. But they didn't expect to meet one another there, you see. That's how the world work, like that.

And I tell you Papa can't be found around there at that moment. There was a little bar in front there . . . Mr Lord's bar. He was a Barbadian. He was from St Joseph, and his wife was a Jamaican. And they give us something to eat, because we hungry you know, travelling the whole day. And a train like that going down, going down, going down to Havana, you know. And Mama didn't have much, and she was weak and so forth and we was hungry, and they give us food.

And a gentleman say, "I going to look for Mr Greaves." And then they find Mr Greaves. And when Mr Greaves was coming to us Mama says, "Look your father coming there." And he says, "Oh Lord, look at my children. Look at my children." And he start to cry. He lift me up and put me on his shoulder, and he received the family, and so forth. And then we move from there the next morning to go down to Mairíque, where all the other Bajans live and so forth, another Bajan town. And that's where I raised up.

In Cuba now, in a place called Ciego de Avila, Barrio Mairíque. I remember when I went to school I didn't know anything about Spanish at all, at all, at all, at all, not even an ABC. And I went to Spanish school and I start to learn between the Cuban children and so forth. I remember that in the school days in Cuba, the schoolteacher put on the blackboard everything – the sums, add, divide and multiply. I could do it because that is international ways, you see, but I could not speak Spanish. I remember she used to say, "How it is that little boy can write and can do other things and can't speak?" I started to learn until I came up speaking Spanish. I don't know if I speak it correctly, but I know I speak it and I can understand. In the school days now, you can imagine how much blows I get. They beat me every day. I fight them too, and they fight me. As schoolchildren, you know.

In Baraguá you find that 80 per cent of the West Indians are Barbadians. They had St Lucians and Jamaicans and other people, but the greatest per cent are Barbadians. They are and was, because right now the descendants of Barbadians, the grandchildren, speak English and Spanish. They got the town there, Bajan Town, where every year they make the carnival and so forth. English Barbadian-raised children have the man with the donkey. He in the centre dancing, and they sing "Sly Mongoose". I remember also they have the song too "Millie Gone to Brazil" about a young man they had here in Barbados. His sweetheart was going to Brazil. He didn't want she to go, he so in love with she, because he think he going to lost her. And he kill her, cut off she neck and throw her down in a well. And they sing this song:

Oh, poor Millie, Millie gone to Brazil.
She ain't tell nobody, but she gone to Brazil.
The razor cut up her neck
And put it down in a well.
Oh, Millie gone to Brazil.

I remember those days. "Sly Mongoose" and all of those songs that they had here, and they have here, they had down in Cuba, in Baraguá. Baraguá was a second Bajan town in Cuba. Yes, you find all the West Indians there. Central Baraguá development build up through West Indians, Barbadians, you see?

I used to go to Baraguá every Sunday, man. Every Sunday. Because from Ciego to Baraguá was only forty-eight miles. I was going to the dance, man, oh Lord, and play cricket and all of those things. Look, they had a cricket game in Baraguá that people come from Jamaica to beat them, and can't beat them never until today. They had a cricket game in Baraguá, I tell you, they come from Jamaica, from Demerara, but I don't remember any coming from this country [Barbados]. But I tell you, every Sunday they had various games, and boxing and so forth.

And I decide one day to go in the boxing line. Listen to this now. Huh, huh. And I going to be a boxer, and I learn a little. But you know, I was strong in those days and I was developed, and muscles, and strength. And I made a couple fights and I win, and sometimes I lose. So one day, I went to fight a fellow from Spain and he beat me. He swell up my face. And Mama saw that and Ma say, "Oh Lord." I'll never forget, she say, "Don't do that again. I ain't want no richness from your body. Don't go and fight nobody again. Don't go fight nobody." And I forget it.

But I like the boxing and I want to continue. Now listen to this one now. They had a heavy, heavy, heavy boy, Bajan boy from the Nelson family. He was a fighter from Baraguá. He defend all the Bajan fights in Baraguá. He was the champion at that place, and I want to fight him. And they says, "No, no, no. Don't meet Mateo Gomez, man. Mateo Gomez is a man that went all over America Latina and fight. You can't beat Mateo, man." But I feel like I would do it. Even if he had beat me, I would have got fame, because I fight the man that have, have, have. . . . You see I get a little fame. But that's not the thing, he would have beat me. He was a terrible, terrible, terrible Bajan boy. He was from Barbados.

In loving affairs and so forth, as young men all over, you know, I was attracted, very attracted to a girl that down there – she old now, just like me. Olga Mauri, she's from Barbados. She wasn't born here, but her mother was from Barbados and her father was a Cuban, a Spaniard. She had a doctor shop, two doctor shops. And she was the one who told me, "Don't go and match Mateo; he going to kill you." And I forget, you know.

We used to keep in contact with family in Barbados. Florence St Hill was my aunt from St Philip. James Campbell, my grandmother, is his grandmother. Eleanor, that's another one. Brenda Licorish. I always, I always, I always write all the time and I could not even receive the answer completely; especially in 1986, when I write my aunt Florence St Hill. I get in contact with she. I have letters here, my son find them. Because I don't know if she was so old she could not even answer. But when I go into the room, the old house that was there, he start to search and find them. Now listen, why we kept in contact all the time, is that in those days she write me a letter one time and told me that she was very sick in the hospital, and she came out of the hospital and was still feeling ill.

We had a piece of land here that she was taking care of while my mother and father was down in Cuba. She was paying the land taxes. She wrote to say, "Now I'm old I cannot take care of the land and the youngsters don't want to work, so what you think I must do with the land? The government going to take it over, because I owe the government." I says, "Oh dear me, the best thing that I could do is tell she sell the land." How could I expect to sell she, my family? The government can't take it over. Papa and Mama sweat to get that land from Panama. Papa sweat and Mama sweat and come to Barbados to buy the land. Who could I expect to give this to? To she, not the government. And I write a letter from Cuba, and here all get together, both governments got together lawyers, and she sell the land.

Now my father, Oliver Gladstone Greaves, he died in Cuba in 1981. My father worked in the cane field, that's number one. Because you couldn't get a permanent job in the mill because the mill was crowded with people, and he had to do something. So he went and cut cane, and so forth, and from then he developed himself and he bought three pair of bulls – two, four and six. And he get a cart to carry the cane then from the farm to the mill.

I'll never forget the name of the bulls; he called them by their names, you know. Yes. One was named Doublon, Flor de Mayo and Acabache. Papa with a rod in the hand and he guiding them, you know. And that's how he developed more and more, until he bought a piece of land in Ciego de Avila and he built his house there and brought all his children together. And he lived there comfortable, comfortable until he died in 1981. After he died, a year after, Mama died. Yes, man, that was a history. It is. Not it was. It is a history, and a truthful history. Very sorrowful sometimes, I remember.

My parents never came back to Barbados. Never. Papa always say, tell my mother, in Spanish "Yo me voy para mi país," "I going home," "I going to Barbados." But I tell you the truth, plenty of Barbadians, old people that are there now still until now, they would be glad to come back to Barbados. Because they hear how Barbados develop.

Well, I learn mechanic trade. I am a mechanic. And I learn it. I think I know it, because you should never finish learning, you know. Mechanics and doctors never finish work. They always striving. And I was working there 'til 1942. I decide to move then from Ciego de Avila to Guantánamo, and is there when I began to work as a mechanic in the naval base at Guantánamo. I work with them until 1962. The United States naval base at Guantánamo. Years after, years after the war declare. In 1938 was a terrible, terrible war between Hitler, England and so forth.

I don't know if you all ever heard, or know, about a submarine that develop and was killing out all the people down there. So one afternoon about half past four o'clock the alarm went off that they was in danger. I was there. In those days I was married and my daughter was a small, little baby. Yes, yes. And everybody stay. And the next morning about half past four o'clock, they catch the submarine. England hit the submarine, and lick it up, and that was the end of the destruction around there.

My dear friend, I had a lot of trouble there, working between two languages – English and Spanish. But I know the Americans and they know us, although some of them – you'll find them all over the world – good and bad. But I tell you the truth, I was accommodated. I was accommodated until I decide then to marry this lady here, Carmelina Greaves García. She is my wife, and my first daughter, Aida Greaves, she's over there, and my son, George Greaves. And another son I got in the United States of America, Raoul Greaves.

During the war, two or three days I couldn't see my wife, because you had to leave the base and come over to Guantánamo. Transportation carry you and bring you, buses. If you want to go by ship, you can go too. After I left the base, then I went and work with the Red Cross.

I was in Cuba from 1925 all the time until the other day when things begin to change, change plenty. I came back to Barbados. I had a very strong desire to see it again, to step on the land where I was established before. I feel myself comfortable here. Where I supposed to be more comfortable than here? This place where my mother was born, and my father, and my great grandfather, all the descendants was born from Africa come down until today. This is the best place for me, Barbados. I'm not saying that Cuba is not a good place, because I raise up there. I have experience in Cuba.

They got plenty churches down there. I think they got about five or six churches in Guantánamo. People go there now. Oh on Sunday, or especially when you see they have a wedding or a baptism. Yes, man. Everybody, those that belong or don't belong, they go and watch from the window. Beautiful, beautiful thing. The same way you see the people here going to church, they goes well dressed in their hat and with their Bible. The same way, the same way my friend, it is down there. We don't stop travelling. *"Onward Christian soldiers marching on to war, with the cross of Jesus going on before."* Nobody molest them.

I have a couple relatives from both sides in Barbados, Papa side and Mama side. Anyway, Olga Bailey, through she I find all of them others. And I expect to find more, because up to today. . . . They call me every day, every day, every day. They ask me how I feeling, from one thing to the other. You see that they interested in me. And if I find five of them, I find sufficient.

Earl "Panama" Greaves was interviewed at his home in Barbados on 7 February 1999. Mr Greaves had returned to Barbados from Guantánamo with his wife, Carmelina, on 6 March 1997, to enjoy his retirement. Their children have visited the island since then to spend time with them, and to become acquainted with the land of their father and paternal grandparents. Mr Greaves died in 2008, and his wife in 2010.

CHAPTER 12

~~~~~~~~

RUFUS HOYTE

"I hold on on the rope and I climb up on the ship, gone right up. I say, 'When you go home, tell my mother I gone to Cuba.' Just like that, nothing in my hand; nothing, nothing, nothing."

I WENT TO CUBA IN 1925. AT THAT time there was emigration. They was emigrating people, but I was nineteen years of age at that time. But I never been because I had no reason for going, and had no idea of going.

But they had a gentleman here that lived in the next gap there – Licorish. His son had been there, you know. He say, "You go on the emigration and come back." But I had no right to go because I used to take charge of the marlhole that my father had. I didn't had no reason to go. But you know young people and so on . . . get caught up . . . and then he came. And the truth is this, when he came here I see the silk shirts that he had on. At that time they had a class of silk in Cuba that was very pretty, and it draw my attention. I saw him and I said, "I would like to go to Cuba and get some of these silk shirts," nothing more than that you know.

So I decide then that when he was going the next time, I would go too. Well, unknown to my mother, because I used to run the marlhole, see, because my father died and I took it over. Well, when that time come I been and I bought a permit. The permit at that time had cost a guinea – twenty-one shillings. I bought a permit to go to Cuba. So when I come home now and I show my mother, I said, "Look, I going to Cuba now." She said, "Do what?!" I said, "I going to Cuba."

She took the permit from me and she went right back to the gentleman, Nightengale I think his name was. Yes. She say, "Listen. This is my son. He's no man. He's only eighteen, running nineteen years of age." I didn't even nineteen. I complete nineteen in February in Cuba. "He's isn't twenty-one, and you can't sell him no permit to go to Cuba. He's not a man." And she tell him, "You give me back my money." And she give him back the permit and he give back the money, because the law was under twenty-one, you know.

So the morning when they were about to go. Let me see, it was the twenty-third of January 1925. I remember the day good. He come to me and say, "Hoyte, so you ain't going?" I said, "No, my mother won't let me go." He said, "Alright, goodbye." So when I turned to her I said, "Kit." We used to call her Kit. I said, "Kit, let me go and see the boys sail out to go to Cuba, nuh." She say, "Alright." And I put on a suit that she had given me for the Christmas, a pair of brown shoes and a brown hat, because I never was without hat. And I went and say, "Alright Kit, I going and see the boys off," and she say, "Alright."

So I went with nothing at all in my hand, only the bare clothes I leave with. So when I get there now and the boys going the last hour, the same boy Licorish . . . at that time you know there wasn't no wharf like now. The ships got to go outside. So he said, "Hoyte, I gone. See you when I come back." He going to spend six months, make the crop, six months.

Well after he gone I felt so lonely, so the same fellow that had the boat, that carry them on the boat, I know him too, Mitch. I said, "Mitch, come here man. Give me a tour outside to the ship where the boys is." He said, "Well get in." So the detective now on the gangway where the people going up. I tell him, "Carry me round to the back." So he carry me round to the back of the ship, and when he carry me to the back of the ship now, in those days you know the ship tall, but they had a rope. I hold on to the rope man, I was real thrifty. I hold on on the rope and I climb up on the ship, gone right up. I say, "When you go home, tell my mother I gone to Cuba." Just like that, nothing in my hand; nothing, nothing, nothing.

When I get board the ship now the same very boys that board the ship say, "Hoyte, you here!" I say, "I here." They say, "How you get here?" I say, "I here." The ship now, we sail out. Night. The ship sail out. When we get to a place . . . God is great man. I have to say I believe God threw me from my mother's womb. When we get to a place between Santo Domingo and Cuba the captain tell everybody, "Below from off the deck. Everybody below." We didn't know what going on. He sent everybody below. I went below too. When I get below I see the people seasick, they casting you know, throwing up. They did puking. And I say, "I ain't stanning down here man." I gone right back up.

When I get right up on the deck of the ship a tide take the ship and hit it forward. It throw me forward, when I get now to the edge of the ship to fall over. . . . God is good man . . . like someone put my two hands on the edge of ship, otherwise I would have gone right over and no one would know. All the boys down below. There wasn't no one to say, "A man overboard." But God is good. Every time I think on that, I shiver. I would have died and my mother wouldn't know, no one would know what become of me. But God is good. My mother was a Christian, belonged to the Christian Mission. God saved me through my mother.

Well when my hand hold on, then the tide come back and lick me back. When it lick me back, then I hear a voice say, "Lay down." And I lie down. If I did still standing up it would have throw me over. I look up now and I saw a ring, and I hold on on this ring and steady myself a little bit; lying down. And then I look and I saw something like a fishpot, but it was a life raft that was a stairs they got for saving you if anything. The mind tell me go inside and I went in there. And I was there till the morning.

In the morning the others see me. They didn't know what happened; I sleep there. They know I aboard the ship because they see when I come, but they didn't know what happened. If I had dead they wouldn't be able to give no one no account of me. Well in the morning I come out this place like a lifeboat and I told them what happened. They say, "Boy, if you had get drown we wouldn't even know to tell nobody nothing." I said, "No one at all. God is good." Anyway, the next day we reached Cuba.

It was a port called Cayo Juan Claro. When we get in Juan Claro, the Cubans that come to take charge of us, you know, we on land now, and they line us up. Two men was checking on the permit that we had. Now I ain't got no permit or nothing, but I was very thrifty man. God was with me too. So when they get about four people off of me, I watching the man, you know; the man that taking the permit from the people. And whilst he taking the permit of others, when it was about two before me, I just slip out the line and gone the next side with people that had passed the people. He ain't see me, you know.

Then someone come with a truck and carry us down to the farm. On the farm they give us a hammock to sleep in and give us food and all such, and all such. After that they give us now a collins and carry us out to cut canes. I went out and had about a week cutting cane. Then they had a strike. This is 1925. Well we was there during the strike. I believe it was about two weeks the strike was on, no working.

But then I heard that a next place, Manatí, my brother was there, and when he write he used to . . . the direction was Central Manatí, and I remember the direction. Through the strike, the strike going on and men they didn't working and they hear Manatí. They say, "We going down Manatí, man. Cut cane and get money, man." I tell them, I say, "You all going Manatí?" They say, "Yes." But those men had went to Cuba already and know the place, you know. I say, "You going to Manatí?" They said, "Yes." I said, "Look. I got a brother in Manatí. When you all going you can carry me with you?" They say, "Yes, you can come." But they got to steal away to go, you know, because this is contract. So they get up about two o'clock in the night and come and shake my hammock. "Get up. We going." I get up and put my clothes in the hammock, wrap the hammock, put the hammock over my shoulder and we gone.

When we get now to Manatí, the walk, they know the road. When we get there now it was morning. It was day. So when we get there now they going to a farm, they know the farm too because they was there already. They went to the farm. When they get to the farm now they say, "Look, you going to the factory, nuh?" I say, "Yes. My brother works in the factory, according to . . ." I show them the address Central Manatí. *Central* is the factory. And they carry me; they bring me on the rail line. They say, "Look, now we stopping here." It was about ten kilometres from where they were. They say, "Now you walk the straight line, only when you see the train coming come off the line. But if there is no train walk the straight line and this here will carry you straight into the factory." Because the same train carry the cane right in the factory. And you know, I was very thrifty, you know.

I take their word and walk, walk, walk . . . get in the factory. When I get there now, a fella had came down with me too, belongst to Manatí, Barbadian too, name was Livy Hoyte; he was there. So when I get there now the first body saw me and know me was he. He say, "Rufus, what you doing here?" I say, "Livy?" He say, "Yes, it's me Livy." He say, "What you doing here?" I say, "Well I was over in Chaparra and they had a strike in Chaparra, and two men walked from Chaparra to Manatí and brought me on one the farms about ten kilometres. Because they had the kilometre mark, you know. So they tell me to walk the straight line and I would find where my brother is in Manatí." So he say, "Yes man, come." Lester here and Garfield and all of them. Man when they see me, my brother knew me, yes, but Garfield and the others didn't know me. Garfield said, "Which one you are?" I said, "I is Rufus." So I say, "I am one of the twin. I'm Rufus."

Then my brother came. He say, "Boy, what you doing here? How you come? Why you come to Cuba?" My brother say, "Look, my mother write and tell me how you used to spend up all the money from the business with your friends; carry your friends at the shop and eat it out; eat out all the money and all such." About my bad behaviour, you know. I ain't say a word. This teenage, you know. I ain't say a word.

At that time anyone could get work in the factory. Well they carry me in the factory and apply for work for me and I get work in the factory. And I was there in the factory working all the time.

Well, I was there until 1968. I leave Cuba in 1968 back for here. I never came back before. Others came back; I never came back. I get Cubanized now; I wasn't coming back neither. Didn't intend to come back. That is forty-three years. But sixteen years before I came here, then I accept the Adventist message and I was a changed man.

I pass eleven years with an ulcer in my stomach. And I pray to God, because I hear someone speak about "the power of faith healeth". And these Pentecostal people was praying and I said, "Lord if I can get on the breach up here, I believe you will hear my prayer and will heal my ulcer." You know God hear my prayer and the people came where I was. In three days' time they was where I was at Central Manatí. From Santiago de Cuba, that's about six hundred miles. And at the service in the stadium, I come out there believing that God would heal me, and he heal me. That's how I come to accept Christ.

When the ulcer leave me now, I say, "Wait, you mean to say that I heal?" I hear a voice say, "Yes, I have healed you. With what are you going to show me some recompense?" I say, "Lord, you don't want money?" I speaking now to myself, you know. "Lord you don't want money. You want my life, I will give you my life." Then I heard the voice say, "Well, look, if you going to give God your life, you is a sinner. You got to stop gambling. You is a drunkard; you got to stop drinking. I stop drinking. And he touch one after the other. And as the voice speak, the Lord give me power to stop it, you know.

Then through a book called the Marked Bible speak about the Sabbath. Because at that time I used to go to the Anglican church. The Anglican minister was telling me about confirmation. But when I see this book I went back to the Anglican minister and I say, "Look, Mr Als, look at this book about the Sabbath. We keep it a Sunday, but Saturday is the right day." He tell me, "No,

the Sabbath for the Jews. We ain't Jews. And the Sunday for the Gentiles." I say,
"What part of the Bible, Mr Als?" He couldn't bring it, but I could bring the text
and show him about the Sabbath. So I beat him.

So when I beat him now, he said, "The truth is this, I can't stop working on
Saturday and let my wife and my two children dead from hunger." And I hear
a voice say like this, "The blind can't lead the blind. Otherwise all two would
fall." I say to myself, "Look, you remember that when you was a member of the
cricket club . . . I like cricket, still like cricket. . . . Manatí had a team that used
to play Baraguá and other teams? You in there dancing and drinking your
rum, and he in there too with the wife. He in there also drinking . . . minister
you know . . . drinking with you. And you going to let a man like this lead you?
The blind can't lead the blind." And then the voice say, "Leave him." Well I left
from there and went over to the Adventists one Sabbath.

It was a communion Sabbath, and when this white man come with a basin
to wash my feet, he said, "You don't mind if I wash your feet?" I said, "Wash my
feet?" A white man, you know. And I looked at the man with disdain, because
I had hate everything name white, down to a white sheet. I had liked to wear
white because I wanted to know that I wearing white. And I grin and say,
"*Lavarme los pies*?" When I grin, the man laugh. The man smile, and I watching
him. And when he smile, he smile bring me right down.

He said, "Today is communion Sabbath. I want to wash your feet." And I
said, "What must I do?" He said, "Take off your shoes and your socks." I take off
my shoes and my socks, and whilst the white man washing my feet, is the Holy
Spirit that spoke to me. It said, "This is love. In which other church you meet a
white man washing a black man feet? You know that white men discriminate
against you all." They discriminate and brought us out of Africa. That was me.
And the Holy Spirit take me on my own grounds.

When they done wash my feet and they done take communion, I went and
looked for him. I say, "Sir, can I join you all?" He jumped back, surprised,
because he know what class of man I is. He said, "You want to join us?" I say,
"Yes, I want to join you all. What must I do?" He give me then a Sabbath school
book and tell me, "Go and study the lesson and come back the Sabbath."

When I get back the next Sabbath and they take the lesson, I could answer
all the lessons, thirty-three of them. Everybody stop and watching me to know
how I can answer these things. Impossible! But it was the Holy Spirit. Anyhow,
I went on and I going every Sabbath.

Well it come to about this time of the year, February, when we have what they call the ingathering. That is a time when, once a year, all the members of the church goes out soliciting from everybody to help the needy. So the elder of the church, he came out, and they had a chart where they put down your name and the amount that you give. And he asked, "Who want to work in the ingathering?" I raise my hand, ready to work for God. Because God did so much for me. So he give me a card. Well, through the gambling, I used to go inside the people house with this gambling business when you see they selling the lotto here. Well this one was against the government, so we used to do it secretly, and I used to go in the people house. All the people in the same Manatí, all them know me.

From there then they name me deacon and then lay active leader. They ask me if I would do it. I say, "I don't know what it means." They ask me, "Are you willing to do anything God tell you to do?" I say, "Yes, I'm willing." They say, "Well look, the Holy Spirit tell us to nominate you as deacon. Would you do it?" I said, "If you all would teach me what to do." They said, "We will teach you." And sixteen years in the church, you hear me? Sixteen years as deacon and sixteen years as lay active leader. Every year they change the officers. They never change me yet. When I accept that church, they take me then as an idol. I remember in 1957 they had a congress in Havana, and they choose a delegate for the young people. I wasn't young then, at that time I was fifty-something years. Because I baptize in 1952. I was forty-six years when I baptize. I was fifty-one years of age, but the young people take me through the Bible. I could give all the texts. We had a competition in the class whosoever could give the most texts would be the head. So the class that I was in, through me, they came out ahead.

So now with the congress, when we went to Havana, there were three delegates. Two white men, and me. When we get to the hotel now, one say, "Rufino got to sleep with me." The other one say, "No, he going to sleep with me." And they don't want me sleep alone, you know. You know what they do? They ask for a bed that can sleep three. I sleep in the middle. How can I do without loving white people? The people idolize me as a black man. There was no difference. And love. I see real love in Cuba.

But then the country changed from what it was to Communism. Castro took over. And after Castro took over, there was a law against religion. Yuh hear me? You can't go nowhere out the church and preach. If they catch you out the church, even with a paper or anything, it's five years for you.

Well, I was notified about three times. I remember a lady that we used to go at on a Sabbath and give Bible studies with her children. Her son, he became now a private police, and the head of the police in the same factory, Manatí, told him that he hear that I goes down there and give Bible studies on Saturdays. And they tell him, "Look, anytime, any time at all he come to give Bible study, only ring. Only notify us, and we going to come and catch him on the spot." But when we went there the Sabbath now to give Bible study, the gentleman mother call us and tell us – and he was there too. She say, "Look, my son is a private police, and he was told by the head of the police that he hear that you all does come and give Bible studies, and any time at all you come ring him and he going to come for you."

She say, "But listen, this is my son and he obeys me. We will never do a thing like this. So once you doing something good, no way. If the head of the police want him, come down here for him himself. But I tell my son don't do that." She tell us, "But don't come back." He turn and tell us, "Yes. I have the authority to make you all prisoners right now." It was me, a next fella and a girl – three of us; a girl that I had just brought the message to. Well, I ain't went back.

A next time again, one Sabbath we went to a next place where we had a branch Sabbath school. And I went to the branch Sabbath school to visit the people. And the gentleman that was there, a police too, but he was a black man, and the people that we went to was white people. And when we coming out, he say, "Come here." Me and a next brother, Garfield. Garfield dead now; he dead an Adventist.

He say, "Sit down here." He say, "Look, there is a law that you all cannot go out of the church and do no class of service at all. In the church, we don't have to see with you, but out the church, no service. And here it is, I am commissioned to make you all prisoner. Right now, two of you all, but I will not do that. You see the same house you just come from, white people. I am a Negro and they are white people and we all move together the same very way. Impossible for I to handle you all. But don't come back." We agree.

One Sabbath, we had a mission that baptism was going to go on the Sabbath. But the next place we had some members of the church to be baptized and there was no one to baptize them. But there wasn't no phone, you know, someone got to go and notify. So the elder of the church says, "Look, the pastor coming next Sabbath to baptize the people. And we got some members in, they call it *La Trocha*, and they had some candidates for baptism, but they didn't know what time the baptism. Someone must go and notify them." He asked the question, "Who will go?" I got up. I said, "I will go."

Now the church that I had belonged to was white. They had thirty-three white people. And they had me and a next black fella who was a Cuban that was coloured, see? So I had brought him in too. Only we two black people, all the rest was white people. So I got up and said, "I will go." Then Primitivo got up and said, "If Rufino going, I will go too." And here it is, the two of us start off.

We start off and we walk, because it wasn't too far. It was about ten to twelve kilometres. Whilst we walking, there was a fella who used to work in the factory with us. He know me and he know Primitivo. And he went and tell one of the secret guards that we going this place. And he and the secret guard came on horseback. And whilst they came on horseback now, Primitivo was in the yard stanning up and I was inside the house overseeing some lessons, Voice of Prophecy lessons that the children had done. But I was waiting now for the people to gather. They didn't gather yet. If the people had gathered, they would come and catch me, because I was going to direct the service. But God is good man. God is a loving God.

When these two men come, well, I know one. Primitivo knew him too, because we work in the same factory. But we didn't know the other fella. Two white men on horses. So the one that we didn't know turn to Primitivo and said, "*Ven aca.*" And Primitivo went to him, and he tell him, "Consider yourself under arrest." And then he look up, and I saw him. I sitting down now in the house with the children, and he said, "*Ven, tu tambien.*" He say, "You come too." I went. So when I get to him now, I say, "*Que pasa?*" "What's the matter?" He said, "Consider yourself under arrest." I said, "May I ask for what?" He said, "I don't know. All I know is that the head of the police in Manatí tell me to make you all prisoners." I said, "Alright, let us go."

So when we get to a certain part, that time I took my Bible and my hymnbook. Primitivo had his Bible and his hymnbook too. Well, when we get to a certain part, they say, "Wait here. Don't go nowhere." They on horseback, we walking. Well after they say so, Primitivo say, "Wait? I going, man. Rufus I going. Rufino, I going, man. I ain't stopping here." I say, "Primitivo, don't go nowhere, man. We ain't do nothing wrong. Primitivo, why you going to run?" And I coax him, and he didn't go.

Well they come back on horseback. They went and tell the people that we say to give the lessons and so on that I was overlooking. We ain't carry those lessons. The children carry those lessons at home, because you can't carry nothing out the church. They want to make it look like we carry these lessons. But God is God. So, we get to the factory now. They carry us and put us in a cell, on the cement. We pass the Sabbath there, but when our members heard, they brought lunch for us. Well, we slept there on the cement the night.

Well, the following day, they tell us come, and they put us on a truck and carry us to a next town. Well, they put us in custody in the next town too. This is the Sunday now. Nothing to eat. Primitivo tell the people that we hungry and asked if they had anything to eat. I said, "But Primitivo, this is no time to look to eat, man." He was afraid too. Well, they had a little white rice, bare rice without flesh or sauce or anything, and they bring it. He eat some, I ain't eat none. I couldn't eat none. He ate some.

And he was there, he was so frighten, he say, "Look, the money that I have on me I'm going to give it to you so that when you go back home you can give my wife." I said, "Primitivo, what's the matter?" I figuring now that he going to kill heself, you know. And that's what he thinking to do, kill himself. I said, "Primitivo, You going to kill yourself? If you kill yourself you don't have any pardon, man. What you going to do?" Anyhow, I coax him and . . .

Well, we sleep there the night, sitting on a chair. In the morning, they take us again on a next truck, and carry us now to a next town. This is three days now. We turn to the indoor sargeant and say, "Look, we hungry. Today is three days that we in custody and they ain't give us nothing to eat. We have money. Would you send someone to buy something for us to eat?" The indoor sargeant call one of the police. He say, "Look, go here and buy some sandwiches for these two men." He went and he bought some sandwiches, but they was pork chops. But this sargeant knew the message. So when he brought the pork chop sandwiches he ask, "*Carne puerco*? These people don't eat hog meat. Go back and ask them to give you lamb, *carne chivo*." So said, he went back and bring it. So when he brought it now, we eat.

When we done eat now, he was an Adventist, man; got to be an Adventist. He turn to me and ask, "You all are Seventh Day Adventists?" We said, "We are." He said, "You all has a belief in God, but not we. We believe in the good works of Castro." Anyhow, we didn't say nothing. So he say, "You all speak about the Bible, and you believe that the Bible is God's word, and it is true." I say, "Yes, it is God's word, and it is true." He say, "I going to demonstrate to you right now that the Bible ain't true. It speak against it own self." I say, "That is not true." He say, "Don't the Bible say that in the first day God said, 'Let there be light and there was light'?" I said, "Yes, the Bible said it."

He said, "And don't the Bible say also that on the fourth day God create two great lights, one to rule the day and one to rule the night?" I said, "Yes, the Bible said it too." Then Primitivo say, "No." And he look at Primitivo with a very straight look. I said, "Primitivo, the gentleman is right. The Bible said it." He ask me, "Wait, he does preach?" I said, "No." He said, "But you does preach?" I said, "Yes, I do." He said, "You have credentials?" This time I take out my credentials and show him. If I didn't have my credentials, I would have get burn. The first thing I carry is my credentials. At that time I had twelve years in the message, but Primitivo only had two years. I brought him in, see? So he look at the credentials and all was right.

So he said, "And what do you say?" I said, "Yes, the Bible said that the fourth day He created two great lights." He said, "Well if it said that on the first day He said, 'Let there be light' and there was light. And now the fourth day He create two lights, don't you see that one contradict the other?" I said, "There is no contradiction at all." He said, "But if the first day He created light, there wouldn't be any need for the two big lights."

I don't know where I get it from, but God is God. The Holy Spirit put this in me. Now, I accustomed that at that time I used to stay in a place that I used to go in the countryside and if night catch me there I got to walk at night, and walk all through the woods. All through the woods dark, but you could see the trail. So I say, "Look, you don't see that in the darkest night, and you're in the mountains, if there is a trail, you can see the trail? And there ain't no moon or no stars?" He ain't say a word; couldn't say a word.

Anyhow, we were there and about ten o'clock the night a police came and he unlock the door and come in. He didn't knock, because he had the key too. So when he came in he said, "Which of you all is Rufino Hoyte?" I said, "*Yo soy.*" "I am." He said "*Ven conmigo.*" "Come with me." And I walk out with him and get in a car.

When we get to a certain place now, this place was dark. But they had a building and light in the building. So when we get there he said, "Get out here." When I get out now, I look, the place don't seem. . . . I said, "Lord have mercy. You mean to say that this man bring me here to do with me as Batista used to do with them." Because in the war between Castro and Batista, who was at that time president, whenever Batista catch the rebels, soldiers used to carry them in an abysmal place and kill them. You find them next morning dead. And sister, I get so frighten, I felt to pass water. And I felt to ease my bowels the same time.

But it is good when you walk with God and you know God's word. You hear me? The word said when the Spirit come it will teach you and will cause you to remember. And whilst I was afraid, I ask the police, "They has a toilet here?"

He said, "Look the toilet there." And whilst I go to the toilet with intentions to pass water, I heard a voice telling me, "Don't be afraid. Don't be afraid. Come out. I will put words in your mouth." Then I remember a text in the Bible that says that they will carry you before magistrates, but when they carry you before magistrates, don't be afraid. He will be there to put words in your mouth.

And when I come out of the toilet the police say, "Come." And I walk with him and then we went up a stairs. When we went up the stairs, a door was open there, and the first thing I saw was this big, fat white man sitting down in the middle in front of a table. And in front him I saw my hymnbook, my Bible, Primitivo hymnbook, his Bible and ninety-eight – almost a hundred – Voice of Prophecy lessons that the children was doing. And they put a chair right in front of him and told me, "*Sientate aqui.*"

Then when I sit down now, he start on me. "*Parece mentiro. Mira como usted, despues que Castro hiso tan buenas cosas con ustedes, y los Estados Unidos hiso tan mal con ustedes negros.*" He said, "You choose to do all these things. Look at these lessons." I said, "No." He said, "You fighting against this country." I said, "No. It ain't so." He said, "What about these lessons?" I said, "Those lessons, I didn't have them." He said, "You don't know there's a law that says you can't walk with them?" I said, "I didn't bring them. All I had was a hymnbook and a Bible. And him too that is there. We didn't have these lessons."

He said, "Look these lessons here. And you all teaching the young people these lessons and you turning these children heart from us." I said, "No sir, it isn't so." But then he going on in such a way, I turn to him in Spanish now. I don't know where the voice come from, I said, "*Pero señor, no me insultas tanto.*" I said, "But sir, don't insult me so much." When I said so, he fixed his eyes on mine, and his eyes make four with mine. I don't know what he see, but he saw something.

When he take his eyes off mine, he call to the police that was standing there and said, "Bring me four cups of coffee." The police brought the four cups of coffee. He put one before me. I said, "*Muchas gracias, pero no tomo café. Yo soy Adventista.*" He said, "You want to drink something soft?" I said, "Yes, bring me a soft drink." When I done drink the soft drink, he was a different man. He start to talk now calm, calm. It was the fifteenth of December, 1965. I'll never forget that date.

He look at me, he say, "You got a child?" I said, "Yes, I got a child, girl child. *Hija.*" He say, "How old she is?" I said, "She's fourteen years." He said, "It is a pity that you going to pass you Christmas in prison and you can't eat your

Christmas meals with your child." Man, my heart break. I said, "*Pero, señor, tenga compasión de mi.*" He said, "Aaah. There's compassion, but under certain circumstances." I said, "What is the circumstances?" He said, "Now listen, I am the judge who's going to judge you. And you see the gentleman there at the typewriter? That's my secretary."

They investigating now to see if what I say is true or not. He said, "I can set you free, or I can imprison you. But I will have compassion on you under certain circumstances." I said, "What the circumstances are?" He said, "Now, when you go home, I going to send a man to you, and if you hear anyone speak anything concerning this government, you will tell him. If you don't tell him, you write it on a piece of paper and he will collect it. You will give him your telephone number and he will call you by phone." But before he finish I say, "Sir, that will never happen. My pastor is Seventh Day Adventist like us, and he teaches us the Bible, and the Bible said, 'Let everyone be obedient to all authority, because there is no authority without God.'" I said, "Let me show you in the Bible. It come in Romans, chapter 13. 'Let everyone be subject unto the high authority, for there is no authority without God.'" He said, "No, no, no. Don't touch the Bible."

Anyhow, when I said that, he said, "Alright, but if your pastor don't, then what about either one of the members?" I said, "The pastor teach us also that we must be obedient. It will never happen." He says, "Suppose you meet one that is not a member, would you speak anything?" I said, "I would not do that either because I would be a busybody. But they had a word in Spanish called *chibata.*" They ask me where I get that word from. I said, "I don't know, but I heard it." He said, "What it mean?" I said, "I don't know." But I knew what it meant. Man, the white man in front me get so vexed he get up. He turn red like a cherry. He tell the police that was standing up, "Get this man from here. Get him from here! Two hours and a half I with this man and can't get nothing out of him. Get him from here!"

Anyhow, the police carry me back. Well, in the morning – midday – our pastor came. He tell me, "Look, don't be afraid. We spoke to the high authority and they told us that they going to let you all go." Because they didn't find no charge. Then the indoor sargeant, about six o'clock he call Primitivo. He said, "Primitivo, should there be war here, you know, if those people that went over to the States come back and make war, what would you do? Would you join them, or join with us?" Primitivo said, "*Yo soy cubano.* I got to be with you all." Then he call me and ask me. I said, "Yes, if there is any kind of war, I would join you all, but under certain circumstances." Primitivo didn't give any circumstances, but I give circumstances. They ask me, "What is the circumstances?" I said, "I am Seventh Day Adventist, and if you call me, and ask me to work on the Sabbath, I wouldn't work."

Then one of the police say, *"Eh!"* He call me a Jehovah's Witness. "What this other *Testigo* Jehovah mean? You want we to stop working and let the Americans come and take over this country?" He say, "Man, you talking nonsense. You got to work." Then I says, "The next circumstances is this. If you give me arms, I would not take it." Man the police say, "Look man, Rufino, if war break out here and we give you arms and you refuse to take it, myself will shoot you." I said, "Well, I'm not afraid to die, but I'm afraid to kill, because the Bible say, 'Thou shalt not kill.'" He was rash, but he was calm. Well the time come that they have us to let go.

I working with the factory now. One day when they let us go for lunch at eleven o'clock. Just as I come out now I hear a man behind me saying, *"Rufino. Rufino."* I stop. It was this white man, and I look good at him. And he say, "You don't know me?" I say, "No, I don't know you." He say, "I know you though." "How you know me?" He say, "You don't know me? You wasn't in trouble some time back with the law?" I said, "Yes, I was. But I wasn't found guilty, and that's why I'm here." He said, "Nevertheless, don't be afraid. I come to arrange certain things with you. Listen, I want you, if you hear anyone speak against this government, I will send someone here and you will tell them. And listen, I'm going to give you a gun and thirty-two dollars a month." I said, "Don't worry with that."

He said, "But the bigger boss . . ." I said, "Yes I was in jail. I spend four days." And when he put this proposition to me I told him, "No. It can't happen. It will never happen." He says, "What happen? Don't come back?" I said, "Don't come back!" So he never come back. But then the spirit tell me, "Look, you going to get kill, you know. Because you ain't going to stop. You will still be carrying on with this business of going out and evangelizing, and you going to get jailed." I couldn't stop evangelizing.

They had a little girl who would tell me, "Rufino, you going to get five years." I said, "No, daughter, God going to keep me, man." Because I went down there by her to a Barbadian fella who had a stroke. Afterwards he died too. And I carry the Voice of Prophecy lessons. It was forty lessons. In his home, I used to sit down and study with him. The girl tell me, "You going to get five years." I say, "No, God will keep me. God will keep me." You know I went so far with the man that the man did accept. He was to be baptized the Sabbath, but he died the Wednesday. But I know that when Christ come, I will see him.

Anyhow, I knew that jail was up and I asked for my repatriation. I send in here to Barbados. I pass three visas, you hear me? From 1965 to 1968 before I come out. When the letter come for my leave, the first thing is, they stop me from working. "If you're planning to go, you can't work anymore." And I pass three years without even working. Well, the church used to sustain me. When now I get my leave to come, the first elder he got me hug up and he crying and I crying too. Two of us crying. He say, "Rufino, you can't leave us man." He say, "We ain't bring you in this church, the Holy Spirit brought you. You don't see that we change everybody every year, different to you. We never change you, we couldn't change you. You can't leave this church. This is your church."

So I then turn to him, a man named Rigoberto Hernández. I say, "Rigo, don't be selfish. I got brothers and sisters in Barbados, and I hear a voice tell me, 'Go home and tell your brothers and sisters, and show them what God has done for you.'" Then he let me go. He stopped crying. He understood my mission. Then after they tell me that I can't go about selling no more, I then decide to put in my petition. It was three years before I get out. Until then the visa come one day for Havana. I fly to Havana and rest there a few days. The twenty-seventh of October, 1968, I get the flight from Havana. But I stop at the pastor home days before I get the flight out. But I couldn't bring nothing though, you know. You must know that, brought nothing. They said, "*Cuba para los cubanos*. So you brought nothing, you carry nothing." All I brought was a Bible and thirty pounds of clothes. But the love that I see in the Adventist church there, I don't see it in Barbados.

I used to write my mother. I'm sure I'm going to see my mother when Christ comes. All her letters come with, "Rufus, if I don't see you any more, I hope to see you in the new world." All her letters come with that. God is great. And a next sister of my own, she died. The same day she died she told me that she dreamed about her death. And I know I'm going to see her.

On his return from Cuba in 1968, Rufus Hoyte lived with relatives in Barbados. He became blind. However, he remained an active member of the Seventh Day Adventist Church up to the time of his death at age 99 in 2005. Mr Hoyte was interviewed at his home in Barbados on 21 January 1998.

CHAPTER 13

DELCINA ESPERANZA MARSHALL

"So that first night we didn't go to sleep at all. We all crowded around our mother crying, saying, 'We want to go back to Cuba.' But she said no, we can't go back, that we're here to stay."

MY FATHER WENT TO PANAMA TO WORK ON the canal, and when that was finished he went to Cuba in 1914 and later sent for my mother there with two daughters. One was born in Panama, and one was born in Barbados.

My parents settled in a place called Central Hershey. It is now called Central Camilo Cienfuegos. We had a lot of West Indians on our street. We had Jamaicans, Grenadians, Barbadians that I can remember. Oh, and Vincentians. There was Mr Skinner, he was a Barbadian. Mr Carrington, he was a Barbadian. Mr McDonald was a Jamaican. Mr Wilson was a Jamaican. We had two Wilsons who were Jamaicans. Mr Wilkinson was a Barbadian. Mr Daniel was a Barbadian. My father, Marshall, was a Barbadian. And then across the street, they had a Vincentian family and a Jamaican family, and the others were Spanish, Cuban people.

There was a Cuban family who had a very strange name – Kanaki – so I was wondering if they were Africans, from Africa. They had Chinese next door to us. They used to do laundry, and they used to cook some sweet food.

The other names that I can remember are Brown, Lincoln, Cane, Walls, Clarke, Trotman, Skinner, Greenidge, Bellman, Williams, Johnson, Forde, Lewin, Austin, Moore, Charles, Allman, Ricketts, King, Quarles, Yearwood, Cumberbatch, Smith and Laudrison.

We had lots of children, and we used to play. I don't remember any kind of racial discrimination at all. Because I had a friend Milagros, she lived in the street behind us, and we were good friends, and we used to play together. Another girl named Ubelina, her parents were Spaniards. Her father was a policeman. And we used to play, all black and white children played together without any sense of difference, you know. And we used to visit each other's home and eat food and that sort of thing.

My sister and I used to go to my brother Rennie's godmother and play until we heard the horn blow in the evening at four o'clock. We used to call it the "corchie". And we would scamper back home, trying to get home before Papa got there. Papa loved horses. Once he had three horses, and my brother, my little brother Rennie, got on one a Sunday morning and went cantering and it took him across the train line. Luckily no trains were passing. And someone beyond the train line stopped him and brought him back home.

My father was chief smith at the factory, and Mr Ince was his second in command. Next door, my sister's godfather he was an engineer. He was from Jamaica. Most of the work was centred around the sugar factory. The men also worked as masons, on railroad trains, as porters, tailors, barbers, factory engineers and blacksmiths. Most of the women were housewives, but some worked as domestics, some cooked and others took in laundry to help. We used to go to the hotel with Ms Dan's sister. She used to do laundry for the hotel, and she would go every Monday night and collect the sheets and so on, and bring them home to wash. She was from Barbados, Ms Wilkinson. My mother just kept house. We had a lady by the name of Del who came in to take care of us, and do the laundry, but my mother did the cooking because my father insisted that she cook his meals.

From what I've heard from older people living there, the West Indians began arriving in the 1890s. In 1912 the United Fruit Company had brought some. They later contracted others to work on plantations with cane, coffee, cutting down trees, on the railroads and all the hard work on plantations. They came with the purpose of earning and saving money, because in their homeland there was scarcity of work due to the failure of the sugar industry and overpopulation. Some came from Panama, where conditions were insanitary and malaria prevailed. In the years of the second decade, after 1912, greater quotas began to arrive from Panama. Most of them hoped to return home on retiring therefore they never became citizens of Cuba. They thought that if they changed citizenship, they'd disgrace their flag. On Sundays, they would visit friends where they discussed local events and gave each other news from home.

In every home there was a Bible and a hymnal. The church was Methodist Episcopal and sometimes services were held at members' homes. We went to a place named Santa Cruz to a church there in the mornings, and there was a Catholic church in Central Hershey itself. We went there in the evenings, and I was even on the confirmation class. And my father said, "No. No. No. She's an Anglican. She's not going to become a Catholic at all." And he stopped me from going there.

Weddings were held in church. They intermarried in order to carry on customs and names. They cried when a baby was born and placed a Bible at its head. When someone died, they informed the neighbourhood who gathered at the house. Hymns were sung until midnight. After that, they told stories and played games. They ate and drank until morning. The radio was covered with a white sheet for nine days.

At Easter, eggs were coloured and hidden. The children would search for them and had lots of fun. December twenty-fifth was a big celebration with whole pigs or goats baked, dark cake, coconut bread, pone, and drinks were made from fruits. Before starting to eat, the father would say grace thanking God for the food.

Other West Indians used to come from Baraguá and different places. They came down on Saturday nights and played cricket on Sunday and then they left on Sunday nights to get back home to their jobs on Monday. And sometimes cricketers from Hershey would visit other provinces in turn. They came from Camagüey, Pinar del Rio, Matanzas, Santa Cruz and Havana. Almost every Caribbean island was represented. They stayed with different families. On these occasions, large tables were laid out with food, homemade drinks and cakes. We cooked Barbadian food. My mother cooked Barbadian food because I remember one of the guests writing her and telling her that he still had the taste of her gravy on his tongue.

We used to go to an English school in the morning from 8:30 until 10:30, and then from 11:00 to 3:00 o'clock we went to the Spanish school. In the English school there was just one teacher, Mr Hugh Holder from Barbados. He gave classes in English in the morning and we attended public school in the afternoon. Another man, Mr McBurney – he was from Jamaica – he had his own English school. His children used books sent from Jamaica, while we used the Royal Reader. So there were two English schools. The Jamaican children went to McBurney's and the Barbadians went to Mr Holder.

There were some men, about fifty of them, who used to live in some barracks behind our house on Thirteenth Street, where the black people were placed. They were from all over the Caribbean. They were bachelors, of course. But a lot of them used to come to my mother's place for food. They used to get paid fortnightly, and every time they got paid they would dress up and go to Havana and spend all of their money, and then on Monday mornings they would hitch a ride on the cargo trains to get back home to go to work. But my father said she was to stop feeding them, because they were wasting their money, they never sent back anything for their family. They never wrote their families. There wasn't much entertainment in Hershey, that's why the fellows used to go to Havana.

I know my mother kept in touch with a nephew of hers in Barbados, Hilton Lawrence. She always used to write him. But I never heard her mention writing anyone else. And my father wrote to his mother and sister, Aunt Betty. They always sent money. They never wrote without putting money in the envelopes, and they got it safely. It wasn't like today when people were breaking into letters or anything like that.

In '35 my father became ill and he died in '36, and our mother decided to bring us home to Barbados, because she had nothing in Cuba, but she had land in Barbados. The two oldest daughters were already married and starting families, so they decided to stay in Cuba.

We came by two different boats. One was a cargo boat, the first one was a cargo boat. And the second was a cruising steamer that brought us from Guadeloupe to Barbados in 1936. The cargo boat stopped in St Thomas and let off cargo and picked up lumber and different things to take from one island to the other. First they let off people in Haiti, because there was a big bunch of them going home for good. Then we passed by St Kitts, but not close enough to stop. We stopped in St Thomas, in Guadeloupe, in Martinique, and then we came on to Barbados. It took us twenty-six days to get here, stopping here, there and everywhere. There were six of us, three boys and two girls, and my mum.

There were a few of the Barbadian men who came home for good at that time too. My mother lent a pillow to one of them, and when we were coming off she took the pillow and feeling in it she found a gun. So she told him, "Take that out of there at once. I'm not bringing in illegal guns for you." And he took it out of the pillow.

We were very well received by some people. But other people said my mother shouldn't have brought these mudhead children here. But we cried because we were accustomed to lights in the street and where we were living in Barbados there were no lights in the street. So that first night we didn't go to sleep at all. We all crowded around our mother crying, saying, "We want to go back to Cuba." But she said no, we can't go back, that we're here to stay.

The interview with my mother, Delcina Marshall, was recorded at our home in Barbados on 27 December 1998. She had returned to Cuba for the first time in fifty-three years in 1989, and I made my first visit to Cuba with her then. My mother died in 2007.

Figure 13.1. The sugar mill and mill town in Central Hershey, 1920. *Courtesy of the Hershey Community Archives, http://www.hersheyarchives.org/.*

Figure 13.2. Residences on Seventh Street in Central Hershey, 1920. *Courtesy of the Hershey Community Archives, http://www.hersheyarchives.org/.*

Figure 13.3. Delcina and Zoila Marshall at school in Central Hershey, 1930s

Figure 13.4. Isaac Newton "Bonnie" Marshall, patriarch of the Marshall family, was chief blacksmith at Central Hershey factory

Figure 13.5. Delcina Marshall and her younger sister, Zoila, outside their childhood home in Central Hershey

Figure 13.6. Miriam Delcina Marshall (*second from right*), with five of her children in Havana, prior to their twenty-six-day sea voyage to Barbados, which began on 29 May 1936. The children are (*clockwise from her right*) Zoila Celestina (7), Rupert Newton (18), Isaac Reynold (11), Livingstone Wakefield (13) and Delcina Esperanza (9).

Figure 13.7. Mercedes Marshall, Delcina's elder sister, with (*from left to right*) her son Alberto Moore Marshall, her husband Fitz Albert Moore, and son Rolando at their home in Santa Cruz del Norte, Cuba, in 1956

Figure 13.8. Mercedes Marshall (*centre*), flanked by her older sister Clotilde and her brother-in-law, Keneth Ford, and their children (*from left to right*) Frances, Migdalia, Arturo, Antonina and Wilfredo

CHAPTER 14

GLORIA NELSON

"Church used to play a very great deal in our society. We had the Adventist church, we had the Salvation Army, the Episcopal Church and the Christian Mission. Then they had the Catholic up the road. We used to go to all."

MY FATHER WENT TO CUBA IN 1920. MY mother went to Cuba about 1917. My mother when she left Barbados was three years old. My grandmother took her to Panama. My grandmother's husband, he worked on the Panama Canal and when the work ended, there were three sisters – my grandmother and two other sisters. When the work was ended, two went to New York and my grandmother went on to Cuba, so my mother was raised in Cuba.

My father left from Barbados and went direct to Cuba, because they were recruiting people to go to work in sugar cane factory and things like that. So he went down there. But when he got there, instead of staying in Oriente where they landed, he went directly to Baraguá, and there he build his own business and he worked there.

He met my mother, and grew up and got married and what's not. My mother never worked in her life; she was always a housewife. My father used to be a building contractor; he used to build houses and what's not. He also used to work at the *playa* where the boats come in, building boats and things like that.

My grandmother came back to Barbados after my mother married. She came back to Barbados, so they used to correspond. And we actually, we used to correspond with my Aunt Mary and Aunt Vi, and Aunt Gloria in New York also.

Growing up in Baraguá was fun. When we were young, we were a family of eight children. And it was a community like . . . mostly Barbadians, Antiguans, Jamaicans. We had one or two Trinidadians living there, but they were more Barbadians. And we were divided like into like Jamaica Town and Bajan Town, and we lived in Bajan Town. It was like a community, close community. Everybody knew everybody. There were lots of West Indian families, as I said before, like the Jamaicans, even from Montserrat they had people there. And we all lived together.

Where we lived in Baraguá, they had, we called it the Spaniards' quarters up the road. They used to have the Americans living in that area. Most Americans that owned the *central* and the sugar factories and what's not; they used to be living in those quarters. And I can remember vaguely . . . not the names or anything like that . . . around Christmas they used to bring like, they used to call them *aguinaldos*. They used to bring like gifts and fruits and apples and thing to the people that work in the sugar factory, and bonus.

English was spoken in the community, and as a matter of fact, we used to go to school when we were children. We were small like four/five years old. Before we go to public school we used to go to English school. And we used to learn English, then after we go to public school you start with your Spanish. But some parents used to maintain that their children go to private English schools up to sixth standard.

And I remember clearly that there was a headmaster from the school, the private English school that they used to go to by the name of Santiago from Antigua, and he used to make sure that that most of the West Indian parents send their children to learn English first, and then Spanish.

In Baraguá where we lived they had . . . I wouldn't say it was like racial discrimination or anything so, racism or anything so. But they used to have two sets of people living in Baraguá – black and white, right? And they used to have like a social, what should I say, like climbing the social ladder. They had people up there and down there. And they had a black society and a white society, with two clubs. The black people could not go into the white people club, the white people could not come into our club.

Yes. There was racism and it still exists. I was kind of young then, but I found out then that my father, he was a man respected in the community and a lot of white people used to come at my house, and he used to visit a lot of white people. And my mother used to exchange gifts with some of them. We used to live good with the white people, but they still had people that showed their racism towards blacks and so on.

So we used to have like dances. Every Sunday evening we used to have dances. They used to have like meetings, like an association in a hall to do our activities. And they used to play cricket against the West Indian children. People used to come from Manatí in Oriente and Camagüey and all those places we used to go to and have like weekends, you know. And they used to have like banquets and dances, and matinee for young people. And they used to have like concerts. In our society they used to have that. And they used to have like queen shows, beauty shows, the best-looking girls, black girls.

Church used to play a very great deal in our society. We had the Adventist Church, we had the Salvation Army, the Episcopal Church and the Christian Mission. Then they had the Catholic up the road. We used to go to all. We had to go to all. Our parents force . . . first and foremost, we used to go to Sunday school on most Sunday mornings. Sunday evening, we go to Sunday school at the Episcopal, and then at night-time, we go to church at the Christian Mission. And Saturdays, we had to go to the Seventh Day Adventists.

When the Salvation Army having their programmes, we used to sing and recite there. When the Christian Mission having their programmes, we used to sing and recite there. When they having a programme at the Episcopal, we do the same thing. Our mother used to sing at all the churches also. Like in the community when we having our concerts, they used to have like mostly religious concerts, they used to have all the elders and all the pastors and preachers and whatever come and assist and help out with everything. It used to be a tight community. They used to come together and help everybody.

The Episcopal Church used to be responsible for the Emancipation Day that we used to have every first of August. But they used to have like a committee from all the churches, and they would like donate things. And then they would have like a big picnic. They used to play rounders on that day. And they used to have like great cake, and they have sweet bun and sugar water, lemonade. Everybody used to come and they used to give out these things to the people. And they used to come and eat and have fun, like a big picnic. Everybody from the community, not just from that church, but everybody from the community used to come and participate. And they used to have like maypole dancing on that day. They used to have a cricket match on that day, playing games and what's not.

After my father died, my mother was going to come back. My grandmother was ill, and she was going to come back. But she took ill and she died also. So she was going to bring the three youngest children, which is myself, Julia and

Yoly, the two under me. And after my mother died, they decided that they weren't going to leave the others and come. But my eldest brother, he said that he's going to come. So I said, if he's coming, I'm going to come too. So then he fixed my papers, and I came on the thirteenth of August 1970. But he decided that he would stay on.

This interview was conducted on 2 October 1997 at Gloria Nelson's home in Barbados. Gloria worked for several years at the leading department store in Barbados. She was an active member of the Cuban-Barbadian Friendship Association, and served as its president. She died in 2006.

EPILOGUE

~~~~~~~~

CUBA CONNECTIONS AND CONTINUITIES

CUBA WAS INDEED A "LAND OF OPPORTUNITY" FOR Barbadians and other British West Indians. It is also unquestionable that the migration to Panama and Cuba influenced the economic development of the migrants' home countries by way of the foreign currency remittances which they sent or brought back. While valuing their membership in the British imperial club, it was in these countries too that a sense of West Indian identity was nurtured.

However, many of the migrants paid a high price for the chance to work in Panama and Cuba. The language barrier, the lack of proper education, cultural differences and the social and political circumstances prevailing in Cuba in the early part of this century made the adjustment to their new environment difficult for some migrants who made the journey to Cuba.

The evidence demonstrates that while in many respects the migrants were victims, they were also actors who constructed communities of some permanence in the host country, and also that women contributed to the creation and maintenance of family and migration networks.

Charles Ray sums up the immigrant experience in Cuba by saying: "When we first came we had a hard time. When we first came to Cuba, the West Indians had a hard time in Cuba. But strangers is all time strangers in a country. In any country you go, as long as you're a stranger, is a stranger they call you. But not everybody, not everyone."

CULTIVATING CARIBBEANNESS

While the British West immigrants were resented in some quarters, this reaction was not universally true. José Millet and Julio Corbea view the West Indian interaction with Cuban society, particularly in the eastern part of the country, quite positively. They write in *Presencia haitiana en el oriente de Cuba* that the open cultural interchange between Santiago and other parts of the Caribbean "created in the people of the southeastern part of the country a sense of belonging to or being immersed in the Caribbean".[1]

Millet and Corbea observe that there were historical factors which contributed decisively to this sense of "Caribbeanness" and belonging to a greater entity than Cubans in this part of the country had identified with previously. They cite the renewed trade in black labour which, in the first three decades of the twentieth century, "brought hundreds of thousands of workers from Haiti, Jamaica, Barbados, Granada [*sic*], St Vincent and elsewhere in the Caribbean who integrated themselves into the Cuban society and culture".[2]

Rolando Alvarez Estévez also views positively the interaction between black working-class Caribbean peoples of the two language groups, stating in *Azúcar y inmigración* that "West Indian migration to Cuba represented, from the beginning of this century, an element of the highest importance in the search for confirmation of a real identification between Caribbean peoples; despite the language barriers, they all had a common denominator in their history: they had suffered under a regime of relations dictated by slave production".[3]

THOSE WHO STAYED

In his 1985 article, Basil Maughan lists some of the Barbadians who remained in Cuba, and, in his view, prospered there:

> Mr. Leroy Springer, brother of the former Commissioner of Police, Mr. Girwood Springer, left Barbados in the 1920s and has lived comfortably in Cuba ever since. He regards Cuba as his home.
>
> Mr. Oliver Nelson prospered in Cuba, himself becoming a property owner and *colono*. He was active in the Masonic Lodge and founded a newspaper in Baraguá, where the family lived. One daughter even won a beauty contest in 1953, not a mean feat in racially conscious Camagüey. . . . A son works with the British Embassy in Havana. Mr. Nelson died in 1959.
>
> Dr. Louis Wiltshire of Trinidad visited Cuba in 1981 on business. While there

he was assigned an interpreter by the Cuban Foreign Ministry, a young man by the name of Edghill. He spoke English fluently, with a Barbadian accent. He said his parents were from Barbados and had gone to Cuba in the 1920s. There are undoubtedly others who have done well.[4]

Joseph Nathaniel Best was one Barbadian who stayed on in Cuba. Born in Belleplaine, St Andrew, on 1 July 1901, he made his way to Cuba in 1921. He settled initially in Puerto Padre, and then in Manatí. He later moved to the municipality of Las Tunas, where he remained until his death in 1978.

Best's daughter Aleida Best Rivero worked for more than five decades as a domestic to help support her family. Today she has a PhD, is a university professor and researcher, and a renowned speaker. She is assistant professor and president of the chair of Caribbean studies at Las Tunas University. Best Rivero told an interviewer, "My father came to Cuba in the early 20th century with the idea that money ran through the streets, and he had to work very hard. He met my mother, a descendant of African slaves, and I was born the youngest of five children in the family."[5]

Las Tunas province has eight municipalities, and in all there is a presence of Caribbean immigrants and descendants of Barbadians. However, it is in the north where they are most abundant. This is where the old *centrales* of Manatí, Chaparra and Delicias are located. There is a sociocultural project in Chaparra involving descendants of Barbadians allied to the chair of Caribbean studies which Dr Best Rivero heads. She is also a member of the Nicolás Guillén Foundation, and directs an academic project on the Presence of Guillén, featuring papers about the contact of the national poet with the Caribbean and Latin America.

In addition, she directs a sociocultural project with children and adolescents in schools as well as students of sociocultural studies, law, social communication and artistic education in the faculty where she works and in coordination with the Instituto Cubano de Amistad con Los Pueblos. They develop monthly activities with the African and Caribbean students studying medicine in the Faculty of Medical Sciences.

My maternal aunts, Clotilde and Mercedes, were also among those who remained in Cuba. Their offspring form an extended family of second, third and fourth generation cousins whom I have in Cuba.

I was privileged to go with my mother on my first to Cuba, when she returned there in 1989 for the first time in fifty-three years. It was the first of

Figure E.1. The author (*centre*) on a visit to Havana in May 2015 with (*to her left*) friend Pat Bynoe-Clarke and relatives (*clockwise*) cousin Migdalia, Migdalia's daughter Liana and son Eduardo

many visits for both of us. I became acquainted with numerous relatives of whom I had only heard before. Some of my Cuban cousins have also visited us in Barbados.

ASSIMILATION AND ETHNIC RESILIENCE

On this question of assimilation and ethnic resilience, Edward Shils, in his essay "Roots: The Sense of Place and Past", suggests that "the assimilation of the culture of the host society by the offspring of immigrants can never be complete because they cannot lose all of the culture of their ancestors. They might in the second generation, at least for a time, be ashamed of this, but the fact is that they do retain some of the old culture."[6]

In order to analyse the status attainment of British West Indians in Cuba, one needs to examine the status of the black or Afro-Cuban population into which the West Indians were subsumed. One Cuba watcher who has done precisely that is Carlos Moore.

In his book *Castro, the Blacks, and Africa*, Moore states, "Since the second half of the nineteenth century, as some analysts have shown, the chief spokesmen of middle class nationalism in Cuba have been first-generation white Cubans."[7] With regard to the situation of blacks in the 1940s and 1950s, Moore makes the following report:

> According to the 1943 Cuban census, there were at least 560 black lawyers; 424 doctors, a fifth of the total in the country, were black, as were 3,500 teachers, compared to about 16,000 white teachers. Blacks were said to be well represented in the arts, dominated laundering, sewing, shoemaking, woodcutting, and tailoring, and were on a level with whites as barbers, bakers, carpenters, coopers, and blacksmiths. The political, economic, and cultural influence of the black middle class was still negligible. Blacks in middle class positions numbered approximately 300,000 in 1959, roughly one-third of their white counterparts. The black middle class was virtually absent from the higher and middle levels of management, business, commerce, the armed forces and from the white preserve of government administration.[8]

Moore charges that after the triumph of the revolution in 1959, Cuban leader Fidel Castro confronted the issue of racial discrimination by focusing exclusively on the public segregation which had existed at that time. The government claimed that an egalitarian society – which had no regard for race or class – had been ushered in with the end of capitalism in Cuba.

Tomás Fernándes Robaina appears to share the revolutionary government's view. He indicates that with the 1959 revolution and the elimination of the imperialist regime, "racial discrimination was struck a mortal blow and the objective struggle began against the inherited prejudices of many years of colonization. It is only from 1959 that the struggle could begin to realise the ideals of [José] Martí: To be Cuban is more than white, more than mulatto, more than negro."[9]

This approach of national integration, in Moore's view, neglected the questions of political power and cultural dominance in a society which privileged the Hispanic element of its culture. He argues that the breakdown of racial segregation within such a narrow context, however, left only one way open to

Cuban blacks: uncritical adoption of the cultural outlook and lifestyle of the politically dominant Hispanic revolutionary elite.[10]

Aline Helg also addresses this issue when she makes the charge that "the myth of Cuban racial equality continues to be used to prevent Afro-Cubans from voicing discontent or organizing autonomously".[11] Helg notes, "This myth also allows the new ruling elite to ignore the issue of racism in socialist Cuba. But the fact that Afro-Cubans even today remain largely underrepresented in the upper spheres of power and overrepresented in the lower strata of society indicates that the Afro-Cuban struggle for equality has yet to be fully won."[12]

Moore comments that "from the mid-1920s onwards, the Cuban Communist party found its most receptive, durable, and enthusiastic clientele among Blacks. They formed the backbone of the Party right up to Castro's accession to power."[13] What Moore describes as Cuba's "African Decade", the period beginning with Castro's first visit to the African continent in 1972, saw changes in the status of some black Cubans. "For the first time, Blacks were appointed ministers: Nora Frometa (Light Industry), Armando Tórres Santrayl (Justice), and Rafael Francia Mestre (Agriculture). However, the chief beneficiaries were appointees to the secret services, the diplomatic corps, the armed forces, and the police. Black manpower was needed for deployment in Africa and, increasingly, the Caribbean. . . . By 1980, out of twenty-one Cuban ambassadors sent to Africa, more than two-thirds were Black."[14]

The first hint that Cubans of anglophone Caribbean descent were being elevated in the Communist Party hierarchy came in February 1986, when President Castro addressed the Third Party Congress, promising to pursue a conscious relentless drive to bring blacks, women and youth into the leadership: "The appointments of Estéban Lazo Hernández to the exclusive fourteen-man Politbureau, and of Gladys Robinson Agramonte and Juán Robinson Agramonte to the Central Committee, said Castro, were indicative of a new 'injection of Blacks' into the Party."[15]

Juan Carlos Robinson, who served at one point as first secretary of the Cuban Communist Party, is in fact a descendant of Jamaican immigrants, and took great personal interest in the work of the British West Indian Welfare Centre in Guantánamo. Another example of a West Indian descendant involved in the political hierarchy is Aleida Best Rivero.

In 1976, when the first elections for the National Assembly of People's Power were held, she was elected as a delegate in her constituency and held this role for twenty-five years. In addition, she served two terms as a member of parliament from 1998 to 2008. Best was also part of the provincial direction of the Committees for the Defense of the Revolution.

At the end of the 1980s, the Cuban government began developing the tourism sector in the wake of the collapse of the former Soviet Union, which had been the main source of support for the island for many years. In the decade which followed, the industry surpassed sugar as the mainstay of the economy. The government's policy of pursuing tourism as a major foreign exchange earner may well have a positive influence on the preservation and continuation of British West Indian culture there.

Cultural heterogeneity is being embraced, even if only as an asset in the attractions which the country can provide for visitors. As members of the West Indian community in Baraguá attest, their First of August celebration is supported by the Communist Party leadership, and it was the party which, in fact, resuscitated the celebration when it was in danger of dying out.

Then there is the role of La Cinta, the musical troupe from Baraguá, which has travelled abroad to represent Cuba in at least one festival in Guyana. The group also provides entertainment for tourists at resorts in Cayo Coco on the northern coast of Ciego de Avila province. They are able to communicate with English-speaking visitors at these resorts. Facility with English, the language of their parents and grandparents, also represents a potential passport to employment in the more lucrative tourist industry for the descendants of the British West Indian migrants.

Teófilo Gay, a community activist in Baraguá, views this activity as part of the process of preserving British West Indian culture: "To me culture is a person, and a person is culture. And that is something that we keep over here, keep in the memory of our foreparents. Our parents teach us that, and we believe it is a way of remembering them, the way of thinking sometimes where they came from, the way we celebrate First of August."

How did the distinctly West Indian survivals endure for so long among the immigrants and their descendants in Baraguá? We might turn to Ewa Morawska for a possible answer. Morawska posits: "Activated by external conditions, ethnicity is at the same time created, sustained, and used by the immigrants themselves as a resource to cope with the environment. Seen in this perspective, the ethnicization of personal identities, social bonds, and institutional networks becomes an important, and sometimes preeminent, mechanism of social and cultural adaptation to the host society."[16]

If we accept this view, then the passing on of the traditions to the younger generation which Teófilo Gay regards as a way of honouring their foreparents can also be interpreted as a method of coping with an alien environment. Morawska outlines the conditions which engender this strong ethnic identity, conditions which certainly existed in Baraguá for the immigrants and the first generation of descendants: "Particularly conducive to 'emergent ethnicity' – that is, to the crystallization of strong enduring ethnic identities and cultural bonds, informal social networks, and ethnic institutions – is the concentration of immigrants in segregated residential neighborhoods, combined with their condensation in the same labor segment and (to a significant degree responsible for this) the exclusionary practices and attitudes of the dominant groups."[17]

Some migrants who had earlier left Cuba have been encouraged to return to visit relatives there. Increasingly, they have been able to renew familial and cultural ties through reciprocal visits, a factor which should strengthen and reinvigorate British West Indian culture in Cuba well into the foreseeable future.

Andrea Queeley argues that Cuba's changing economic circumstances – from the first decades of the twentieth century, when English-speaking skills could be an employment advantage, through the revolution of 1959, when a new era which promised to end racial discrimination was ushered in, and to the period of post-Soviet support to the island to the present – have forced West Indians and their descendants to navigate the shifting terrain in relation to their race and their ethnic origins.[18] Descendants of West Indian immigrants in Cuba began embracing their ethnic heritage in the wake of the Special Period. She observes that "nearly seventy years after the bulk of these immigrants arrived in Cuba, people of English-speaking Caribbean origin began establishing – in some cases, reestablishing – ethnic associations in an attempt to 'rescue their roots' ".[19]

On 3 July 1993, the Young People's Department of the British West Indian Welfare Centre was formed to ensure the continuation and invigoration of the centre for future generations. Eixa and Croos Valiente and Margarita Lewis explained the significance of this development in a paper presented at the first international symposium on the British West Indian presence in Cuba mounted by the centre in March 1996. "Our parents and grandparents, men and women of strong personality, of high moral values, devoutly religious, stubborn of habit, respectful and disciplined citizens, have left us an inestimably rich culture which present and future generations should know and preserve."[20]

A November 1999 report on the British West Indian Welfare Centre by Alberto Jones indicated that its membership stood at some six hundred, "among them 39 of the original emigrants, two of whom are over 100 years old, a few in their 90's and most others in their 80's".[21] The countries of origin given are Jamaica, St Kitts and Nevis, Barbados, Antigua and Barbuda, St Thomas, St Lucia, Grenada, the British Virgin Islands, Guyana, Martinique, Trinidad and Tobago, and the Turks and Caicos Islands. The report also asserts that

> descendants of the community have attained high levels of education and professional training, though less so in the arts and cultural fields than in other areas. Nonetheless, the Center's cultural activities have expanded in scope, depth and diversity; and a serious effort is underway to document and preserve all aspects of what was for many a painful history. A recently revived English-language school has produced its first graduates. Center physicians, dentists and nurses offer health care services free of charge for members and also dispense medicine free of charge, when available.[22]

Among the other achievements listed are the organization of a twenty-voice chorus, soloists, a dance group, arts and craft activities, a cricket team and a softball team.

The culture which the immigrants took with them had some influence on the wider Cuban society. While it does not rival the national pastime of baseball, the game of cricket, avidly played by the early migrant community, is enjoying increasing popularity in Cuba. In 2002 Cuba became an affiliate member of the International Cricket Council:

> Cricket was enjoyed in Havana by Cuban high society around the beginning of the 20th Century, but with the arrival and settlement of West Indian immigrants during the 1920s, the sport developed around the sugar mills in the Eastern zones, such as Banes, Baragua, Manati, Guantánamo and others.
>
> Since 1998 cricket was resurrected in Cuba, through a rescue programme among West Indian descendants, inspired in 1997 by Leona Ford, daughter of an outstanding player who was founder of the Guantánamo Cricket Club, and coordinator of several tours between Jamaican and Cuban clubs, especially during the 1940s and 1950s.
>
> In 1998 the Cuban Cricket Commission was founded with the support of the Havana Provincial Direction of Sports Activities and the President of the Sports Historian Commission, Olegario Moreno. Outstanding assistance also came from Michael White, British Consul in Cuba at the time.[23]

Assistance in providing equipment for the Cuban cricketers has also come from individuals and organizations in the Caribbean countries from which the West Indians migrated.

RETURNING NATIONALS

Some of the Barbadian emigrants did achieve their dream of returning home with more than they had on leaving, while others were forced to go back because of difficult circumstances. Returning emigrants increased the island's population by 8 per cent in just five years from 1932 to 1937.[24]

Cleophas Belgrave spent fifty years in Cuba, remaining there up until the 1970s. In 1973 he decided to return to his homeland, Barbados, bringing with him his Cuba-born son, Edwin. Another son, Colbert, who was also born and raised in Baraguá, followed in 1979 when he came with his mother. For Colbert, the transition was an easy one:

> In that community, the same traditions that we see here now in Barbados, living here now, I realize that we had them back home there also. Like it wasn't anything strange to me when I came here to eat cou cou . . . well not the flying fish, because the flying fish is only here in Barbados . . . but we had cou cou. We had the sorrel that we would have at Christmas time, so it was kind of more or less the same environment coming here.

He has been employed for many years as a music teacher at the West Terrace Primary School, and also as a church organist.

CONNECTIONS AND CONTINUITIES

Cuba has been enjoying economic and diplomatic cooperation with the former British West Indian territories for some time. In 1972 the four recently independent countries of the English-speaking Caribbean – Barbados, Guyana, Jamaica, and Trinidad and Tobago – established diplomatic relations with Cuba at a time when it was not a popular course of action. Other former British colonies in the region followed suit on gaining their independence.

President Fidel Castro visited Barbados on at least three occasions. I had the opportunity to interview him in May 1994 when he attended the UN Global Conference on Small Island Developing States, and to serve as mistress of ceremonies when he spoke at the dedication of the Cubana monument in 1998.

Direct air links between Barbados and Cuba had been established in the 1970s. Cubana de Aviación, Cuba's largest airline and flag carrier flew between Bridgetown and Havana. On 6 October 1976, anti-Castro terrorists planted and ignited two bombs on board Cubana flight 455. It crashed off the coast of

Figure E.2. President Fidel Castro being interviewed by the author in Barbados, May 1994

Barbados shortly after taking off from the airport. All seventy-three passengers and five crewmembers on board were killed. The Government of Barbados erected an obelisk at Payne's Bay, St James, on the coast nearest the crash site to commemorate those killed in the bombing. It stands as a visible reminder of this tragic link between the two countries.

Some of the milestones which mark the progress of official bilateral relations between Barbados and Cuba include the opening of a Cuban embassy in Barbados in 1994, the establishment of a Barbados-Cuba Joint Commission in 1997, and the opening of a Barbados embassy in Havana in 2010.

Among the cooperation programmes is an agreement with the National Sports Council of Barbados in which a number of Cuban athletics coaches have been serving at schools on the island. Following the signing of the initial bilateral sports agreement in December 2002, eight coaches started a four-year period of technical assistance from Cuba. The disciplines were swimming, boxing, track and field, hockey, table tennis and volleyball.

An assessment by the Sports Council at the end of the initial four-year period asserted that the coaches brought new approaches to the local sports landscape, especially in swimming, and that the schools have benefited immensely from their presence. This cooperation programme was later extended; new batches of coaches are working in Barbados up to the present time. In addition, Cuban swimming coaches have been engaged privately by individual swim clubs.

Barbados was also a beneficiary of Operación Milagro, the free eye-care programme offered by the Cuban government with support from the government of Venezuela. In October 2008, 450 eye patients in Barbados were assessed and by January 2009, the first group of patients arrived in Havana.

People-to-people contact has been facilitated by organizations such as the Cuban-Barbadian Friendship Association, the Clement Payne Movement, the National Union of Public Workers in Barbados and the Caribbean Association of Cuba.

Hundreds of young West Indians have been awarded scholarships to study a wide variety of academic disciplines in Cuban universities, and CARICOM counties have benefited from Cuban technical expertise in a range of areas. Between 2007 and 2008, Barbadians accounted for twenty-four of these scholarships, and that number increased to sixty-eight in 2010.

More young, and not-so-young, Cubans of Barbadian descent are interested in securing official documents which authenticate their heritage claims. Some have used their ancestral and familial ties to visit Barbados at the invitation of relatives. Some of them have settled in Barbados, forming part of the Cuban community there. At one point, fifteen of the eighteen teachers in the Ministry of Education's Primary Spanish Programme were Cuban Barbadians. Among them is Gloria Nelson's sister, Yolanda, another daughter of the late Oliver Nelson, a respected member of the community in Baraguá.

In 2015 the Cuban embassy in Barbados celebrated Cuban Culture Day on 20 October. The programme included a musical performance by Cubans and Barbadian descendants resident in the island. It also featured the Barbados Community College Cuban Ensemble, made up entirely of Barbadian students. Their music was warmly embraced and enjoyed by the Cubans present, especially an extended rendition of the classic "Guantanamera", which delighted the audience.

In November 2015, the Barbados embassy in Havana celebrated Barbados's Independence anniversary with a series of activities to which Barbadian descendants were invited. In Las Tunas, there were three Barbadian students in the Faculty of Medical Sciences at Las Tunas University, and Dr Best Rivero planned an activity for 30 November in tribute to Barbados.

Clearly the story of the Barbados-Cuba connection is one which is to be continued.

A PERSONAL NOTE

During the research for my doctoral thesis on British West Indian migration to Cuba, I had conducted several research visits to Cuba, specifically to Havana and Santiago de Cuba. When I thought that my research work was completed, and I could begin the writing process, I was advised that my work would not be complete if I did not visit Guantánamo. I had just finished an interview with Earl Alonzo "Panama" Greaves, when I got this advice from his son, Jorge.

I made that visit to Guantánamo in August of 2000. William Hope's son, Pedro – a trained graduate teacher – was one of the descendants of British West Indian migrants whom I met there. Like other professionals in Cuba, he was attracted to a more lucrative living in the tourism sector. At the time, he was employed as public relations manager with the hotel where I stayed. His facility with French and English were being used to good advantage in dealing with the hotel's foreign guests.

Pedro was of invaluable assistance to me in making appointments for my research work. We discovered through conversation that we were both grandchildren of Barbadian grandfathers who had been migrants to Cuba. His father had stayed, and Pedro was born – three months before me – and raised in Cuba, while my mother had been taken to her mother's home country and I was born and raised in Barbados.

We discovered that we had other things in common, such as our love for Bob Marley's music and the French language. He invited me to his home to meet his mother and sister, and took me to a club, now converted to a café, where his father used to play piano.

On my return home, I invited him to Barbados to see the land of his grandfather, Edmund Lee Hope. He accepted the invitation, and he arrived in Barbados in December 2000. He was granted permission to reside outside of Cuba, and has remained in Barbados. He began his working life in Barbados teaching in the Spanish Primary Programme. One of the first schools to which he was assigned was St David's Primary, a stone's throw from St David's Chapel where his grandfather was baptized. He is now head of the foreign languages department of a secondary school.

Pedro and I were married on 26 May 2001.

Our house is in the parish of Christ Church, not far from Warners, where his grandfather was born. The name of our house is "Esperanza" – my mother's middle name, and the Spanish translation for Pedro's paternal surname – Hope.

Figure E.3. Pedro Hope Jústiz and Sharon Marshall on their wedding day, 26 May 2001

NOTES

PREFACE

1.   Kathryn Walbert, "The Value of Oral History", Learn NC, www.learnnc .org/lp/pages/762.
2.   Jorge Giovannetti, "Black British Caribbean Migrants in Cuba: Resistance, Opposition, and Strategic Identity in the Early Twentieth Century", in *Regional Footprints: The Travels and Travails of Early Caribbean Migrants,* ed. Annette Insanally, Mark Clifford and Sean Sheriff (Kingston: Latin American–Caribbean Centre, University of the West Indies, 2006), 115.

CHAPTER 1

1.   F.A. Hoyos, *Barbados Our Island Home,* 4th ed. (London: Macmillan Caribbean, 1989), 129–30.
2.   Hilary McD. Beckles, *Great House Rules: Landless Emancipation and Workers' Protest in Barbados, 1838–1938* (Kingston: Ian Randle, 2004), 88–89.
3.   Ibid.
4.   Bonham Richardson, *Panama Money in Barbados, 1900–1920* (Knoxville: University of Tennessee Press, 1985), 43.
5.   Ibid., 77.
6.   Ibid.
7.   Ibid., 19.
8.   Ibid., 81.
9.   "Emigration from Barbados to British Guiana", *Barbados Herald,* 10 May 1919, 4.
10. "Workers from Barbados", *Barbados Herald,* 6 September 1919, 3.
11. Richardson, *Panama Money,* 108.
12. Ibid.
13. Elaine Pereira Rocha, "Another Black Like Me: Strategies of Identification in *Afrodescendientes* in Latin America", in *Another Black Like Me: The Construction of Identities and Solidarity in the African Diaspora,* ed. Elaine Pereira Rocha and

Nielson Rosa Bezerra (Newcastle upon Tyne: Cambridge Scholars Publishing, 2015), 9.

14. Richardson, *Panama Money*, 108.

15. Ibid., 107.

16. "Barbadian Ubiquity", *Barbados Herald*, 6 September 1919, 3.

17. G.W. Roberts, "Emigration from the Island of Barbados", *Social and Economic Studies* 4, no. 3 (1955): 247.

18. Ibid., 247–48.

19. Ibid., 248.

20. Pedro L.V. Welch, "Post-Emancipation Adjustments in the Urban Context: Views from Bridgetown, Barbados", in *In the Shadow of the Plantation: Caribbean History and Legacy*, ed. Alvin O. Thompson (Kingston: Ian Randle, 2002), 274.

21. Mary Chamberlain, *Narratives of Exile and Return* (New York: St Martin's, 1997), 22.

22. Elizabeth Thomas-Hope, "The Establishment of a Migration Tradition: British West Indian Movements to the Hispanic Caribbean in the Century after Emancipation", in *Caribbean Social Relations*, ed. Colin G. Clarke (Liverpool: University of Liverpool Centre for Latin American Studies, 1978), 75.

23. Velma Newton, *The Silver Men: West Indian Labour Migration to Panama, 1850–1914* (Kingston: Institute of Social and Economic Research, University of the West Indies, 1984), 93.

24. Ibid., 74.

25. Roberts, "Emigration", 270.

26. Richardson, *Panama Money*, 136.

27. Ibid., 106.

28. Ibid., 146.

29. Ibid., 234.

30. Ibid., 219.

31. "Emigration", *Barbados Herald*, 26 July 1919, 4.

32. Jerome Handler, "Plantation Slave Settlements in Barbados 1650s to 1834", in *In the Shadow of the Plantation: Caribbean History and Legacy*, ed. Alvin O. Thompson (Kingston: Ian Randle, 2002), 124.

33. "Diary of Major Joseph Gorham", *Cinco Diarios del Sitio de La Habana* (Havana: Empresa Consolidada de Artes Gráficas, 1963).

34. Jonathan Curry-Machado, "How Cuba Burned with the Ghosts of British Slavery: Race, Abolition and the *Escalera*", in *Slavery and Abolition* 25, no. 1 (April 2004): 71–93.

CHAPTER 2

1.   Daniel E. Bender and Jana K. Lipman, "Through the Looking Glass: US Empire through the Lens of Labor History", in *Making the Empire Work: Labor and United States Imperialism*, ed. Daniel E. Bender and Jana K. Lipman (New York: New York University Press, 2015), 23.
2.   Ibid., 19.
3.   Franklin Knight, *Slave Society in Cuba during the Nineteenth Century* (Madison: University of Wisconsin Press, 1970), 20.
4.   Leland Jenks, *Our Cuban Colony* (Havana: Editorial Alfa, 1939), 31.
5.   Ibid.
6.   Louis A. Pérez Jr, *Cuba between Empires, 1878–1902* (Pittsburgh: University of Pittsburgh Press, 1983), 349.
7.   Ibid.
8.   Ibid., 347.
9.   Ibid.
10. César Ayala, *American Sugar Kingdom: The Plantation Economy of the Spanish Caribbean, 1898–1934* (Chapel Hill: University of North Carolina Press, 1999), 58.
11. Ibid., 77.
12. Ibid., 78.
13. Pérez, *Cuba between Empires*, 357.
14. Jorge Ibarra, *Prologue to Revolution: Cuba, 1898–1958* (Boulder: Lynne Reiner, 1998), 11.
15. Louis A. Pérez Jr, *Lords of the Mountains: Social Banditry and Peasant Protest in Cuba, 1878* (Pittsburgh: University of Pittsburgh Press, 1990), 102.
16. Pérez, *Cuba between Empires*, 360.
17. Albert G. Robinson, *Cuba Old and New* (1915; reprint, Westport, CT: Negro University Press, 1970), 210.
18. Ibid.
19. Ibid., 214.
20. Knight, *Slave Society in Cuba*, 33.
21. Ibid., 13.
22. Pérez, *Lords of the Mountains*, 162.
23. *Asociación para el Fomento de Inmigración* (Havana: Rambla y Bouza, 1917), 5.
24. Ibid., 6.
25. Alejandro de la Fuente, "Immigration and Race in Cuba", in *Work, Protest, and Identity in Twentieth-Century Latin America*, ed. Vincent C. Peloso (Wilmington, DE: Scholarly Resources Inc., 2003), 6.
26. Ibid.

27. Marc McLeod, "Garveyism in Cuba, 1920–1940", *Journal of Caribbean History* 30, nos. 1–2 (1996): 136.

28. Alistair Hennessy, "The Imperatives and Complexities of the Cuban Labour Movement", in *Labour in the Caribbean: From Emancipation to Independence*, ed. Malcolm Cross and Gad Heuman (London: Macmillan, 1988), 245.

29. McLeod, "Garveyism in Cuba", 136.

30. Basil Maughan, "Some Aspects of Barbadian Migration to Cuba, 1919–1935", *Journal of the Barbados Museum and Historical Society* 37, no. 3 (1985): 245.

31. Hugh Thomas, *Cuba: The Pursuit of Freedom* (New York: Harper and Row, 1971), 543.

32. Ibid.

33. "The Bursting of a Bubble", *Barbados Herald*, 18 June 1921, 4.

34. *Barbados Herald*, 4 February 1922, 3.

35. "Cheap Passages on Commodious Steamers Each Fifteen Days, to Cuba", *Barbados Herald*, 7 October 1922, 4.

36. *Barbados Herald*, 6 January 1923, 4.

37. Ibid.

38. Ibid., 31 October 1923, 4.

39. British Consul, Santiago de Cuba, to Chargé, Havana, 22 December 1925, FO 277/201, Public Records Office (PRO).

40. "Immigrant Boat Wrecked", *Barbados Herald*, 2 January 1926, 4.

41. "Return of Immigrants from Cuba", *Barbados Herald*, 14 May 1927, 5.

42. "Cuban Immigration", *Barbados Advocate*, 12 July 1926, 5.

43. Ibid.

44. Mark J. Smith, "Nature and Profit: A Cuban Sugar Plantation in the Early Twentieth Century" (MA thesis, University of Florida, 1993), 2.

45. Barry Carr, " 'Omnipotent and Omnipresent?' Labor Shortages, Worker Mobility, and Employer Control in the Cuban Sugar Industry, 1910–1934", in *Identity and Struggle at the Margins of the Nation State: The Laboring Peoples of Central America and the Hispanic Caribbean,* ed. Aviva Chomsky and Aldo Lauria-Santiago (Durham, NC: Duke University Press, 1998), 267–68.

46. John Dumoulin, *Azúcar y lucha de clases, 1917* (Havana: Editorial de Ciencias Sociales, 1980), 47.

47. Cuba, Central Hershey, 1916–1946, www.hersheyarchives.org, accessed 21 March 2015.

48. Ibid.

49. Jenks, *Our Cuban Colony*, 220.

50. Ibid.

51. *Barbados Herald*, 16 September 1922, 2.

52. "The Past and the Present: A Warning", *Barbados Herald*, 28 April 1923, 4.

53. Ibid.

54. Editorial, *Barbados Advocate*, 23 October 1922, 5.

CHAPTER 3

1. Wayne Smith, *Portrait of Cuba* (Atlanta: Turner, 1991), 57.

2. Ibid.

3. Ibarra, *Prologue to Revolution*, 141.

4. Pérez, *Cuba between Empires*, 385

5. Ibid.

6. Ibid.

7. Ibarra, *Prologue to Revolution*, 141.

8. Vera Kutzinski, *Sugar's Secrets: Race and the Eroticism of Cuban Nationalism* (Charlottesville: University of Virginia Press, 1993), 139.

9. Ibid., 143.

10. Elizabeth McLean Petras, *Jamaican Labor Migration: White Capital and Black Labor, 1850–1930* (Boulder: Westview Press), 236.

11. Pérez, *Lords of the Mountain*, 144.

12. Robert Nairne Lauriault, "Virgin Soil: The Modernization of Social Relations on a Cuban Sugar Estate" (PhD diss., University of Florida, 1994), 298–99.

13. Aline Helg, *Our Rightful Share: The Afro-Cuban Struggle for Equality, 1886–1912* (Chapel Hill: University of North Carolina Press, 1995), 228.

14. Melina Pappademos, *Black Political Activism and the Cuban Republic* (Chapel Hill: University of North Carolina Press, 2011), 5.

15. Helg, *Our Rightful Share*, 228.

16. Aviva Chomsky, " 'Barbados or Canada?' Race, Immigration, and Nation in Early-Twentieth-Century Cuba", *Hispanic American Historical Review* 80, no. 3 (2000): 420.

17. Ibid.

18. Jason Colby, *The Business of Empire: United Fruit, Race, and U.S. Expansion in Central America* (Ithaca: Cornell University Press, 2011), 3.

19. Ramiro Guerra y Sánchez, *Sugar and Society in the Caribbean: An Economic History of Cuban Agriculture* (1927; reprint, New Haven: Yale University Press, 1964), 144–45.

20. Rolando Alvarez Estévez, *Azúcar y inmigración, 1900–1940* (Havana: Editorial de Ciencias Sociales, 1988), 67–68.

21. Oscar Zanetti, *United Fruit Company: Un caso de dominio imperialista en Cuba* (Havana: Editorial Ciencias Sociales, 1976), 216.

22. Noel Navarro, *Marcial Ponce: de central en central* (Havana: Union de Escritores y Artistas de Cuba, 1977), 57–58.
23. Zanetti, *United Fruit Company*, 303.
24. Jenks, *Our Cuban Colony*, 226.
25. Editorial, *Barbados Advocate*, 27 October 1924, 5.
26. "Undesirable Immigration", *Havana Post*, 2 August 1924, 4.
27. Ibid.
28. Pablo Llaguno de Cárdenas, *Asunto cubano: Problemas sobre inmigración deseable e indeseable y las industrias nacionales* (Havana: Rambla y Bouza, 1917), 5.
29. Ibid., 17.
30. "Barbadians in Cuba", *Barbados Herald*, 15 June 1929, 6.
31. McLeod, "Garveyism in Cuba", 134.
32. *UNIA and ACL petition to the League of Nations* (London: Vail, 1928), CO 323/1004/8, PRO.
33. "West Indians in Cuba Organize New Religious Body", *Barbados Herald*, 12 May 1928, 5.
34. Alejandro de la Fuente, "Immigration and Race in Cuba", 14.
35. Ibid., 15.
36. Lauriault, "Virgin Soil", 338.
37. Estate manager, Manatí, to Manuel Rionda, New York, 18 October 1924, Braga Brothers Collection. University of Florida, Gainesville.
38. *Barbados Herald*, 26 September 1925, 4.
39. de la Fuente, "Immigration and Race in Cuba", 16.
40. Ibid.
41. Pérez, *Lords of the Mountains*, 163.
42. Roberts, "Emigration", 284.
43. "Population, Unemployment and Emigration", *Barbados Herald*, 24 January 1925, 4.
44. British Consulate, Santiago de Cuba, to British Legation, Havana, 28 July 1926, FO 277/202.
45. "West Indians Ill-Treated in Cuba", *Barbados Advocate*, 27 October 1924.
46. "Jamaican Murdered by Cuban Mob in Town Near Havana", *Barbados Herald*, 6 September 1919, 3, 6.
47. Ibid.
48. Raoul Piedemonte, "Cuban Answers Jamaican's Defence of Immigration", *Havana Post*, 29 July 1924, 2.

CHAPTER 4

1.   Godfrey Haggard to Carlos Manuel de Céspedes, 3 January 1924, *Correspondence between His Majesty's Government and the Cuban Government Respecting the Ill-Treatment of British West Indian Labourers in Cuba* (London: Great Britain Foreign Office, 1924), 4.
2.   Ibid., 5.
3.   Godfrey Haggard to Carlos Manuel de Céspedes, *Correspondence*, 22 January 1924.
4.   Donald St Clair Gainer to Carlos Manuel de Céspedes, 23 April 1924, *Further Correspondence between His Majesty's Government and the Cuban Government Respecting the Ill-Treatment of British West Indian Labourers in Cuba* (London: Great Britain Printing Office, 1924), 5.
5.   Carlos Moore, *Pichón: Race and Revolution in Castro's Cuba: A Memoir* (Chicago: Lawrence Hill Books, 2008), 6–7.
6.   Godfrey Haggard, Havana, to Sir Leslie Probyn, Governor of Jamaica, 7 January 1924, FO 277/200, PRO.
7.   Aurelio Portuondo, Havana, to Manuel Rionda, New York, 25 January 1924, Braga Brothers Collection, Box 33, Series 10.
8.   Haggard to Probyn, 7 January 1924.
9.   Sir Leslie Probyn to Godfrey Haggard, 23 January 1924, FO 277/200, PRO.
10. Gainer to J. Ramsay MacDonald, 25 June 1924, *Further Correspondence*, 16.
11. T.J. Morris, British Chargé d'Affaires, Havana, to Principal Secretary of State, Foreign Office, London, 12 March 1925, FO 371/106018, A1667/22/14, PRO.
12. T.J. Morris, British Chargé d'Affaires, Havana, to Principal Secretary of State, Foreign Office, London, 23 December 1924, FO 277/200, PRO.
13. Ibid.
14. Robert Vansittart, Foreign Office, to Under-Secretary of State, Colonial Office, 30 January 1925, FO 277/201, PRO.
15. Morris to Principal Secretary of State, 23 December 1924.
16. Ibid.
17. Ibid.
18. Ibid.
19. Godfrey Haggard, Havana, to Principal Secretary of State, London, 8 April 1924, FO 277/200, PRO.
20. Telegram from Donald St Clair Gainer, Chargé d'Affaires, Havana, to Foreign Office, London, 31 July 1924, FO 277/200, PRO.
21. Donald St Clair Gainer, Chargé d'Affaires, Havana, to Foreign Office, London,, 19 August 1924, FO 277/200, PRO.

22. Ibid.

23. Ibid.

24. *Annual General Report of Jamaica Together with the Departmental Reports for 1924* (Kingston: Government Printing Office, 1924), 4.

25. Telegram from T.J. Morris, Havana, to Foreign Office, London, 29 January 1925, FO 277/201, PRO.

26. T.J. Morris, Havana, to Secretary of State, Austin Chamberlain, London, 31 March 1925, FO 277/201, PRO.

27. "West Indians in Cuba", *Barbados Herald*, 3 January 1925, 4.

28. "The Problem of Migration", *Barbados Herald*, 2 March 1929, 18.

29. *Minutes of the Jamaica Legislative Council for 1926*, Tuesday, 2 March 1926, 71.

30. British Consular Agent, Camagüey, to British Embassy Consular Section, Havana, 10 August 1951, FO 277/263, PRO.

31. British West Indians, Elia, to British Consular Agent, Camagüey, 15 May 1951, FO 277/260, PRO.

32. Daril Allen, Las Villas, to British Consular Agent, Camagüey, FO 277/260, PRO.

33. Marcus Francis, Las Villas, to British Consular Agent, Camagüey, 7 August 1951, FO 277/260, PRO.

34. Thomas Aiken, Las Villas, to British Consular Agent, Camagüey, 20 August 1951, FO 277/260, PRO.

CHAPTER 5

1. Andrzej Dembicz, *Cañeras y poblamiento en Cuba* (Havana: Editorial de Ciencias Sociales, 1989), 38.

2. Alvarez Estévez, *Azúcar y inmigración*, 21.

3. "William Preston Stoute, Native of Barbados Passes Away", *Barbados Herald*, 31 March 1923, 2.

4. G.B. James, Camagüey, to British Consul, Havana, 16 May 1949, FO 277/255/66, PRO.

5. Maughan, "Some Aspects", 263.

6. Michael Anthony Pettitt, "Social and Economic Change in the Community around a Sugar Mill in Cuba" (MA thesis, University of California, Berkeley, 1973), 125.

7. Alfred Sauvy, "Pyscho-Social Aspects of Migration", *Economics of International Migration: Proceedings of a Conference Held by the International Economics Association*, ed. Thomas Brinely (London: Macmillan, 1958), 299.

CHAPTER 6

1. "Arrival of Immigrant Ship from Cuba", *Barbados Herald*, 8 October 1921, 4.
2. Ibid.
3. "Labour Conditions in Barbados", *Barbados Herald*, 15 October 1921, 4.
4. Ibid.
5. "Repatriation from Cuba", *Barbados Herald*, 11 November 1922, 4.
6. "The Webster SS Company: Bi-Monthly Sailings for Cuba", *Barbados Herald*, 21 October 1922, 4.
7. "Emigration to Cuba", *Barbados Herald*, 17 February 1923, 8.
8. Cable from M. Rasco-Portuondo, Cuba, to Higinio Fanjul, New York, 22 October 1926, Braga Brothers Collection, Box 32, Series 10.
9. Salvador C. Rionda, Cuba, to Manuel Rionda, New York, 3 November 1926, Braga Brothers Collection, Box 32.
10. UNIA Havana Branch to British Chargé, 29 October 1926, FO 277/203, PRO.
11. Ibid.
12. Governor A.R. Slater to the Jamaica Legislative Council, 5 December 1932, enclosure no. 3, in *Minutes of the Jamaica Legislative Council for 1932*, 6 December 1932, 151.
13. Telegram from British Minister at Havana to Governor of Jamaica, 10 December 1932, ibid., 13 December 1932, 168.
14. "Week's Telegrams", *Barbados Herald*, 9 March 1929, 14.
15. *Barbados Herald*, 23 November 1929.
16. Malcolm J. Proudfoot, *Population Movements in the Caribbean* (New York: Negro Universities Press, 1970), 15.
17. *Jamaica Annual Report for 1929* (Kingston: Government Printing Office, 1929), 4.
18. *Jamaica Annual Report for 1930* (Kingston: Government Printing Office, 1930), 4.
19. Francis Maxwell, "The Sugar Crisis: How It May be Solved", *Barbados Herald*, 11 January 1930, 11.
20. Louis A. Pérez Jr, *Cuba and the United States: Ties of Singular Intimacy* (Athens: University of Georgia Press, 1990), 181.
21. Alan Dye, "Cuba and the Origins of the US Sugar Quota", *Revista de Indias* 65, no. 233 (2005): 202.
22. Ibid., 203.
23. Pérez, *Cuba and the United States*, 194.
24. Maughan, "Some Aspects", 262.
25. Ibid.
26. Thomas Brimelow, British Consul, Havana, to Acting Colonial Secretary, British Honduras, 2 March 1949, FO 277/255/66, PRO.

27. Colonial Secretary, Barbados, to British Consul, Havana, 14 June 1949, FO 277/255/66, PRO.

28. G.B. James, Camagüey, to British Consul, Havana, 16 May 1949, FO 277/260, PRO.

29. G.B. James, Camagüey, to Hugh Coxe, Kingston, Jamaica, 26 January 1949, FO 277/260, PRO.

30. G.B. James, Camagüey, to Hugh Coxe, Kingston, Jamaica 8 March 1949, FO 277/260, PRO.

31. John Rahr, Trinidad, to British Consul, Havana, 27 December 1950, FO 277/261, PRO.

32. G.B. James, Camagüey, to British Consul, Havana, 30 June 1949, FO 277/255/66, PRO.

33. Memorandum from Jeffrey Jackson, Foreign Office, London, to British Consul, Havana, FO 277/255/66, PRO.

34. G.B. James, Camagüey, to Thomas Brimelow, Havana, 11 October 1949, FO 277/260, PRO.

35. Circular to British West Indians from G.B. James, Camagüey, October 1949, FO 277/260, PRO.

36. G.B. James, Camagüey, to British Consul, Havana, 27 October 1949, FO 277/260, PRO.

37. Ibid.

38. G.B. James, Camagüey, to British Consul, Havana, 23 September 1949, FO 277/255/66, PRO.

39. British Consular Agent, Camagüey, to Consul, J.W. Pethybridge, Havana, 29 November 1951, FO 277/261, PRO.

40. Ibid.

41. Minute by Thomas Brimelow, British Consul, Havana, 16 September 1949, FO 277/255/66, PRO.

42. Raoul Piedemonte, "Cuban Answers Jamaican's Defence of Immigration", *Havana Post*, 29 July 1924, 2.

43. L.E. Gill, Havana, to Dolores Jústiz Collymore, Guantánamo, 6 September 1973.

CHAPTER 7

1. *Bye-Laws for the Government of the British West Indian Welfare Centre* (Guantánamo: La Universal, 1949).

2. Minutes of the British West Indian Welfare Centre, Guantánamo, General Meeting, 27 February 1955, 452.

3. Ibid., 12 February 1956, 493.

4. Ibid., 1 December 1945, 5.
5. Ibid., 2 December 1945, 10.
6. Ibid., 14 July 1946, 37.
7. Ibid., 12 January 1947, 61.
8. Ibid., 28 July 1946, 41.
9. Ibid., 9 November 1947, 67–68.
10. Ibid.
11. Ibid., 18 April 1948, 82.
12. Ibid., 9 July 1950, 147.
13. Ibid.
14. Ibid., 26 January 1947, 64.
15. Ibid.
16. Ibid.
17. Andrea Queeley, "El Puente: Transnationalism among Cubans of English-speaking Caribbean Descent", in *Rewriting the African Diaspora in Latin America and the Caribbean: Beyond Disciplinary and National Boundaries*, ed. Robert Lee Adams Jr (New York: Routledge 2013), 110.

CHAPTER 8

1. "Cuban Revolt Is Spreading", *Los Angeles Herald*, 1 October 1907.
2. Jorge I. Domínguez, *Cuba: Order and Revolution* (Cambridge, MA: Harvard University Press, 1978), 46.
3. Ibid., 46.
4. Ibid., 16.
5. Gillian McGillivray, *Blazing Cane: Sugar Communities, Class, and State Formation in Cuba, 1868–1959*, (Durham, NC: Duke University Press, 2009), 89.
6. Jorge L. Giovannetti, " 'Usual Suspects': The Racial Fear and the 1917 Massacre of West Indians in Jobobo, Cuba", paper presented at Twenty-fifth Annual Conference of the Caribbean Studies Association, Castries, St Lucia, 2000.
7. Ibid., 44.
8. Ibid.
9. Ibid., 46–47.
10. Moore, *Pichón*, 55.
11. Ibid., 54.
12. Oscar Zanetti and Alejandro García. *Sugar and Railroads: A Cuban History, 1837–1959* (Chapel Hill: University of North Carolina Press, 1998), 371.
13. Ibid., 395.

14. Ibid., 397.
15. Ibarra, *Prologue to Revolution*, 151.
16. Queeley, "El Puente", 110.
17. Carlos Moore, *Castro, the Blacks, and Africa* (Berkeley: University of California Press, 1988), 5.
18. Samuel Furber, *Cuba since the Revolution of 1959: A Critical Assessment* (Chicago: Haymarket, 2011), 167.
19. Ibid., 168.
20. Moore, *Castro, the Blacks, and Africa*, 5.
21. Zanetti and García, *Sugar and Railroads*, 370.
22. Jeffrey Sachs, "Twentieth-Century Political Economy: A Brief History of Global Capitalism", *Oxford Review of Economic Policy* 15, no. 4 (1999): 95.
23. Harvey Neptune, "The Twilight Years": Caribbean Social Movements, 1940–1960, http://exhibitions.nypl.org/africanaage/essay-caribbean-40.html.

EPILOGUE

1. José Millet and Julio Corbea, *Presencia haitiana en el oriente de Cuba* (Santiago de Cuba: Casa del Caribe, 1987), 73.
2. Ibid.
3. Alvarez Estévez, *Azúcar y inmigración*, 16.
4. Maughan, "Some Aspects", 262–63.
5. José Armando Fernández Salazar, Aleida Best: una mujer valientemente negra, http://periodico26.cu/index.php/es/de-las-tunas/1826-aleida-best-una-mujer -valientemente-negra, 21 August 2015. Accessed 4 November 2015.
6. Edward Shils, "Roots: The Sense of Place and Past – The Cultural Gains and Losses of Migration", in *Human Migration: Patterns and Policies*, ed. William H. McNeil and Ruth S. Adams (Bloomington: Indiana University Press, 1978), 422.
7. Moore, *Castro, the Blacks and Africa*, 39.
8. Ibid., 46.
9. Tomás Fernándes Robaina, *El Negro en Cuba, 1902–1958: Apuntes para la historia de la lucha contra la discriminación racial* (Havana: Editorial de Ciencias Sociales, 1990), 94.
10. Moore, *Castro, the Blacks and Africa*, 39.
11. Helg, *Our Rightful Share*, 248.
12. Ibid.
13. Moore, *Castro, the Blacks and Africa*, 51.
14. Ibid., 324.

15. Ibid., 345.

16. Ewa Morawska, "The Historiography and Sociology of Imigration", in *Immigration Reconsidered: History, Sociology, and Politics*, ed. Virginia Yans-McLaughlin (New York: Oxford University Press, 1990), 214.

17. Ibid.

18. Andrea Queeley, "Somos Negros Finos: Anglophone Caribbean Cultural Citizenship in Revolutionary Cuba", in *Global Circuits of Blackness: Interrogating the African Diaspora*, ed. Jean Muteba Rahier, Percy C. Hintzen and Felipe Smith (Urbana: University of Illinois Press, 2010), 204.

19. Ibid.

20. Eixa Valiente, Croos Valiente and Margarita Lewis, *Estudio preliminar de aspectos sociales de algunos de los inmigrantes y descendientes del Centro de Bienestar Antillano Guantánamo*, 1996.

21. Alberto N. Jones, "Report on the West Indian Welfare Center", AfroCuba Web, www.afrocubaweb.com/wiwc.htm#letter. May 1996. Accessed 27 April 2000.

22. Ibid.

23. International Cricket Council, www.icc-cricket.com/about/183/icc-members/affiliate -members/cuba. Accessed 25 February 2015.

24. Proudfoot, *Population Movements*, 77–78.

SELECTED BIBLIOGRAPHY

OFFICIAL DOCUMENTS

Anglo-American Directory of Cuba 1960. Marianao, Cuba.

Annual General Report of Jamaica Together with the Departmental Reports for 1924. Kingston: Government Printing Office, 1924.

Asociación para el Fomento de Inmigración. Havana: Rambla y Bouza, 1917.

Barbados Blue Book. 1909–1910.

Barbados Blue Book. 1930

Censo de la República de Cuba, Bajo La Administración Provisional de Los Estados Unidos 1907. Washington, DC: Office of the Census of the United States of America, 1908.

Jamaica Annual Report for 1929. Kingston: Government Printing Office, 1929.

Jamaica Annual Report for 1930. Kingston: Government Printing Office, 1930.

Universal Negro Improvement Association and African Communities League Petition to the League of Nations. London: Vail, 1928.

NEWSPAPERS AND PERIODICALS

Barbados Advocate

Barbados Herald

Havana Post

La Discusión

Los Angeles Herald

Nation (Barbados)

BOOKS AND JOURNALS

Alvarez Estévez, Rolando. *Azúcar y inmigración, 1900–1940.* Havana: Editorial de Ciencias Sociales, 1988.

Ayala, César. *American Sugar Kingdom: The Plantation Economy of the Spanish Caribbean, 1898–1934.* Chapel Hill: University of North Carolina Press, 1999.

Beckles, Hilary McD. *Great House Rules: Landless Emancipation and Workers' Protest in Barbados, 1838–1938.* Kingston: Ian Randle, 2004.

Bender, Daniel E., and Jana K. Lipman. "Through the Looking Glass: US Empire through the Lens of Labor History". In *Making the Empire Work: Labor and United States Imperialism*, edited by Daniel E. Bender and Jana K. Lipman, 1–32. New York: New York University Press, 2015.

Bustamante, Ramón. *Cuba: "The Pearl of the Antilles".* Saint Louis, MO: Foreign Publishing, 1916.

Carr, Barry. "'Omnipotent and Omnipresent?' Labor Shortages, Worker Mobility, and Employer Control in the Cuban Sugar Industry, 1910–1934". In *Identity and Struggle at the Margins of the Nation State: The Laboring Peoples of Central America and the Hispanic Caribbean*, edited by Aviva Chomsky and Aldo Lauria-Santiago, 260–91. Durham, NC: Duke University Press, 1998.

Chamberlain, Mary. *Narratives of Exile and Return.* New York: St Martin's Press, 1997.

Chomsky, Aviva. "'Barbados or Canada?' Race, Immigration, and Nation in Early-Twentieth-Century Cuba". *Hispanic American Historical Review* 80, no. 3 (2000): 415–62.

Colby, Jason M. *The Business of Empire: United Fruit, Race and U.S. Expansion in Central America.* Ithaca: Cornell University Press, 2011.

Curry-Machado, Jonathan. "How Cuba Burned with the Ghosts of British Slavery: Race, Abolition and the *Escalera*". *Slavery and Abolition* 25, no. 1 (April 2004): 71–93.

de la Fuente, Alejandro. "Immigration and Race in Cuba". In *Work, Protest, and Identity in Twentieth-Century Latin America*, edited by Vincent C. Peloso, 1–23. Wilmington, DE: Scholarly Resources, 2003.

Dembicz, Andrzej. *Cañeras y poblamiento en Cuba.* Havana: Editorial de Ciencias Sociales, 1989.

Domínguez, Jorge I. *Cuba: Order and Revolution.* Cambridge, MA: Harvard University Press, 1978.

Dumoulin, John. *Azúcar y lucha de clases, 1917.* Havana: Editorial de Ciencias Sociales, 1980.

Dye, Alan. "Cuba and the Origins of the US Sugar Quota". *Revista de Indias* 65, no. 233 (2005): 193–218.

Fernándes Robaina, Tomás. *El Negro en Cuba, 1902–1958: Apuntes para la historia de la lucha contra la discriminación racial.* Havana: Editorial de Ciencias Sociales, 1990.

Furber, Samuel. *Cuba since the Revolution of 1959: A Critical Assessment.* Chicago: Haymarket Books, 2011.

Guerra y Sánchez, Ramiro. *Sugar and Society in the Caribbean: An Economic History of Cuban Agriculture.* 1927. Reprint, New Haven: Yale University Press, 1964.

Giovannetti, Jorge L. "Black British Caribbean Migrants in Cuba: Resistance, Opposition, and Strategic Identity in the Early Twentieth Century". In *Regional Footprints: The Travels and Travails of Early Caribbean Migrants*, edited by Annette Insanally, Mark Clifford and Sean Sheriff, 103–20. Kingston: Latin American–Caribbean Centre, University of the West Indies, 2006.

———. "'Usual Suspects': The Racial Fear and the 1917 Massacre of West Indians in Jobobo, Cuba". Paper presented at the Twenty-fifth Annual Conference of the Caribbean Studies Association, Castries, St Lucia, 2000.

Handler, Jerome S. "Plantation Slave Settlements in Barbados 1650s to 1834". In *In the Shadow of the Plantation: Caribbean History and Legacy*, edited by Alvin O. Thompson, 123–61. Kingston: Ian Randle, 2002.

Helg, Aline. *Our Rightful Share: The Afro-Cuban Struggle for Equality, 1886–1912*. Chapel Hill: University of North Carolina Press, 1995.

Hennessy, Alistair. "The Imperatives and Complexities of the Cuban Labour Movement". In *Labour in the Caribbean: From Emancipation to Independence*, edited by Malcolm Cross and Gad Heuman, 234–57. London: Macmillan, 1988.

Hoyos, F.A. *Barbados Our Island Home*. 4th ed. London: Macmillan Caribbean, 1989.

Ibarra, Jorge. *Prologue to Revolution: Cuba, 1898–1958*. Boulder: Lynne Reiner, 1998.

Jenks, Leland. *Our Cuban Colony*. Havana: Editorial Alfa, 1939.

Knight, Franklin. *Slave Society in Cuba during the Nineteenth Century*. Madison: University of Wisconsin Press, 1970.

Kutzinski, Vera. *Sugar's Secrets: Race and the Eroticism of Cuban Nationalism*. Charlottesville: University of Virginia Press, 1993.

Lauriault, Robert Nairne. "Virgin Soil: The Modernization of Social Relations on a Cuban Sugar Estate, the Francisco Sugar Company, 1898–1921". PhD dissertation, University of Florida, 1994.

Llaguno de Cárdenas, Pablo. *Asunto cubano: Problemas sobre inmigración deseable e indeseable y las industrias nacionales*. Havana: Rambla y Bouza, 1917.

Maughan, Basil. "Some Aspects of Barbadian Migration to Cuba, 1919–1935". *Journal of the Barbados Museum and Historical Society*, 37, no. 3 (1985): 239–75.

McGillivray, Gillian. *Blazing Cane: Sugar Communities, Class and State Formation in Cuba, 1868–1959*. Durham, NC: Duke University Press, 2009.

McLean Petras, Elizabeth. *Jamaican Labor Migration: White Capital and Black Labor 1850–1930*. Boulder: Westview Press, 1988.

McLeod, Marc C. "Garveyism in Cuba, 1920–1940". *Journal of Caribbean History* 30, nos. 1–2, (1996): 132–68.

Millet, José, and Julio Corbea. *Presencia haitiana en el oriente de Cuba*. Santiago de Cuba: Casa del Caribe, 1987.

Moore, Carlos. *Castro, the Blacks, and Africa*. Berkeley: University of California Press, 1988.

Morawska, Ewa. "The Historiography and Sociology of Immigration". In *Immigration Reconsidered: History, Sociology, and Politics*, edited by Virginia Yans-McLaughlin, 187–238. New York: Oxford University Press, 1990.

Newton, Velma. *The Silver Men: West Indian Labour Migration to Panama, 1850–1914*. Kingston: Institute of Social and Economic Research, University of the West Indies, 1984.

Pappademos, Melina. *Black Political Activism and the Cuban Republic*. Chapel Hill: University of North Carolina Press, 2011.

Pereira Rocha, Elaine. "Another Black Like Me: Strategies of Identification in *Afrodescendientes* in Latin America". In *Another Black Like Me: The Construction of Identities and Solidarity in the African Diaspora*, edited by Elaine Pereira Rocha and Nielson Rosa Bezerra, 1–23. Newcastle upon Tyne: Cambridge Scholars Publishing, 2015.

Pérez Jr, Louis A. *Cuba between Empires, 1878–1902*. Pittsburgh: University of Pittsburgh Press, 1983.

——. *Cuba and the United States: Ties of Singular Intimacy*. Athens: University of Georgia Press, 1990.

——. *Lords of the Mountains: Social Banditry and Peasant Protest in Cuba, 1878*. Pittsburgh: University of Pittsburgh Press, 1990.

Pettitt, Michael Anthony. "Social and Economic Change in the Community around a Sugar Mill in Cuba". MA thesis, University of California, Berkley, 1973.

Proudfoot, Malcolm J. *Population Movements in the Caribbean*. New York: Negro Universities Press, 1970.

Queeley, Andrea. "El Puente: Transnationalism among Cubans of English-speaking Caribbean Descent". In *Rewriting the African Diaspora in Latin America and the Caribbean: Beyond Disciplinary and National Boundaries*, edited by Robert Lee Adams Jr, 100–117. New York: Routledge, 2013.

——. "Somos Negros Finos: Anglophone Caribbean Cultural Citizenship in Revolutionary Cuba". In *Global Circuits of Blackness: Interrogating the African Diaspora*, edited by Jean Muteba Rahier, Percy C. Hintzen and Felipe Smith, 201–22. Urbana: University of Illinois Press, 2010.

Richardson, Bonham. *Panama Money in Barbados, 1900–1920*. Knoxville: University of Tennessee Press, 1985.

Roberts, G.W. "Emigration from the Island of Barbados". *Social and Economic Studies* 4, no. 3 (1955): 245–88.

Robinson, Albert G. *Cuba Old and New*. 1915. Reprint, Westport, CT: Negro Universities Press, 1970.

Sachs, Jeffrey. "Twentieth-Century Political Economy: A Brief History of Global Capitalism". *Oxford Review of Economic Policy* 15, no. 4 (1999): 90–101.

Sauvy, Alfred. "Psycho-Social Aspects of Migration". *Economics of International Migration: Proceedings of a Conference Held by the International Economics Association*, edited by Thomas Brinley, 297–302. London: Macmillan, 1958.

Shils, Edward. "Roots: The Sense of Place and Past – The Cultural Gains and Losses of Migration". In *Human Migration: Patterns and Policies*, edited by William H. McNeil and Ruth S. Adams, 404–26. Bloomington: Indiana University Press, 1978.

Smith, Mark J. "Nature and Profit: A Cuban Sugar Plantation in the Early Twentieth Century". MA thesis, University of Florida, 1993.

Smith, Wayne. *Portrait of Cuba*. Atlanta: Turner, 1991.

Thomas, Hugh. *Cuba: The Pursuit of Freedom*. New York: Harper and Row, 1971.

Thomas-Hope, Elizabeth. "The Establishment of a Migration Tradition: British West Indian Movements to the Hispanic Caribbean in the Century after Emancipation". In *Caribbean Social Relations,* edited by Colin G. Clarke, 66–81. Liverpool: University of Liverpool Centre for Latin American Studies, 1978.

Welch, Pedro L.V. "Post-Emancipation Adjustments in the Urban Context: Views from Bridgetown, Barbados". In *In the Shadow of the Plantation: Caribbean History and Legacy*, edited by Alvin O. Thompson, 266–82. Kingston: Ian Randle, 2002.

Zanetti, Oscar. *United Fruit Company: Un caso de dominio imperialista en Cuba.* Havana: Editorial de Ciencias Sociales, 1976.

Zanetti, Oscar, and Alejandro García. *Sugar and Railroads: A Cuban History, 1837–1959.* Chapel Hill: University of North Carolina Press, 1998.

ORAL SOURCES

Atwell, Joseph. Interview by the author. Baraguá, Cuba, 11 April 1993.

Belgrave, Colbert. Interview by the author. Barbados, 28 September 1997.

Elcock, Lilian. Interview by the author. Baraguá, Cuba, 19 October 1997.

Gay, Teófilo. Interview by the author. Baraguá, Cuba, 11 April 1993.

Greaves, Earl. Interview by the author. Barbados, 7 February 1999.

Greene, Maradell. Interview by the author. Barbados, 8 December 1996.

Hoyte, Rufus. Interview by the author. Barbados, 21 January 1998.

Hunte, Ruby. Interview by the author. Baraguá, Cuba, 11 April 1993.

Jones, Celia. Interview by the author. Baraguá, Cuba, 19 October 1997.

Marshall, Delcina. Interview by the author. Barbados, 27 December 1998.

Mullings, Rupert. Interview by the author. Barbados, 23 March 1999.

Nelson, Gloria. Interview by the author. Barbados, 2 October 1997.

Ray, Charles. Interview by the author. Guantánamo, Cuba, 22 August 2000.

Scantlebury, Ethelbert. Interview by the author. Baraguá, Cuba, 19 October 1997.

Stoute, William V. Interview by the author. Baraguá, Cuba, 18 October 1997.

INDEX

Fernández, Francisco Maria, 90
Forbes, Sir George, 107
Ford, Keneth, 168
Ford, Leona, 181
foreign contract labour: anti-immigrant
    sentiments, 56; anti-immigration
    legislation, 90–92; assaults against,
    66, 67–69; British West Indian Relief
    Fund, 92–93; diplomatic protest
    over treatment of, 54–56, 57–60;
    discrimination against, 43–44; fines
    for unauthorized labour, 27; railroad
    construction, 24; and sugar industry,
    25–27; surety requirements, 26–27
Francia Mestre, Rafael, 178
Francis, Marcus, 68
Franjul, Armando, 67–68
French West Indies, migration from, 53
Frometa, Nora, 178
Furber, Samuel, 120

Gainer, Donald St Clair, 55,
    57–58; secretary of immigration
    appointment, 61–63
Galloway, Elizabeth, 12–13
García, Alejandro, 119, 120
Garvey, Marcus, 41, 62, 75; Universal
    Negro Improvement Association
    (UNIA), 44–45
Gay, Teófilo, 71, 75, 79, 179, 180
Germany, crop restrictions, 88–89
Gilkes, Eliza, 127
Gill, L.E., 103
Gill-Belgrave, Monica, 73
Giovannetti, Jorge, xvi, 118
Gleamaud, Lidiere, 110, 111
Goddard, Lillian, 12–13
Gomez, Mateo, 144
Goodridge, Joseph, 142
Gorham, Joseph, 16

Grau San Martín, Ramón, 90
Greaves, Aida, 146
Greaves, Earl Alonzo "Panama", 139–46
Greaves, George, 146
Greaves, Jorge, 185
Greaves, Oliver Gladstone, 139–40,
    144–45
Greaves, Raoul, 146
Greaves García, Carmelina, 146
Greene, Maradell Atwell, 12–13, 128–38
Greene, Whittington St Clair, 136–37
Guantánamo: All Saints Episcopal
    Church, 109, 114; British West Indian
    Welfare Centre, 45, 104–9, 114, 115;
    Catalina Lodge, 104, 105; Mechanics
    Lodge, 104, 106; preservation of
    West Indian culture, 104; religion,
    and religious institutions, 109–10; St
    Thomas Catholic Church, 109; US
    Naval Base as employer, 104, 111–13, 117,
    145–46
Guantánamo Cricket Club, 181
Guatemala workers' revolt, 41
Guerra y Sánchez, Ramiro, 41
Gutíerrez, Marcelino, 55
Guyana, diplomatic relations with Cuba,
    182

Haggard, Godfrey, and British
    diplomatic protest, 54–55, 56, 59, 60
Haitian migration to Cuba, 25, 43
Haitian Revolution: impact on Cuban
    sugar industry, 19
Hall, Bernard, 55
Hall, J.B., 67
Handler, Jerome, 16
Hanschell, A.J., 29–30
Hanschell and Company, 29–30
Harding, George P., 30
Helg, Aline, 40, 178

CPSIA information can be obtained
at www.ICGtesting.com
Printed in the USA
LVOW08s1934070417

530038LV00001B/114/P